D1498449

LUXURY BRAND MANAGEMENT
A WORLD OF PRIVILEGE

LUXURY BRAND MANAGEMENT
A WORLD OF PRIVILEGE

Michel Chevalier
Gérald Mazzalovo

WILEY

John Wiley & Sons (Asia) Pte. Ltd.

Other Wiley Editorial Offices

John Wiley & Sons, Inc., 111 River Street, Hoboken, NJ 07030, USA
John Wiley & Sons Ltd., The Atrium Southern Gate, Chichester PO19 8SQ, England
John Wiley & Sons (Canada) Ltd., 5353 Dundas Street West, Suite 400, Toronto,
        Ontario, M9B 6HB, Canada
John Wiley & Sons Australia, Ltd., 42 McDougall Street, Milton, Queensland 4064,
        Australia
Wiley-VCH, Boschstrasse 12, D-69469 Weinheim, Germany

Library of Congress Cataloging-in-Publication Data
978-0-470-823262

Typeset in 11 points, Rotis Serif by Hot Fusion
Printed in Singapore by Saik Wah Press Ltd.
10 9 8 7 6 5 4 3

CONTENTS

INTRODUCTION

The notion of luxury has become so central to contemporary consumption and communication activities that it has generated a whole literature related to it. However, these publications have tended to be largely conceptual and inadequate for practical management purposes. Having identified that a pragmatic and comprehensive approach to the management of luxury brands was missing, and confident of our own professional experience in luxury brand management, we decided to write the first practical guide to the topic.

How might "luxury brand" be defined? Clearly, as we set out to write a book on the subject, we must first answer this question. However, we have found that there is no single, definitive meaning, but rather a large number of alternatives from which to choose.

One could say that *a luxury brand is a selective and exclusive one*; that is, it is almost the only brand in its product category, giving it the desirable attributes of being scarce, sophisticated and in good taste. It also has a slightly understated and aristocratic dimension. Based on this definition, there would be only one luxury car—Rolls-Royce—while a flashy red Ferrari might be considered the epitome of bad taste. If we were to choose one brand from each product category and make it a luxury "icon," we might have Krug or Dom Pérignon for champagne, Guerlain for fragrance and cosmetics, Hermès for leather goods, Armani or Valentino for women's ready-to-wear, Brioni for men's suits, and Van Cleef & Arpels for jewelry.

This restrictive definition of luxury makes sense, but it doesn't represent the situation as we know it today. Even brands such as Hugo Boss and Lacoste will be considered as offering luxury goods, because we believe there is a need for an operational definition that takes into account the location of brands in stores and how they are perceived by the consumer. So, we might say that a luxury brand is one that is selective and exclusive, and which has an additional creative and emotional value for the consumer. This definition is much broader and includes a larger range of fashion products.

There is also some debate about the distinction between luxury and fashion. According to this point of view, a brand in the textile and accessory field, for example, might start out as a fashion brand, and would only be given the status of a "luxury" brand when it has achieved some stability and a quality of being timeless. A new fashion brand has to be creative and come up with new ideas, new concepts and new products for every season, in order to attract the interest of consumers. However, as it develops "classical" models that sell year in and year out, becoming permanent best-sellers with a signature style, its status will move from fashion to luxury. While this distinction between fashion brand and luxury brand is a valid one, it is also misleading and possibly even dangerous. It is misleading because even if it has achieved "luxury" status, a fashion brand such as Chanel or Dior must still come up with new designs each season, and present them in new ways, in order to retain customers' interest. It is also dangerous because it implies that a luxury brand doesn't have to innovate to the same extent as a fashion brand, which is obviously not the case.

This may be an appropriate time to describe the different sectors of activities that we include in our analysis of luxury:

- The exclusive **ready-to-wear** category for women and men includes, of course, all the selective fashion brands such as Chanel, Valentino, Burberry, and Versace, but also more traditional brands such as Jaeger, Daks, and Celine. It also includes brands such as Hugo Boss and Lacoste, as indicated above, because they are still quite selective in their distribution and product approach. In fact, even if they have an accessible price, they still function as luxury brands, sold through selective distribution. One could question the inclusion of Lacoste men's products in this category, given that they are a

luxury **brand** management

basic product with little scope for creativity, but Lacoste for women is certainly creative and sophisticated. Where do we draw the line, then? Obviously, we eliminate brands that don't have a selective distribution. But what about Nike or Zara? In these cases, the brand status and level of sophistication, as perceived by the consumer, set these brands well apart from the luxury brands. Nevertheless, there are still many things that the luxury brands can learn from the likes of Zara and H&M in terms of operations systems.

- The luxury **jewelry** and **watches** segment is clearly part of this world. These brands have their own stores, or are sold through a very limited number of selective jewelers.

- **Perfumes** and **cosmetics**, when sold through selective distribution channels, are clearly luxury products, even if they correspond to low-priced items.

- **Fashion accessories** brands generally run as sister brands of fashion brands. This category includes handbags and leather goods, but also shoes, belts and any other element of the total "look," such as glasses, writing instruments, lighters and so on. For men, it includes ties, shoes, shirts and other elements of their wardrobe, including, for the very sophisticated, outfits for weekend wear.

- **Wines** and **spirits** are problematic as luxury goods given that they are available in supermarkets and other food outlets and could be considered part of a food category or a beverage category that includes beer and Coca-Cola. In fact, in the product concept and positioning of wines and spirits, there is a level of sophistication that sets these products apart from beer. They are also far from these fast-moving, repeat-purchase products because they are expensive, are often gift items and are clearly part of brand identity constructions. This combination of sophistication and selective consumption entitles wines and spirits to be included in the luxury category.

- **Luxury automobiles** are clearly a special category in the world of luxury goods. We mentioned earlier Rolls-Royce and Ferrari. Other luxury brands are Bentley, Maserati, Porsche, Maybach and, possibly, some Mercedes, BMW or Audi models. In a sense, the strength of the brand, the difficulty and exclusiveness of its positioning, the sophistication of the products, and the selective system of distribution and after-sales service would justify a luxury categorization for almost every brand and every product in the automotive category. However, at this stage we can limit it to only those cars that consumers perceive as being very special and different from the others.

- **Luxury hotels** can also be thought of as luxury services, in that guests expect outstanding service and a very special experience. In this field, the brand is only one part (though an important one) of a mix that includes design, atmosphere and the quality of service.

- **Luxury tourism** in general, and cruise activities in particular, is a distinctive category.

- **Private banking** could also be considered a luxury activity through its selectivity, the quality of the service and the importance of branding.

We have not attempted in this book to discuss every one of these categories of luxury goods and services, or others such as home furnishings or airlines not listed above. We may extend our analysis to such categories at a later stage.

The final factor to consider in forming a definition of "luxury" is the level of luxury epitomized by a brand. Danielle Alleres[1]

distinguishes three different levels of luxury. First is *inaccessible* luxury, which corresponds to exclusive models, sometimes hand-made in single units, as in the case of a very expensive, unique combination watch or a special-model Rolls-Royce. Next is *intermediary* luxury, which corresponds to objects that are, in fact, expensive replicas of individual models. In the fashion field, *haute couture* would be the *inaccessible* luxury, while specially made outfits, duplicating all or part of a *couture* model, would fall into this intermediary category. For cars, a catalogue Ferrari or Maserati would be classified as an intermediary luxury item, as would a Porsche 911. Finally, *accessible* luxury represents all those products made in factories or workshops, and in larger series, such as Dior women's ready-to-wear, Ferragamo shoes, perfume or a bottle of whisky.

This analysis is interesting, but in a way it misses the point that 98% of the luxury business today corresponds to the accessible luxury category. Thus, while the classification may be useful for describing the origin and specificities of the field, it is not a very operational one.

The question today is to what extent we can still attach the label "luxury product" to a bottle of wine or a pair of canvas shoes. And unless one invents new subdivisions in the "accessible" category, this three-part categorization doesn't help us to distinguish between an Yves Saint Laurent perfume and a Nivea moisturizing cream in determining which can be labeled a "luxury item."

Having failed to discover a definition that clearly explains what makes a product a "luxury item," we have evolved our own. For us, a luxury good must satisfy three criteria: it must have a strong artistic content; it must be the result of craftsmanship; and it must be international.

The *artistic* dimension of the luxury business is what distinguishes it most clearly from all other activities. A luxury object has always been submitted to a profound and sophisticated aesthetic-research process. The easiest way to light a cigarette is by striking a match or flicking a Bic disposable lighter. A silver

S.T. Dupont lighter is heavy in the pocket and messy to refill, but it is an "object"–not merely a "product"–that is like no other: an object that probably has an emotional content. (It may have been received as a gift or purchased for an important event.) The silver work is perfect, and the shape aesthetically pleasing. It is heavy and durable, and makes a distinctive sound when used. It is almost a work of art.

In this world of objects, the aesthetic characteristics are very important parts of the global impression. A new fragrance bottle and its packaging should make an artistic statement. They should generate a perception of beauty and have an aesthetic appeal. A cocktail dress should enhance the personal charm of the woman wearing it and therefore must be itself an aesthetically researched and refined object.

We will discuss this point when we consider the management of creation and of the design team, but even in products that are less about creativity and more about marketing, as in the case of an after-shave lotion or a bottle of vodka, the artistic elements of the business proposition–for example, the product, the packaging and the advertising execution–must always remain very strong.

So, customers don't purchase products; they purchase objects, and they want those objects to be beautiful.

The *craftsmanship* aspect of luxury is just as important. Customers buy objects that have been designed by Giorgio Armani or John Galliano. Even if the *products* are mass-manufactured, as in the case of a perfume, they want to believe that the *object* comes directly from the designer's workshop.

In the luxury field, it is almost impossible to visit factories. It is possible in Paris, for example, to visit a Hermès production center in Bagnolet or a Louis Vuitton workshop in Asnières, but in both cases customers can see leather specialists working by hand on individual pieces. These are either expensive pieces, in the case of Hermès, or made-to-order items for Louis Vuitton. But it boils down to the same thing: it is difficult to visit automated factories, when and if they exist, because this is not what the brands want the consumer to remember.

The luxury business therefore seems to be a business of designing and hand-producing beautiful, artistic, well-crafted objects that customers love to purchase, to receive as a gift, or to use.

The third dimension is the *international* aspect. When a Canadian buys an Italian or French luxury object that he highly values, he expects the product to be as highly valued by French, Japanese or Chinese purchasers of luxury goods. When a French man or woman walks along Madison Avenue or 57th Street in New York, they may make a mental note of the French brands that have a well-located store and feel a sense of pride. But if these visitors notice the absence of a Kenzo or Givenchy outlet, say, then they may deduce that those brands are less highly valued in New York and may consequently value them less highly as well.

We will see later in the book that a significant part of the luxury-goods business relies on consumers who are far from home, and who consider the purchase as something very special. So, in the luxury business, it is almost essential to have a presence in the world's most fashionable cities, such as Paris, Milan, New York, Los Angeles, Tokyo, Hong Kong, Shanghai, Singapore, London, Geneva and Dusseldorf. In these and other cities, the big brands will try to outdo each other, making it difficult for smaller brands to find a store location in central retail areas where the luxury brands congregate.

Luxury brands must therefore have an international profile and presence, but with a discernible national character. When a Korean woman enters a Gucci store in Seoul, it is with the expectation that the atmosphere will be evocative of Italy, whether it be through the sophisticated use of color, the music or the store fit-out. And when she enters an Yves Saint Laurent boutique, she expects to get a subtle whiff of Paris.

Thus, those beautiful objects, virtually hand-made by artists and craftsmen, must be seen everywhere in the world before customers will accept being part of the deal and purchase them in their home country or elsewhere.

This is the vision of the luxury business that we will deal with in this book. Our analysis will be quite heavily descriptive, as we wish to describe at length what is specific about the luxury-goods business. We will examine brand status, and discuss how it should be handled in this environment. We will then move on to a more normative process and explain how to analyze luxury clients and deal with brand identity. We will then analyze distribution and communication issues, and suggest ways of dealing with them so that all activities are effective and consistent with the brand objectives.

The text has been organized so that it can be read from start to finish, or individual chapters can be studied separately.

Our objective is for the reader to understand the brand potential that exists in luxury activities, and how luxury-goods businesses should be conducted on a daily basis.

Please note that throughout the book financial values are expressed in euros. (At the time of writing, €1=US$1.41 approximately.) Except as otherwise indicated, all tables are of our own devising, based on our own research and on publicly available records.

Some of the material used in this book (principally in chapters 4, 6 and 12) is based on our earlier book *Pro Logo* (New York: Palgrave Macmillan, 2004).

Endnote
[1] Danielle Alléres, *Luxe: Stratégie, Marketing*, Economica, 1990.

chapter 1

SPECIFICITIES OF THE
Luxury
INDUSTRY

Representatives of any business sector are usually eager to assert that their business is different from any other, but managers working in the luxury industry are possibly the only ones who are justified in claiming so. The luxury sector really *is* different. This is due partly to the amount of creative talent needed for a luxury brand to be successful, and partly to the very different way in which a luxury brand with a worldwide market needs to be run. Three major differences will be identified below. We will then briefly examine the major requirements for success in this business. We will conclude by identifying the main companies operating in this field.

WHAT IS SO DIFFERENT ABOUT THE LUXURY-GOODS INDUSTRY?

The three major differences between the luxury industry and the non-luxury segment are: company size, financial characteristics and the time factor.

Company size

In almost every business, size is a major—if not *the* most important—element in comparing firms or industries. But in the luxury world, size doesn't seem to matter that much. In general, luxury businesses are small; but they are respected and have impressive reputations. Dior Fashion has annual sales of approximately €800 million, while the Peugeot Group has annual sales of €56 billion. So, in fact, Peugeot is 70 times bigger than Dior Fashion. General Motors has sales of around €150 billion, 200 times those of Dior Fashion. The number of employees in each case is probably in the same ratio, if not higher.

But if you were to ask an American, a Japanese or a Chinese consumer to name a French product or a French company, they will name Dior before Peugeot. This can be explained by brand awareness: the Dior brand is better known, worldwide, than the Peugeot brand. And this very high awareness comes from the fact that consumers have a genuine interest in luxury and fashion brands. They read about them in magazines and want to know more about them.

LVMH, the luxury-goods giant with a portfolio of more than 50 brands, has total annual sales of approximately €15 billion. Compare this with Gap, with annual sales of €11 billion, or Zara Inditex, with €8 billion. In other words, the average LVMH brand—which incorporates some of the most powerful brands in the luxury industry—is about 10 to 20 times smaller than Gap or Zara.

We can conclude, therefore, that luxury brands are rather small but with very strong awareness among consumers. So, despite their prestige image and their advertising presence all over the world, luxury companies are generally small to medium-sized enterprises (the exceptions being the larger conglomerates of small individual

luxury **brand** management

companies). Some companies are very small. Cardin has worldwide annual sales of only €10 million, and Carven has sales of around €1-2 million. This is much smaller than a Volkswagen dealership in Athens, or a small group of five supermarkets in Birmingham. But, of course, Cardin and Carven remain worldwide brands.

How do such relatively small businesses achieve such a strong presence in the mind of the consumer?

Sales figures are difficult to compare

In the luxury industry, comparing levels of sales across companies can be like trying to compare apples with oranges, as corporate figures may comprise very different elements. If we take the sales figures for Louis Vuitton, things are relatively simple because they include sales in the 400 stores of the group worldwide. But Carven's sales figures, for example, reflect retail sales at its stores, ready-to-wear sales at wholesale outlets, export sales and revenues from licenses given to outside enterprises. As a rule of thumb, wholesale sales are approximately half of retail sales, export sales are generally 20% of retail sales, and license royalties amount in general to 10% of billings, which can in turn come from retail, wholesale and export sales. Thus, it just doesn't make sense to compare the two companies in terms of their sales figures.

To compare the power of two brands, one would have to multiply part of the activity by a coefficient to account for differences in export sales and wholesale sales, for example, so that everything would be computed as a final retail sales amount. But this would still be misleading, because a brand developing essentially through license agreements will be weaker than a brand that controls 100% of its activities at retail. Also, in most cases, the split between retail, wholesale, export and license royalties isn't given, so assumptions are difficult to make.

The fact that some brands are developed through licenses, with royalties from these accounting for only 2–3% of their sales, explains why luxury businesses are sometimes very small, even when the brand has a strong presence worldwide in various stores.

However, a brand such as Hermès, which (except for its perfumes) sells almost exclusively in its own stores, can still have annual sales of €1.4 billion. It may not be as big as Peugeot or Renault, but for a luxury company, it is quite impressive.

The mix of activities makes it difficult to understand exactly what is meant when executives of luxury companies declare sales targets of, say, €100 million in China or Japan. Are they referring to total sales, as will be reported in their consolidated financial statements, or do they mean retail volume, which may earn them only €3–5 million in license royalties? There is a significant difference.

As a rule, these sorts of statements should be considered carefully, given that, as we have seen, comparing businesses in financial terms can be quite difficult.

Limited number of staff

The fact that most luxury-goods companies are small or medium-sized enterprises has an obvious consequence: they also have a limited number of staff. In China, for example, the most successful luxury brands have staff numbers of only 200 or 300, most of them working in stores. The "small enterprise" element is also amplified by the fact that luxury brands must have a global presence. It is probably true to say that there are more marketing executives in companies such as Procter & Gamble or Nestlé than in the total luxury-goods sector. Several elements contribute to this situation.

First, some companies are not just small; they can be very small. They may operate with just a small design studio that monitors trends and designs products, and may subcontract all the other activities to licensees and distributors. So, the next-most important area of activity after the studio is the legal department, or even an outside lawyer, which prepares and follows up contracts with outside partners. Some fashion companies have global headcounts that might not exceed 15 to 30 people. For example, the Ungaro brand has a design studio and a limited number of directly operated stores, while all its manufacturing and distribution are subcontracted.

luxury **brand** management

This tendency to subcontract production activities is the second very particular aspect of the luxury field. Chanel doesn't have its own factories manufacturing all its ready-to-wear items or leather goods. Often, luxury-goods companies have just one or two factories, making prototypes and some product lines. The rest of the manufacturing is carefully controlled, but is done by subcontractors. For example, the various components of most luxury-brand watches are generally produced by different companies, before the final item is assembled in the home country.

An automotive business is all about the factory, machinery and equipment, but luxury brands are about design and communicating a message. Where are the products made? Who manufactures them? How many consumers know that companies in the LVMH Group, Bally or Prada have their goods or product components manufactured in China or India? What challenges does this pose at the production level? It seems that these questions are never raised.

Third, aside from the creative activity, the most important part of the luxury industry process is the sale. At Lancôme, probably 80% of the company's worldwide employees stand behind a counter. At Gucci, a very important part of the process happens in the stores. To make a career at Prada or Salvatore Ferragamo, it makes sense to start out working in a store—because this is where contact is made with the consumer. Very few of a luxury brand's employees will be based at headquarters, as all the investment goes into the stores. Ferragamo's group headquarters, Palazzo Feroni in Florence, also serves as the worldwide flagship store and a museum, an important tool for communicating with consumers.

So, the average luxury-goods company is small. Its sales figures include elements that are difficult to assess and to compare. A lot of activity at the level of manufacturing and distribution is subcontracted. And staff numbers are very limited.

Financial characteristics

In studying the different luxury companies, and as we will confirm later in this book, it quickly becomes noticeable that a significant number of them are losing money. In any other industrial sector, a firm losing money is rapidly eliminated, merged with its competitors or goes bankrupt. In the luxury-goods industry, there are brands that have been losing money for five or even 10 years and that survive as part of a luxury group or as a diversification within another industrial company. Bic, the writing-instruments group, owned the Guy Laroche company for a very long time and probably lost money for more than 10 years in a row before it took steps to sell out. Charles Jourdan also lost money for many years when it belonged to its previous owners (the proprietors of a large Swiss cement company). Christian Lacroix apparently never generated profits while in the LVMH Group.

Why would intelligent and reasonable executives continue to accept losing money for so long? There are probably two reasons for this: the first entails the value of the brand. Despite losing money for many years, Guy Laroche remains attractive to consumers and there is a tremendous brand awareness. The second reason is that successful brands are so successful and so profitable that they can compensate for many years of losses. In 1994, the research group Eurostaf conducted a study of the luxury ready-to-wear companies in France. This found that Chanel, taken alone, was more profitable than the rest of the sector combined. Of 14 companies investigated, 10 were losing money. The fact that Chanel was so profitable could lead any other brand to think that it too had the potential to develop and generate similar returns for shareholders. Furthermore, luxury brands are a very productive path that can lead to becoming a lifestyle brand which, in turn, can lead to enormous growth capacity through product extension. We will look more closely at this phenomenon in Chapter 4.

In this respect, the luxury business is a kind of "jackpot" business: not because it is unpredictable and things come only by chance, of course, but because those that are profitable become extremely profitable.

This incredible spread between unprofitable and extremely profitable companies seems to be the result of two peculiarities.

First, the luxury business is a very high break-even business. Second, cash needs are quite limited.

A very high break-even

In an average sector, break-even is a function of manufacturing investments and of fixed costs. In the luxury sector, even the smaller brands have to pretend they are powerful and rich, and by doing so they end up with a very high break-even.

For example, every brand must be present everywhere in the world. If the Japanese tourist cannot find his Givenchy or Aquascutum store when he visits Milan or New York, he may well conclude that these brands are weak and he might decide to stop buying them in Japan.

At the outset, a brand can be in only one place, like the Café Greco in Rome. But as soon as it starts to become international, the consumers expect to find it everywhere. Each store, wherever it is in the world, has fixed costs—rental, staff and other costs—before it makes its first sale.

But also, in the world of luxury brands, everything from the production process to the sale has to be of top quality. Service has to be perfect, and wherever they are in the world, customers should leave with a special and distinctive carrier bag (for Bottega Veneta, the handles are of leather) bearing the logo and the color of the brand. Even before going into the bag, the product is often expensively packaged and all of the costly glass molds, carton cases, ribbons or bags have to be manufactured. And this is an area where cost-cutting can be extremely dangerous, because all of these factors contribute to the sense of luxury and to the individual purchase experience.

A brand's standing is often determined by expenses that rarely generate an equivalent gross margin. For example, a fashion brand must start the process by holding an expensive fashion show, twice a year, where the products that are presented are not identical to those that will be sold in the stores: for a given model, the shoulders are a bit larger, the waist a bit tighter and the skirt a bit shorter on the runway. The cost of making a particular dress may never be recovered because the dress will probably never be sold. *Haute couture*, in Paris, is another activity designed to promote the image of the brand and to make it stand out, rather than to make money.

Another very expensive investment is to have "flagship stores" in the home town of the brand; these are invariably progressively bigger in a bid to outdo competitors. Of course, for large-volume stores, this is not so much of a problem, but for a middle-sized brand, this is a painful and unprofitable activity.

All of this adds to the very high break-even and to the difficulty for a new brand to establish itself and develop credibility before it has built sufficient volume to balance all the upfront investments.

A limited cash need

As soon as a brand achieves sales above break-even, life becomes much easier. Margins are very high and when all fixed costs are covered, a large part of the margin becomes profit.

In manufacturing, when sales develop it is necessary to invest in new factories. In luxury it is always possible to subcontract the production or the additional production. Accounts receivables is another problem area for most businesses. When the brand operates its own stores, it is paid in cash or other immediately recoverable payment methods.

What about inventory, then? In fact, as the product gross margin is quite high, inventories at cost are not too difficult to finance when the level of sales is satisfactory. The major financial difficulty is to make sure inventory is available everywhere in the world, in all of the brand's own stores or in those of its distributors. But this difficulty is, of course, much higher for newly established companies than for those with a very high and growing level of sales.

Another difficulty in the area of fashion products is that of returns: at the end of a season some items must be either sold or returned. For small brands, this is a major issue because they are obliged to start with a large number of products each season to bring variety to their customers: with a small volume of sales, bargain sales end up very big. For high-volume brands, a fashion distributor will sell 80–85% of the collection at full prices and 15–20% at bargain prices. For difficult brands, the financial picture is not the same: up to 65% of total volume will be at bargain prices. So, small companies have to deal with the issue if they want to ensure that their distributors will buy the next season's products. This often entails giving distributors special discounts if they are to avoid having to take returns, knowing that products that are returned are either sold through factory outlets or destroyed. This is a major issue for small and medium-sized brands. For large brands, returns are a small part of the volume and bargain sales to staff or press are usually sufficient to dispose of any outdated merchandise.

The only very important cash need relates to the opening of stores under the brand name. This need does not exist in perfumes, cosmetics, wine and spirits and watches, but it is an essential part in the development of a fashion or accessories brand.

The conclusion is very simple: luxury is a great and very profitable business for those who are successful. It is a very difficult business for the others. And it is also very easy to go from a very profitable situation to major losses as soon as the sales begin to decrease when products are no longer adapted to the consumer and, for some reason, no longer fashionable.

The luxury-goods business can therefore be summed up as either a "win all" or "lose all." It is great for the top profitable brands. It is difficult for those striving to make an impression. It is a nightmare for those who cannot afford a flagship store in Paris, Milan, New York and Tokyo and who have to keep on losing money in some of their activities to maintain the dream and the glitter around their brands.

Time-frame

In the automotive business, everybody is trying to reduce the time to develop a new car so that the product line can be changed more frequently. In many businesses, it is possible to turn a situation around in little more than a year. Sometimes, for fast-moving consumer-goods products, it is possible to launch a product, have an immediate and clear indication of how well it is selling in the stores and get sales to cover the original investment costs within six months.

In the luxury world, launches often take much more time and investment. To launch a new perfume, it is necessary to come up with a complete line, from extracts to eau de toilette, even a "bath line," and for each item there is a need for a costly glass bottle mold and a plastic cap mold. Such molds can take up to 12 months to make. Then a large quantity of the product has to be manufactured, so that at the time of the launch the new perfume can be immediately available in a large number of countries. So the lead time for a launch can be anything from 18 months to two years. Then in the first year, for major launches, it is not uncommon to spend an amount equal to the first year sales forecast on advertising and promotion. It often takes three or four years to start making money.

In the watch business, too, timing is crucial. The design and manufacturing processes have to be completed in time for the Geneva or Basel watch and jewelry fairs at the end of February or beginning of March each year. If the deadline cannot be met, the launch is delayed until the following year.

Table 1.1: Fashion cycle for a Fall–Winter collection

Exclusive fabric commitments	September–October, year t–1
Development of prototypes and matching with fabrics	September, year t–1, February, year t
Fashion show	February–March, year t
Order-taking from multi-brand stores	March, year t
Delivery to the stores	July, year t
Sale at full price	September–December, year t
Bargain sale	January–February, year t+1

luxury **brand** management

The fashion cycle

In the world of luxury fashion, everything boils down to the fashion cycle, as illustrated in Table 1.1.

The cycle starts when fabric manufacturers present their new samples of materials. They offer new colors, new fabric touches and new designs. Each year, in September or October, designers visit the fabric manufacturers in Paris (Première Vision) and Italy (Idea Como) to select the colors and feel they will use for their next Fall–Winter collection. To get exclusivity on a given design, they have to commit themselves to the purchase of a minimum number of meters of the fabric that will provide the special look of their collections for the next year.

They then go back to their studios and prepare the collections for the February/March fashion shows, which will, of course, be attended by the media and by buyers from department and multi-brand stores all over the world. These buyers come with specific budgets for each brand and make firm orders for the items that they believe they can sell in their stores.

The dresses are then manufactured and delivered, by July at the latest, to be presented in September as the "new Fall–Winter collection." It is only at the end of the bargain period, at the end of February, that they will know how successful they have been with a given collection, how much has been sold at the full price, how much at bargain prices, and how much is left over at the very end of the process.

The fashion cycle lasts 18 months. During that same period, of course, another Spring–Summer collection will be committed, selected, presented and delivered, and results will not be known until the very end of the cycle. This is why, when a company decides to change its designer, the new stylist will need a minimum of two years to impose a new style, to define his personal view of the brand and to make it a success.

Some brands have tried to get out of this "strait-jacket" by having additional, interim collections (the "cruise" collections), but the system remains quite rigid. Some newcomers in the mass-market segment, such as Zara, have rejected the traditional system and develop 26 collections a year. However, unless they deal with very high volumes, they have difficulty purchasing exclusive materials and are forced to present collections produced mainly in plain fabrics.

This time-frame forces the brands to plan a long time ahead and it is a long time before consumers can really see major changes in styles or in brand positioning in their local stores.

Turn-around time

For the reasons mentioned above, in the luxury field there is no short-term impact of major strategic decisions. For a luxury fashion brand, for example, the results of changing the designer might not be seen until two or three years down the road.

Brands themselves cannot be modified overnight. They have a specific identity in the mind of the consumer, and it is difficult to modify this. Nina Ricci, for example, is a very feminine brand and its attempts to launch masculine products have been conspicuously unsuccessful. Paco Rabanne is, curiously, a designer for women, but the brand is mainly known for masculine perfumes: its ladies' perfumes have never done very well. Some brands are modern, others are perceived as traditional. It is very difficult to change such perceptions. Chanel is a brand for women, but it also has fragrances, ties and a watch for men. At the moment, it does not have men's ready-to-wear. In the long run, it probably will. But this is a major change that the brand is preparing for by presenting its masculine products at its fashion shows for women. The idea is to convince the customer that Chanel is a brand for both women and men. This may take some time and its men's ready-to-wear products are not yet available in the stores. When the consumer changes his mind, they will be.

It takes time to turn a brand around, as the experience of Yves Saint Laurent clearly shows. When the fashion brand was purchased by the Gucci Group, everybody thought the turnaround in its fortunes would be rapid. However, with accumulated losses

luxury **brand** management

already amounting to several hundred million euros, the brand will probably continue to lose money for a few more years before it turns the corner.

This has major implications for investors who want to buy and redevelop a brand that has lost its image and sales. This may be possible for watches and for wines and spirits, but for fashion and perfumes it is close to impossible. If a brand is not doing well, its identity must be modified over time. The paradox is that when this is done, customers have the feeling the brand has been mishandled and its history betrayed. In the end, nobody is happy—unless a great deal of time, effort and money are committed to the cause.

Of course, as we will explain later, it has been possible to take brands such as Gucci and Burberry, which were doing relatively well, modify them over time and increase their sales substantially. But when smaller brands such as Jacques Fath or Poppy Moreni have lost their glamour, their interest and their reason for being, there is not much that can be done to bring them back into the limelight.

This time-frame explains why private-equity specialists or private individuals seldom purchase a majority of small luxury brands. There are exceptions—Loewe, Montana fashion and Odiot—but turnarounds are seldom successful.

This is why this activity has been traditionally the field of family firms. Family firms have time and can accept poor results for a few years before growing and making money again. There are many in this situation, including Chanel, Salvatore Ferragamo, Armani, Versace, Laurent-Perrier and Pernod Ricard. And we should never forget that three of the major luxury groups, LVMH, Richemont and PPR Gucci, are also controlled by families.

THE KEYS TO SUCCESS IN LUXURY GOODS

Professor Bernard Dubois would start on this subject by speaking of the paradox of luxury goods (see Table 1.2). To achieve success in this field, he said, it was necessary to do exactly the opposite of what was taught in traditional marketing lessons.

Table 1.2: The paradox of luxury-goods marketing

High price

High cost

Craftsmanship

Limited distribution

Low promotional activity

Advertising with no sophisticated copy strategy

Source: Bernard Dubois[1]

At first sight, high prices, high costs, no manufacturing investment and a limited distribution do not seem to be normal marketing practice. But the process is based on the creation of a well-controlled scarcity. The product must be known and be visible but it should also appear expensive and slightly out of reach. Customers must go out of their way to find it. This is a "niche" marketing approach that can only work when the brand has a strong identity and a reason for being. It also requires a specific aesthetic concept: the product must be easily recognizable and in line with the mood of the time and with the specific fashion trends.

The need for a strong name

We come back again to brand identity. It frequently starts with the name of a person, then must be extended and should always keep bringing additional values and reasons for being.

Most luxury brands start with a person's name; that of a craftsman or a designer who was different from the crowd and who made things differently. Louis Cartier made watches and jewelry. Sotirio Bulgari used Greek and Roman art in his pieces while giving them a contemporary touch. This became a reference for customers and a guarantee that the products bearing the name of the founder remain exclusive high-quality objects. It was Salvatore

luxury **brand** management

Ferragamo who made shoes for the actresses and Coco Chanel who made dresses for her most sophisticated friends. It was Giorgio Armani and Valentino Garavani who started their own fashion collections. Boucheron, Chaumet and Van Cleef & Arpels are all family names.

Some brands do not bear the name of a founder. This is the case of Lancôme, which was created by the Petitjean family. In the case of Ralph Lauren, the name itself is a creation of the founder and little by little it has become his own name. This act itself is a kind of recognition of the importance of a discrete family name and identity for all luxury businesses. Those, like Aquascutum or Escada, which have no such name seem to miss something, to somehow lack identity. The family name embodies a heritage and the fact that products are made just for a very small category of friends, at least at the beginning.

Brand extension and legitimacy

As we have seen, the process of establishing a brand often starts with a name. But the name can limit the scope of the business to the craft of the founder: Ferragamo and Prada make shoes; Gucci makes handbags; Louis Vuitton makes travel bags; Christofle makes silver-plated cutlery...

To develop a fully fledged business, it becomes necessary to enlarge and diversify the product line to increase the sales volume on which to advertise. If Calvin Klein was extremely well known in the United States, he was relatively unknown in Europe and Asia until his perfume line was advertised heavily and became a success. On the back of this success, he was able to open stores for his fashion lines in France and Japan.

This process of line extension—moving away from one product category to another one—is particularly delicate for luxury goods. It took seven years for the first Bulgari watch to be successful. It took approximately the same time for Boucheron watches to start selling. While the psychological distance from jewelry to watches may seem very slight, it still takes a lot of time for the consumer to get used to the shift.

Some extensions have been more rapid and without apparent problems. When Prada went from shoes to handbags and then into the ready-to-wear field for women and men, it worked almost every time. The same thing happened with Gucci in its line extensions.

Other cases have been more delicate. In the 1990s, Christofle decided that tableware was not a fast-growing market. Recalling its origins as silversmiths, it decided to launch a jewelry line, opting for white gold. After the launch of its first collection, it produced a watch, also in white gold. But moving too far away from its traditional area of expertise, and failing to make sufficient investment in advertising and promotion, the extension did not work and proved to be a major setback for the brand.

When Chanel decided to extend into jewelry, it was much more careful, launching a single model of watch from free-standing boutiques set up specifically for this purpose in Place Vendôme and Avenue Montaigne in Paris. The watch was a success. The company waited another four or five years before setting up a very large jewelry store in Place Vendôme, the best location for major jewelers in Paris. This, too, was a success.

Baccarat provides another interesting story. It was selling crystal glasses and facing the same problem as Christofle: the difficulty in the tableware market. The company decided to concentrate on lamps and candle-holders for the home and to move into crystal jewelry pieces. It invested heavily, gave the best locations in its stores to this product line and, today, diversification products represent approximately half of the brand's total sales.

The conditions governing line extensions can be summarized as follows:

- Never believe it will be easy.
- Make a major investment and a major effort.
- Do not start small as a side business.
- Do not believe consumers will be immediately convinced. Give them time.

luxury **brand** management

- Emphasize coherence and style.
- Find a credible reason why the new product line is appropriate for your brand.

Of course, with time and investment, everything is possible. But a careful review at the outset of the differences and the major issues the new product category will bring to the brand is vital.

Identifiable products

A Mercedes sedan or a BMW, whatever the model, is instantly identifiable. There can be no mistaking the design, the workmanship or the overall appearance.

When someone makes the investment to buy a luxury product, it goes without saying that the service should be perfect, the product should be of exceptional quality, and it should be made as if it were a unique object, handcrafted or carefully prepared for the individual purchaser. But it needs something else. It needs to have a high aesthetic value. It should be part of a family of products and be clearly identified. Each brand should have its own aesthetic codes and maintain a strong coherence across its entire range of products. A Chanel perfume bottle is classical, simple and sophisticated. An Yves Saint Laurent jacket should look like no other and its perfume bottles should be romantic, baroque and feminine. There should be instant recognition.

The primacy of design

Design should be considered a priority in almost every luxury activity. This is obvious for a fashion brand, but it is also the case for a watch or for a perfume. In fact, in creating a perfume, two different creative teams are involved: the "nose" that develops the fragrance, and the designer for the bottle in which it is presented. With perfumes, while there should also be a family homogeneity of fragrances within the same brand (Guerlain fragrances, for example, are generally quite heavy, with a vanilla heart note—the fragrance that lingers an hour or two after application), and each product should bring additional value to the total picture. That is to say, an Yves Saint Laurent men's suit should have something in common with a women's dress from the same house.

This is why for a luxury brand, management should be able to communicate with all types of designers. They should have a common language and a common understanding that enables them to discuss all aspects of a new product.

The "raison d'être"

Each object in the collection should add to the brand and have a reason for being. When Armani, for example, makes optical frames, they should not simply be standard glasses with an Armani label: they should have something special. This requires that for each new product line, the product category is reinvented in line with the brand's ethical and aesthetic invariants, the two basic components of any brand identity, as we will explain in Chapter 6.

This is why the licensing of products without the brand studio retaining real control and real guidance is now mostly over. For many years, Rochas, which had been a full fashion line and had become a perfume house, had a women's ready-to-wear license in Japan. Lancel was a leather-goods company in Europe, but in Japan it had a whole collection of licensed products, from women's ready-to-wear to panties, shoes, men's shirts and socks. This was perfectly all right in the 1960s and '70s when luxury consumers were traveling less and when brand information was less available. Today such licensed products have a major drawback. All the customers who are knowledgeable about the brand refuse to buy them and the products slip down to a consumer category less interested, less aware and less demanding: they rapidly become middle-market brands.

In a way, these are simply standard positioning principles, as they apply to any marketing product analysis. For luxury items, however, we must go back to the concept of craftsmanship and what differentiates such items from mass-market products. A luxury object must be crafted and designed carefully. This is as true for a luxury fragrance as it is for a dress or a jacket. The sophistication of a luxury perfume should be matched by that of its presentation. Every element of the product should be carefully thought out—from the bottle to the inner and outer packaging—to give the consumer a sense of quality and perfect design every time. The distinction between a luxury product and a mass-market product is evident in the presentation of the jars of the anti-wrinkle creams of Plenitude de L'Oréal and of Lancôme. They are both manufactured by the same company, yet the shapes, the weights and the finishes are quite different.

However, given that mass-market products are gradually upgrading their appearance and approach, it is even more important for luxury goods to work harder to stay ahead of the pack.

Craftsmanship should be the hallmark of all categories of luxury goods, and any product bearing a particular luxury brand should display all the ethical and aesthetic values that belong to that brand.

The social and cultural environment

This ethical and aesthetic dimension has another effect. It places the luxury industry in the realm of the arts and into the cultural trends of the moment. As it looks for new shapes, colors, feelings or modes of consumption, this industry is much more a part of the cultural scene than any others. Thus, its advertising bypasses traditional processes and looks for a special aesthetic environment and a special artistic connivance with its consumer target. In this, luxury products must function as a cultural mirror.

Keeping up with social trends

The importance of staying in touch with changing social trends is reflected in the experiences of some of the leading brands themselves. For example, at one time the "sexy chic" positioning of Gucci met with strong approval from its target customer. Versace, too, was doing very well with the sexiness of its dresses and in its communication. Today the "sexy chic" theme seems to be less attractive to the consumer and Gucci has come to a much more classic positioning. Versace, however, failed to read the mood in the same way and didn't change, with the result that its sales fell considerably.

Paco Rabanne, with his glittering metallic dresses, was an icon of the spirit of sexual liberation that was all-pervasive around 1968 and met with strong interest from the public. Jane Fonda and Brigitte Bardot had special gowns made for them as a special commitment to a given way of life. Fashion magazines were showing his models and interviewing him for his views on the new social trends. At that time, his point of view mattered to the public. Today, though, few would be interested in his thoughts on what is happening in the world.

In using a luxury product, the consumer is making a claim to being different and very special, at the forefront of social trends rather than appearing to be outside of society.

This fit with social trends and the spirit of the time is a very strong aspect of luxury. When people longed for a return to nature and a simpler society, they loved the Danish designer Per Spook, who was designing natural-looking heavy wool-knit jackets and beige cotton skirts. When they wanted an extremely sexy look, they went for Versace. When the times become more traditional and conservative, with the emphasis on the mature woman, Chanel has a lot to offer.

With hindsight, it is clear that some brands have developed very quickly at one time and then declined, and not necessarily because their management was less effective and their marketing was off-base. It was simply a product of the changing times. Now, of course, good marketing is supposed to remain in line with consumer trends. But how far should a company go to adjust its product and brand positioning to the changes in society?

The response to changing trends
As mentioned earlier, Paco Rabanne's appeal faded when his

philosophy was deemed to be out of step with changing social trends that saw the advent of the sexy society of the late 1990s. He could have come to a "sexy" positioning and, indeed, many of the sophisticated metallic dresses of Versace could have been done by him. But this was not his style and he did not feel the need to do it.

Salvatore Ferragamo provides another interesting case. It developed from high-quality shoes to producing the finest silk ties and scarves on the market. A Ferragamo tie is immediately identifiable by its beautiful colors and its extremely fine prints, which could almost have come from an old Persian manuscript. But, now, the fashion is for plain jacquard silk ties. Should Salvatore Ferragamo change its product philosophy? The fact is that it has indeed introduced some jacquard silk ties, but the company is struggling to differentiate itself from its competitors.

We wanted to finish this section with a note to remind managers of the underlying uncertainty of the luxury business. Often, success (or the lack of it) is as much a product of the changing social environment as it is of individual managerial style.

THE MAJOR OPERATORS

In this introductory chapter, it is necessary to describe the major operators in the field. Various articles say that the tendency is toward large groups and that individual companies don't stand a chance in the luxury market in the long run. Is this really the case?

What is the size of the luxury market?

As we said earlier, in luxury, size is relative. As there is very little data available on the size of the total market, we are obliged to come up with our own "guesstimates" of this activity.

It all depends, of course, on whether we consider luxury in its more limited scope (fashion, accessories including leather goods, cosmetics and fragrances, wine and spirits, etc.) or if we also include luxury cars and travel. In the larger category, the total turnover of the corporations manufacturing products or rendering direct services would be approximately €250 billion. By the more limited definition, we estimate that sales are approximately €190 billion, divided as shown in Table 1.3.

Table 1.3: Estimates of business size, 2006 (€ billion)

Ready-to-wear	20
Leather goods	15
Fragrances and cosmetics	30
Spirits and champagnes	30
Still wines	50
Watches	10
Jewelry	30
Tableware	5
Total	190

Source: Estimates of the authors based on discussions with professionals of the different sectors.

Based on these estimates, we compare the relative size of the French and the Italian companies, as set out in Table 1.4. Again, these figures are our own estimates and have been rounded up.

In the ready-to-wear category, Italy and France between them have 80% of the market, with Italy clearly leading the way. "Others" comprises countries such as England and the United States. However, if we confine ourselves to luxury, and therefore do not take into account brands such as Liz Claiborne, Gap or Banana Republic, the United States is not strong in this category.

For alcohols and spirits, we have not included wine; with sales of around €50 billion, this really forms a category in its own right. Nevertheless, it should be noted that Italy is very strong in this field. Most of the spirits business—vodkas, gins and whiskies—is done in the United States and England, but France keeps its position thanks to cognacs and champagnes and to strong groups that we will study later.

luxury **brand** management

Table 1.4: Estimates of the respective contributions of French and Italian companies

	Total (€ billion)	French (%)	Italian (%)	Others (%)
Ready-to-wear	20	20	60	20
Leather goods	15	60	30	10
Spirits and champagnes	30	30	5	65
Fragrances and cosmetics	30	50	10	40
Watches	10	10	5	85
Jewelry	30	10	5	85
Tableware	5	40	10	50
Total	140			

Source: The figures in Table 1.4 are based on the authors' discussions with different industry specialists.

In the watches category, which is obviously dominated by the Swiss, the French and Italians are merely secondary players.

Of the overall total, French and Italian brands account for €43 billion and €23.5 billion, respectively. France's strong position is built around perfumes. With the exception of Armani, Gucci and Laura Biagiotti, Italy seems to have been unable to impose strong perfume brands, and neither does it have a strong international market in spirits.

However, Italy's strength in fashion is quite visible. Where France has five brands with sales of over €750 million (Louis Vuitton, Cartier, Chanel, Hermès and Dior), with two whose core business is in the ready-to-wear world, Italy has eight (Gucci, Prada, Armani, Max Mara, Salvatore Ferragamo, Bulgari, Dolce & Gabbana and Versace), with seven coming from the ready-to-wear and fashion world.

This pre-eminence of Italian fashion will have unexpected consequences in the long run as perfume brands are often built on the strength of ready-to-wear lines. If one day the Gucci, Prada and Versace perfumes reach parity with those of Chanel, Dior and Yves Saint Laurent, then Italy will become the number-one luxury operator in the world.

For reasons that will be discussed later, the French have been very slow to develop fashion and ready-to-wear brands in the last 20 years. The three major creations of French fashion brands date back to Yves Saint Laurent, Kenzo and, more recently, Christian Lacroix; somehow, this looks like ancient history.

Oligopoly or open market?

From reading the press, it might be easy to form the conclusion that luxury has become the field of large groups and that there is no place for small operators. In fact the real picture is quite different, as Table 1.5 shows.

Table 1.5: The major luxury operators, 2006 (€ million)

Luxury Operators	Sales	
LVMH	11,415	Total 15,306
Diageo	9,000 (E)	Guinness not included (estimated at 1,890)
Pernod Ricard	6,443	
Estée Lauder	5,026	
Richemont	4,827	
L'Oréal	3,773	Total 15,790
Chanel	3,600 (E)	
PPR Gucci	3,568	
Bacardi	3,000 (E)	
Rolex	2,000 (E)	
Fortune Brands	2,000	
Tiffany	1,891	
Valentino Fash. Gr.	1,728	
Hermès	1,514	
Burberry	1,275	
Others	128,940	
Total	190,000	

Source: Annual reports or authors' estimates indicated by (E).

luxury **brand** management

As will be discussed later, small operators, if they have the critical mass to be clearly international, can do quite well in this world.

The "Big Three" Corporations

In the luxury business, people speak generally of the big three corporations–LVMH, Richemont and PPR Gucci. Actually, PPR Gucci's luxury division is smaller than that of L'Oréal, and both Richemont and PPR Gucci are smaller than Estée Lauder and than major wines and spirit companies such as Diageo and Pernod Ricard. However, in this section, we will confine ourselves to these three companies. Other companies will be described at length in the next chapter.

LVMH

In Table 1.5, we took LVMH's sales to be approximately €11.5 billion because we removed the distribution activities from the total of €15.3 billion in 2006. The total picture is presented in Table 1.6.

Table 1.6: LVMH: Sales and results, 2006			
	Sales **(€ million)**	**Operating profit** **(€ million)**	**Profit/sales (%)**
Wines and spirits	2,984	962	32.1
Fashion and leather goods	5,222	1,633	31.3
Perfumes and cosmetics	2,519	222	8.8
Watches and jewelry	500	80	16.0
Selective distribution	3,891	400	10.3
Miscellaneous	(57)	(125)	
Total	15,306	3,172	20.7

Source: LVMH annual reports

As we can see, LVMH is a very impressive group, with nearly one-third of its luxury business done in the fashion and leather division. It is also striking to note that this business provides 53% of the group's total operating profits.

This was clearly a very good year for the group, after several years of limited growth. In 2001 total sales were €12.2 billion; in 2002, €12.7 billion; in 2003, €12.0 billion; and in 2004, €12.6 billion. Some analysts questioned the performance of those years, but there was a similar situation for all the European companies, which suffered from selling largely to U.S.-dollar-based markets. When the dollar weakens, it is very difficult to make a profit and maintain growth. This situation was reversed with the strengthening of the dollar in the years 2004, 2005 and 2006, but was seen again in 2007 when the dollar weakened once more.

LVMH's overall performance for 2004, 2005 and 2006 is summarized in Table 1.7.

Table 1.7: Scorecard of LVMH results (€ million)

	2006		2005		2004	
Sales	15,306	100%	13,910	100%	12,481	100%
Operating profit	3,172	20.7%	2,743	19.7%	2,372	19.0%
Net profit	2,160	14.1%	1,668	12.0%	1,402	11.2%

Source: LVMH annual reports

The net profit of 14.1% on sales in 2006 was one of the highest in the industry. But this percentage is interesting for another reason: Table 1.6 shows that for the perfume business, there were recorded sales of €2,519 billion, with an operating profit of €222 million and an estimated net profit of €56 million.[2] In other words, the perfumes and cosmetics division is almost breaking even.

In the luxury sectors, only two activities were profitable: the fashion and leather goods division, and the wines and spirits division. In fact, in percentage terms, the wines and spirits division (with 32.1% of operating profit on sales, and brands including Krug,

luxury **brand** management

Dom Pérignon, Moët and Chandon, Veuve Clicquot and Hennessy) was more profitable than the fashion and luxury division (31.3%). In the fashion and luxury division, LVMH has many brands, including Louis Vuitton, Donna Karan, Fendi, Loewe, Celine, Marc Jacobs, Givenchy, Thomas Pink, Pucci, Berluti, Rossimoda and StefanoB. The question here is to determine which of these should be given priority. We would suggest that, based on size and potential, Fendi and Donna Karan will be given major resources and develop. But what is the future of the other brands, if they are not profitable?

In geographical terms, the group is well balanced, as can be seen in Table 1.8.

Table 1.8: LVMH geographical split, 2006

France	15%
Rest of Europe	22%
United States	26%
Japan	13%
Rest of Asia	17%
Other markets	7%
Total	100%

Source: LVMH annual report

Of course, this geographical split varies across divisions and brands.

Richemont

The Compagnie Financière Richemont, based in Geneva, with sales of €4.8 billion is the second major operator in the luxury fashion, jewelry and watch businesses. Its results in the past five or six years have been lackluster, probably in part because of the relative weakness of the U.S. dollar. Its sales and profit figures for the last eight years are shown in Table 1.9.

Table 1.9: Richemont historical sales and profit (€ million)

	Sales	Operating profit	Net profit
2007	4,827	916	1,329
2006	4,308	713	608
2005	3,717	505	414
2004	3,375	246	320
2003	3,651	259	728
2002	3,860	489	331
2001	3,684	712	528
2000	2,924	534	357

Source: Richemont annual reports

As the Richemont fiscal year ends in March, its 2007 results are comparable with the 2006 results of other companies. For 2007, the operating profit was higher than the level of 2001. The company's results by product lines are given in Table 1.10.

Table 1.10: Richemont performance by product lines, 2005–2007 (€ million)

	Sales			Operating profit		
	2007	2006	2005	2007	2006	2005
Jewelry houses	2,437	2,227	1,938	667	616	460
Specialty watches	1,203	1,063	870	274	227	148
Writing instruments	583	497	424	110	83	59
Leather and accessories	307	283	259	−11	−38	−40
Other businesses	297	238	226	20	22	13
Unallocated	—	—	—	—	−197	−162
Total	4,827	4,308	3,717	916	713	505

Source: Richemont annual reports

luxury **brand** management

As with LVMH, figures are not given by brand but by category. What can be said is that in 2007 the jewelry houses (Cartier and Van Cleef & Arpels) represented 50% of sales and 73% of operating profit, with Cartier probably being the biggest, if not the only contributor. Specialty watches (which include Vacheron Constantin, Baume & Mercier, Jaeger-LeCoultre, Lange und Söhne, Officine Panerai, IWC and Piaget) also performed quite well.

The performance of Montblanc (with Montegrappa included in the figures) was certainly quite impressive as well. The only bad news was in the leather-goods category (which includes Dunhill and Lancel), which was the slowest-growing category and lost €130 million in a period of four years.

Richemont is both a jeweler and a watchmaker. It has a star brand in Cartier, a very strong brand with Montblanc, and major problems with Lancel and Dunhill. But who knows: those two brands, if well positioned and with a new brand focus, could become the stars of the company in 10 years. This is what is peculiar in the luxury business.

PPR Gucci

This group was created in 1999 by the purchase by PPR of a minority interest in Gucci and the immediate purchase of the YSL fashion and YSL beauty group. Since then the group has purchased many other brands, including Bottega Veneta, Boucheron and Balenciaga, and is one of the few groups that has grown by purchasing existing brands and by developing its own from scratch. This latter category includes, for example, Alexander McQueen and Stella McCartney.

For PPR Gucci's luxury divisions, results are not very detailed. Table 1.11 summarizes the existing data.

Table 1.11: PPR luxury division performance (€ million)

	Sales			Operating profit		
	2006	2005	2004	2006	2005	2004
Gucci	2,101	1,807	1,902	612	485	535
YSL fashion	194	162	196	−49	−66	−71
YSL beauty	626	613	734	32	15	26
Bottega Veneta	267	160	113	55	14	N.A.
All others	378	294	268	38	N.A.	N.A.
Total	3,568	3,036	3,213	565	390	394

Source: PPR annual reports

Aside from Gucci, the figures are not great. Given the non-availability of details for so many of the brands, we think it's fair to assume that all but Gucci and YSL beauty lost money in 2004. In 2005, it seems that Bottega Veneta became profitable thanks to impressive growth, and YSL beauty experienced a strong decline in sales (–16.5%) but was able to break even thanks to cost cutting and restructuring. For YSL fashion, sales were thin, with losses for 2006 at around €49 million.

PPR is a good example of a group with a difficult balance between brands with good long-term prospects and brands with only limited potential.

Can the single-brand company survive?

The answer to this question is quite simple. Yes, it does make sense to be a "pure player" in this industry, to have only one brand and to manage it as well as possible. Armani, Hermès, Bulgari or Tiffany's are prime examples of what can be achieved.

In multi-brand portfolios with a number of star brands, management must decide where to invest and those brands deemed

luxury **brand** management

to be of lower priority have a difficult time. On the other hand, the brands with high potential but which are struggling cannot invest as much as they would need, because they have to balance out the losses of the smaller brands.

Take Tiffany's, for example, whose recent performance is recorded in Table 1.12.

Table 1.12: Tiffany's scorecard (US$million)

	2006	2005	2004	2003
Sales	2,648	1,690	1,556	1,412
Operating profit	415	270	207	251
Net earnings	253	180	215	152

Source: Tiffany's annual reports

In 2006, the company's operating profit was 16% of sales, which was less than that of rival Cartier but quite impressive nevertheless. The difference between operating and net earnings was 6%.

Clearly large and diversified groups are not necessarily more profitable than individual brands (such as Chanel or Prada, for example). It is true that groups provide an opportunity for small brands to find cash to finance their growth. The idea is that the new brands will one day provide future growth and profit to the company as a whole. This may well prove to be true for some but by no means all.

To sum up our findings in this first chapter: the luxury business is a different business from non-luxury sectors and follows different rules. Timing, financial constraints and the effects of size are clearly different. The keys to success are different, and even though the multi-brand groups are powerful, it is possible to remain small, independent, profitable and growing as a single-brand company.

In the next chapter, we will analyze each of the major sectors in the luxury field.

Endnotes

[1]Bernard Dubois, L'art du Marketing, Village Mondial, Paris, 1998, p.292.

[2]Calculated as follows: The difference between operational profit and net profit is 6.6% on sales. For perfumes, sales are €2,519 million and the operational profit is €222 million. If we subtract from the latter amount the average difference between operational profit and net profit (2,519 x 0.066 = €166.25 million), that gives us the net profit for the perfume and cosmetic division: 222–166 = 56 million.

chapter **2**

MAJOR
Luxury
SECTORS

We are so used to the idea of luxury brands that we tend to forget that this is a relatively new concept. For many years, businesses that we now include in the luxury sector were considered completely separate and were represented by different federations: the Federation of Ready to Wear, the Federation of Leather Goods, the Federation of Perfumes and Cosmetics, and so on. On the face of it, in the manufacturing and sales processes, a bottle of champagne and a lady's dress have very little in common. The champagne is produced through an automated system using very modern machinery. It is then sold in special wine stores but also in supermarkets and hypermarkets. On the other hand, a lady's dress is often made by hand and in very limited numbers, and sold in exclusive luxury stores around the world.

The French were probably the first to understand the fact that a bottle of champagne and a sophisticated dress do have something in common, and this is why in 1954 they created the "Comité Colbert," an association to promote the concept of luxury.

The stated values of Comité Colbert could be an introduction to the global luxury concept: its members, it informs us, "share the same ideas of a contemporary art de vivre and constantly develop and enrich this through their diversity. They have a common vision of the importance of international ambition, of authentic know-how and high standards, of design and creativity and of professional ethics." Its members are drawn from the following "metiers," or trade activities:

- *Haute couture* and accessories
- Perfumes
- Jewelry
- Designer homeware
- Hotel and gastronomy
- Great wines, champagne and cognac
- Publishing
- Decoration

When the Comité Colbert was created and the concept of "luxury business" developed, it wasn't immediately obvious that these "metiers" had so much in common. Now, however, the idea is commonplace, as this book can testify.

It is interesting to note that the Comité Colbert does not include luxury automobiles, probably for the simple reason that France does not manufacture any of these. While "hotels" are included, there is no mention of luxury cruises, special airline activities or specific or cultural travel agencies.

In this chapter, we will describe the luxury world by individual sectors, so that their characteristics and key success factors can be clearly identified.

luxury **brand** management

READY-TO-WEAR ACTIVITIES

Under this heading we include both ladies' and men's ready-to-wear and *haute couture*, which in Chapter 1 we estimated to amount to around €20 billion in volume.

While other businesses such as perfumes and cosmetics or wines and spirits may have greater sales, in image terms the luxury fashion business is undoubtedly the most important. Through its fashion shows, its constant renewal and its leadership in new trends, new shapes and new colors, it remains the sector that is most frequently mentioned in the press and that is most closely associated with the artistic world.

While the majority of students in luxury programs want to end up in the fashion business, less than 20% of the "luxury jobs" are in a field where most staff are in stores, presenting and selling the merchandise to the final consumer. As we saw earlier, marketing teams are quite small and production is generally subcontracted. Unfortunately, this is also a field where profitability is not always easy to achieve. For many brands, the fashion business remains unprofitable, and we will try to explain why.

In this section, we will describe the specific fashion market, the key management issues and the most common organizational structure found in this sector.

The fashion business and its operation
The players

The Italian business is by far the strongest, with worldwide sales that we estimate at around €12 billion.

The Italians arrived on the luxury fashion scene later than the French, with Armani, Gucci, Prada, Valentino and Versace, for example, coming to the fore in the mid 1970s and the 1980s. In some ways they are better positioned than the French in that they are still perceived as new, and they provide a very large diversity, opening new stores in the major cities of the world. Customers love the appearance of "newness" that the Italians have been able to build in their brands. While 20 years ago in the top luxury shopping complexes, such as the Imperial Tower in Tokyo or the Peninsula Hotel in Hong Kong, most stores were presenting French fashion brands, today Italian brands are much more present and much more powerful. Customers are attracted by their sophistication and the quality of their products.

It's worth reminding ourselves that many of the top Italian brands did not start out in the fashion business. Guccio Gucci, for example, was a handbag manufacturer; Salvatore Ferragamo was a shoemaker; Edoardo and Adele Fendi were fur specialists; and Mario Prada designed and sold handbags, shoes, trunks and suitcases. But from their craftsmanship base, they were able to start ladies' ready-to-wear lines that were interesting, creative and fashionable.

Take Fendi, for example. As a fur brand, Fendi was much less known and less powerful than Revillon. But while Revillon stayed as a "pure player," selling fur almost exclusively in a declining market, Fendi began to distribute shoes, then leather ready-to-wear, then very successful ladies' handbags. In the 1970s, it hired Karl Lagerfeld to design a ladies' ready-to-wear collection. At first it sold very little; but it persisted and now, with sales around €400 million, Fendi is a fully fledged brand, strong in both handbags and ready-to-wear. For its part, Revillon began to move away from fur, but not until the 1990s. But its approach lacked strength, intelligence and consistency and today the brand has almost disappeared.

As they moved away from their original businesses and into ready-to-wear, the Italian brands found a very receptive local community with strong fabric creators, with many ready-to-wear manufacturers and subcontractors and a creative, open environment that was ready to take risks. For many years, the Fendi ready-to-wear was produced through an outside licensing agreement and sales were very small. While it was not always profitable, it received strong and intelligent support from the company and, over time, this support has paid off.

Italy has never promoted *haute couture*, even if brands like Armani or Valentino are happy to be part of the Paris fashion shows. They believe in creative ready-to-wear lines that sell in the

luxury **brand** management

stores, and put all their efforts into lavish twice-yearly fashion collections. And the products sell.

Though the Italians have fewer licensing deals than the French, they still have many selective licenses, as we will explain later. The market is very open, without any one brand claiming an exclusive position. The industrial sector is open and fast. Though Prada has been producing ready-to-wear collections for less than 20 years now, it is perceived as a very strong fashion brand, as if it had always been that way.

From the start, the Italian brands were run with a mix of creative talent and strong business competence. Franco Moschino developed his own business with a very strong manager, Tiziano Gusti; Gianni Versace first developed his brand with a strong businessman who was one of his classmates, Claudio Luti; and Giorgio Armani started his business in 1975 with the late Sergio Galeotti and has become a very rare breed—a designer who is also a businessman.

The French business is more traditional, with the strongest brands such as Chanel and Dior being created before or immediately after the Second World War. The French were innovators at that time, with Christian Dior inventing the licensing business that later became the *raison d'être* of many brands, including Pierre Cardin. In addition to creating *haute couture*, they were the first to develop perfume businesses, using their name and their image: first, Coco Chanel in 1921, then Carven and Dior immediately after the war. To this day, French fashion brands have a strong presence in the perfume business.

But the French, in a traditional Gallic way, also invented barriers to entry. In the 1970s and '80s, it was quite difficult to create a new fashion brand in France. Launching an *haute couture* collection was expensive and difficult. French ready-to-wear manufacturers were very few and did not want to handle small or upcoming brands. New brands were thus obliged to subcontract their ready-to-wear lines in Italy.

The newcomers then began to position themselves as "creators," making dresses that would command immediate notice; but this did not work well either. In the last 25 years, only Kenzo and Jean Paul Gaultier have been able to create fully fledged brands. Thierry Mugler has developed awareness and a thriving perfume business, but not a strong, viable fashion business. Claude Montana was certainly one of the most gifted creators of his generation, but his business is no longer strong. Other gifted creators such as Angelo Tarlazzi, Myrène de Prémonville, Azzedine Alaïa and Hervé Léger have a reason for being but have been unable to establish lasting fashion brands.

A new generation of designers with a strong business sense, such as Regina Rubens or Paul Ka, is now emerging. In the long run, they may well create strong worldwide brands.

Table 2.1 highlights the brands that have achieved sales of over €500 million. They have managed to do this because they can invest heavily in advertising, have the necessary volume to open stores almost anywhere in the world and have the customer attractiveness necessary to reach break-even. These are the brands that can generally be found in the major luxury shopping galleries of the world.

Table 2.1: The fashion mega-brands (sales above €500 million)

FRANCE	ITALY	
Chanel	Armani	Max Mara
Dior	Dolce & Gabbana	Prada
Hermès	Ermenigildo Zegna	Salvatore Ferragamo
Louis Vuitton	Gucci	

luxury **brand** management

Table 2.2 illustrates what we might call the "second-tier" companies: those that have achieved sales in excess of €100 million. (Below this level, brands can only be national or strong in two or three countries, but they cannot have a direct presence in the major markets of the world.) With this size, it is possible to have profitable stores, perhaps not in every major city of the world, but certainly in those such as New York and Hong Kong where there are enough luxury specialists to make it profitable.

Unfortunately, companies with sales below €100 million cannot easily afford to open stores around the world, and even if they could, they probably don't have the awareness, the potential or the merchandise attractiveness to make those stores profitable.

We had originally intended to include only fashion brands, but then only Chanel and Dior would have been included on the French

Table 2.2: Second-tier fashion brands (sales of €100–€500 million)

FRANCE		ITALY	
Agnès B.	Lanvin	Alberta Ferretti	Les Copains
Celine	Longchamp	Bottega Veneta	Mariella Burani
Chloé	Sonia Rykiel	Blumarine	Mariella Rinaldi
Jean Paul Gaultier	Yves Saint Laurent	Brioni	Marni
Kenzo		Etro	Missoni
		Fendi	Miu Miu
		Ferre	Moschino
		Furla	Nazareno Gabrielli
		Krizia	Roberto Cavalli
		La Perla	Trussardi
		Laura Biagiotti	Valentino
		Loro Piana	Versace

side of Table 2.1. But this would have been unfair on Louis Vuitton and Hermès, which are among the most powerful French brands and which are also engaged in ready-to-wear activities. For this same reason, we were forced to add Longchamp, Furla and Bottega Veneta to Table 2.2.

In doing so, we clearly show the strong advantage in size, diversity and power the Italian brands have over their French counterparts. We ought not to forget, though, that in leather goods the French have a very strong advantage, with their two major brands being above anybody else in this product category.

Other nationalities are also part of this business, but they cannot be compared with either the French or the Italians. The Americans Ralph Lauren, Calvin Klein and Donna Karan have done quite well in developing a new concept of "lifestyle brands"—products geared to a specific style. The creator in each case is also a businessperson and has developed ready-to-wear products addressed to a specific type of clientele in their stores. Ralph Lauren does this beautifully with his Old England and New England traditional style that fits a certain type of wealthy clientele looking for nostalgic products and a country atmosphere for clothing to be worn in an urban environment.

But to be effective, the American "lifestyle" concept requires heavy advertising budgets, and this has created a barrier to entry that makes it difficult for newcomers to be part of this very sophisticated crowd.

Perhaps because of its climate, Britain is home to two very important businesses that were first built around raincoats: Burberry and Aquascutum. It is also successful with strong men's wear brands such as Paul Smith, Dunhill and Daks. It also has Jaeger, a knitwear brand positioned at a middle range. Newcomers like Vivienne Westwood bring something interesting but are still small by world standards.

Germany has Escada and Hugo Boss (which used to belong to the Italian group Marzotto). Two of its brands are particularly interesting because they are different: Jil Sander, because she

luxury **brand** management

first developed a strong collection for executive women; and Joop, because he developed a very strong name in German-speaking countries on the basis of licensing deals.

Spain is home to the internationally renowned brands Loewe, Purificación Garcia and Adolfo Dominguez. Other creators like Pertegaz, Victorio y Luchino, Roberto Verino and Toni Miro are strong at home but have never been able to develop outside of their own country.

The Belgian designers Ann Demeulemeester or Dries Van Noten should also be included on the list, as should Switzerland's Akris.

The reason for speaking of nationalities and looking at overall business volume is because luxury fashion is a business and should be considered as such. The objective of a ready-to-wear luxury brand is to become a worldwide success. As we will discuss later, the nationality of the designers has a strong impact on the positioning of the business outside of their respective national territories.

How to develop a brand

As a brand starts locally and develops, it needs to do things correctly from the outset. This process requires both a strong creator and a strong business person. The creator has to develop a unique style, but should also have someone close by who can be relied upon to take care of business development and channel that creativity into areas that translate into sales at the cash register without constraining the designer's creativity. The partnerships of Giorgio Armani and Sergio Galeotti and of Yves Saint Laurent and Pierre Bergé are object lessons in the kind of teamwork that is required for success. A strong and trusting relationship, with complementary styles and instincts, is very important to the development of a ready-to-wear brand.

The ladies' ready-to-wear line is what gives a strong identity to many successful brands. It provides press coverage worldwide and creates an awareness in retailers and consumers alike. As brands develop the "total look" concept, ready-to-wear acts as the anchor: it is very difficult to sell branded belts, panties or shoes without a strong image for dresses or ladies' suits.

To develop a brand, it is necessary to have a presence in many large cities around the world, and ladies' ready-to-wear is the way to go as it enables the creation of a network of retail stores under the brand name. These stores often sell more accessories and handbags than ready-to-wear, but it is the ready-to-wear line that makes the shop window attractive and creates a fashionable store environment. It's a bit of a chicken-and-egg proposition, really: to sell accessories and handbags requires a strong name and a strong ready-to-wear line. To be able to develop and promote a strong ready-to-wear line requires the volume obtained through the sales of handbags and accessories.

How to make money

The paradox is that many ladies' fashion activities are unprofitable. As we will see later, the set up of a new ladies' ready-to-wear collection requires expensive prototypes, runway products and showroom collections that are only profitable when the volume is there. This is also the case for men's ready-to-wear lines, which are often difficult to differentiate from one brand to another one. Store activities are also very dependent on the level of sales that can be achieved. In other words, as mentioned earlier, it is not possible to make money opening a store for a brand that is not well known and not "fashionable" and attractive enough.

In fact, as we will discuss later, the best way to finance the start-up and development of a ladies' ready-to-wear collection is to develop license deals in other product categories.

What must be said here is that many brands are losing money in this area. Eurostaff undertook a study of the profitability of 21 French ready-to-wear brands in 1994. Of these only seven showed significant profits; three just broke even; and 11 lost money. And Chanel, with a net profit equivalent to €67 million on ready-to-wear sales of €570 million, was more profitable than the rest of the sector combined.

Key management issues
The creative process

We return here to the most important element of style: the creator. The role of management within this area is to organize a workable plan that sets out the requirements for the coming season: How many suits with pants? How many suits with skirts? How many cocktail dresses? It will also specify retail price targets and the target cost of the fabric to be used. The designer must then perform and create within these precise guidelines that ensure that the final product will sell at an acceptable price in the stores.

Similar planning is also required for accessories and other products, each of which must be coherent with the rest and readily identifiable with the brand. A Dior tie should be distinguishable from an Yves Saint Laurent tie, and each product bearing a brand name should bring a specific quality and an added value to the total product group. This can only be realized through coordination and clear design directives.

While management should not be directly involved with the creative process, it must set the rules and the processes for planning and reviewing, for harmonizing the different product lines, and for analyzing what has/has not been selling. Management should also take charge of ensuring the quality of raw materials (fabrics, buttons, technical materials, lining and so on) and of manufacturing.

The creativity of people such as Karl Lagerfeld and Giorgio Armani should not be controlled. It is simply a matter of setting guidelines, objectives and reviews so that the creative process can be used to improve the brand's standing in the marketplace.

A worldwide presence

The balance of activity for a fashion brand takes into account image-creation items (such as free-standing flagship stores in major cities) and image-consumption activities (such as licensing deals for secondary products).

The distribution of ready-to-wear fashion products varies in accordance with the particular needs of specific markets. In the

United States and Japan, for example, luxury fashion brands are distributed mainly through department stores. The buyers of the different stores visit the Milan and Paris fashion shows and buy by brand in accordance with their "open to buy" budgets. This is the most important engine of brand development. But if the brand wants to create a special strength or awareness on its own, it must also build its own flagship stores in New York, Los Angeles, Tokyo, Osaka and other main cities.

In other countries, European brands use an importer or a distributor to take charge of developing sales in a given territory. This requires a showroom and a showroom collection whose products end up in multi-brand stores and local department stores that do not buy direct.

In countries such as Hong Kong or Singapore, the business is run in part by individual fashion retailers such as Joyce in Hong Kong or Glamourette in Singapore. These retailers are strong at identifying new brands with potential and buy them before anybody else in the country.

Why is it difficult to make money?

In this ready-to-wear activity, it all boils down to the volume of business created and sold. In fact, when the volume is not there, the cost of manufacturing a dress becomes extremely high.

If we take the example of a women's suit sold at retail for €950, the wholesale price will be about €395 (that is, a mark-up coefficient of 2.4). Table 2.3 gives an indication of how manufacturing costs vary with volume.

Table 2.3: Cost of making a women's suit in France (€)		
	If large volume	If small volume
Manufacturing cost	100	300
Accessories (buttons, lining, etc.)	50	60
Fabric	100	115
Total Cost	**250**	**475**

The manufacturing cost can be multiplied by two or three if the item is to be made in small volumes. In such cases, it becomes too expensive to use a laser cutter and the way in which individual pieces are located on the fabric may not be as economical as with larger volumes. The process of making the suit may then become entirely manual, with no guarantee that the quality is much better at the end of it all.

The economic picture is also dependent on whether the products are all sold at full price, or some have to be sold at bargain prices, with discounts that can range from 30–70%. When production runs are small and most products are only sold at bargain prices, profitability is certainly no longer in the horizon, keeping in mind that in a good season only 50% of the collection is normally sold at full price.

This is where license deals come into the picture, as they provide the cash necessary in the early days to invest heavily in these ready-to-wear activities and to ensure they are successful.

The most common organizational structure

It is a fairly common feature within many luxury fashion brands that the position of marketing manager does not exist. The reason for this is that the role of the marketing manager is to find out from the consumer what the brand should be, and that could be in direct conflict with the designer, whose job is to create what the consumer should have. Nevertheless, it is extremely necessary to have one person whose rare competence is to be able to provide unobtrusive guidelines that force the designer to look at what happens in the stores. This position is generally referred to in the U.S. and U.K. fashion circles as the "Merchandiser."

Another specific role within luxury fashion is that of the Communications and/or Public Relations Manager. This person generally reports to the General Manager and acts as a very important conduit between the GM and the designer.

Luxury fashion structures seldom have factories (there is generally a Purchasing Manager or a Supply Chain Manager in charge of products). So the most important jobs fall within the field of store activities: Store Managers, of course, but also Area Managers, Country Retail Managers, Regional Retail Managers and Retail Merchandising Manager worldwide.

As mentioned earlier, the number of staff is limited and these are in direct contact either with the designer or with the final consumer.

PERFUMES AND COSMETICS

As we saw in Chapter 1, this is one of the largest luxury sectors, with total sales estimated at around €30 billion. It is also the largest in staff, as it employs probably more than 30% of all luxury-goods employees. It is also relatively concentrated, with Paris, New York and Geneva being major headquarters.

This business entails selling standardized products in large quantities at low unit prices and, in this, is somewhat reminiscent of the fast-moving consumer-goods market. But, as we will discuss, this is a very different market because the consumer expects to find a product with a very high aesthetic content and something that is special every time.

The market

This is, strangely enough, a relatively recent market. For many years individual perfumers would extract fragrances from flowers through an alembic, as described in Patrick Süskind's novel (and subsequent film) *Perfume*. Perfumers generally had another activity: they also sold gloves. This is why a French perfumer is now developing retail stores under the name "Parfumeur et Gantier" (Perfume and Glovemaker). The mass-market business of selling the same standard product over time to a larger population started in the eighteenth century in the city of Köln, where they developed the "Kölnish Wasser" or "Eau de Cologne" under the German brand 4711. Guerlain came into being at the end of the nineteenth century. All other brands were started in the twentieth century: Caron, then Chanel, Patou, Lancôme and Lanvin. Most of the major brands such as Estée Lauder, Dior, Armani and Ralph Lauren were created after 1950.

luxury **brand** management

Given the fact that the average product is sold at retail for less than €50 and that the total sales of €30 billion includes products sold at wholesale and export prices, it is likely that as many as two billion units of luxury products are manufactured and bought every year. In major developed markets, product penetration reaches 80% of households, with a minimum purchase of one to two units a year for perfumes and much more for cosmetics. This a very large market.

Consumer expectations

When they buy a perfume, consumers are looking for an intensely personal, sensuous, almost narcissistic, pleasure (which comes from holding and opening an aesthetically pleasing bottle and breathing in a sophisticated scent that conveys a sense of luxury and personal satisfaction). But they are also looking for social reassurance: they want to appear sophisticated and to have "good taste." Perfumes provide a personal dream of luxury at a reasonable price. It is great to be able to afford the luxury and sophistication of Chanel or Yves Saint Laurent for less than €50.

For cosmetic products, customer expectations are quite different. For make-up, which women often carry in their handbags, products have strong social connotations: there is a much greater degree of sophistication conveyed by opening a handbag and taking out a Chanel lipstick than there is in pulling out a mass-market product from the same handbag. For skin-care products, expectations are again different as they deal with a long-term investment in personal appearance—the need to look good and the hope of remaining good looking for a long time.

What is clear is that consumers are looking for much more than is actually contained in the bottle. This is why "knock-offs" (those cheap perfumes sold for a couple of dollars in U.S. supermarkets with the claim "if you like Youth Dew from Estée Lauder, you will love this perfume number 17") have never done well. Of course the fragrance is an important part of the deal, but the perceived quality of the bottle, its aesthetic value and the social reinforcement it provides is certainly much more important.

In fact, consumers are much more interested in what we might call "the environment" of the product than in the product itself.

Product types

For perfumes, the mass-market segment has never really worked. Only 20% of perfume units are sold through mass markets and this has not changed in the last 25 years. Major mass-market merchandisers have offered extended low price ranges but without significant success. Most women, whatever their level of income, prefer to buy a €50 Dior perfume in a sophisticated perfumery or department store than spend €10 on a little-known brand in their supermarket.

The make-up category is divided into two sub-segments. For "social" make-up (lipstick or touch-up products that they carry in their handbags and use in front of others), women buy—and will continue to buy—the right brand and in a sophisticated environment. On the other hand, for "personal" make-up products (such as nail polish), most of the buying is done in supermarkets or other mass-markets distributors, which represent around 75% of unit volume.

Skin-care products are a different case again. In the 1950s and '60s, most products were sold through department stores and perfumeries, as the consumers were looking for advice on which products were suited to their specific skin type. Today, consumers are much more knowledgeable about skin-care products. Most of the units purchased (around 80%) are bought through mass-market distributors. Mass-market brands such as Plénitude de L'Oréal or Procter & Gamble's Oil of Olay have done a very good job in catering to such a market.

Of course, the €30 billion we mentioned relates only to the luxury part of this market. How this will evolve over time remains to be seen, but it will all depend on the quality of the products and the diversity of the luxury segment. What we can say is that for a perfume or a cosmetic product, consumers are very interested in the aesthetic values of the bottle or the jar, of the top, of the outer carton box, of the specific luxury positioning of the selective products, and of the dream conveyed by the concept, which all

luxury **brand** management

combine to enrich the purchasing experience and the pleasure to be had from using the products.

They are also very interested in the sophistication of the purchasing environment. They want the products to be available but they value an impression of scarcity, as if the products were available only to them. Of course, this is not easy to achieve for products that are sold by several billion units every year.

The concept of "affordable" luxury for top exclusive brands in a sophisticated environment will remain the key to the development of the market for years to come.

The financial aspect

The basic principle of luxury perfumes and cosmetics is that the same product, generally manufactured in one single location or, at most, in two or three locations, must be available everywhere in the world, with the same luxury presentation to the different national customers.

Products must therefore be shipped everywhere, and the necessary customs duties must be paid everywhere in the world. The same product must therefore go through different distribution phases depending on the markets in which it is to be offered, as illustrated in Table 2.4.

We have taken the example of the same product that would be sold in France and in Chile at the same retail price. In France, things are simple: the company operates with its own sales force and the billing is done at the wholesale level: the company nets €50 for each product that is sold for €100 retail. In Chile, things are a bit more complicated. The product is generally sold by a local distributor who works on a margin of 50% of the wholesale value. Also, a special local budget of 15% of wholesale (i.e. €8.25) is set aside for local advertising and promotional activities. The landed cost is therefore €19.25, on which duties, freight and insurance have been paid. This means that the French manufacturer will receive only €14.80 for each €100 of retail sales in Chile. Thus, the system requires very high gross margins in France for the Chilean

Table 2.4: Comparison of cost structures for a product sold in different countries (based on an assumed retail price of €100 in the French and the Chilean markets: figures could equally be in US$ or any other currency)

	France	Chile	Coefficients for Chile
Retail price	100	100	675.76
Wholesale price	50	55	371.62
Distributor or agent's margin		27.5	185.81
Local advertising budget		8.25	55.74
Landed cost		19.25	130.00
Paris ex-factory		14.80	100.00

business to be profitable. In this case, a gross margin of at least 70%, and probably 80%, is necessary.

While the figures may differ according to the country being targeted, very high margins are generally necessary in the perfumes and cosmetics category. Bear in mind, too, that advertising and promotional budgets (incorporating media advertising, samples, testers, in-store displays and other PR activities) are very high and can be anything from 15% to 25% of wholesale prices.

The major operators
The major brands
To be strong on a worldwide level, sales of €300 million are necessary. The brands that have achieved this level are listed in Table 2.5.

Table 2.5: Brands with sales above €300 million

Armani	Gucci
Biotherm	Guerlain
Calvin Klein	Hugo Boss
Chanel	Lancôme
Clinique	Sisley
Dior	Yves Saint Laurent
Estée Lauder	

Of these 12 brands, five (Estée Lauder, Chanel, Dior, Armani and Lancôme) have sales exceeding €1 billion. All have large advertising budgets (in most cases, above €100 million) and have established a strong presence everywhere in the world.

Also, most of these brands operate in the different segments of the industry. Half—Estée Lauder, Chanel, Clinique, Dior, Guerlain and Lancôme—operate in all three segments (perfumes, skin-care and make-up); just two—Gucci and Hugo Boss—deal exclusively in perfumes.

Table 2.6 lists the second-tier brands (that is, those with sales between €100 million and €300 million), which also have a strong presence.

Table 2.6: Second-tier brands (sales €100–300 million)

Azzaro	Kenzo
Bulgari	Lacoste
Burberry	Lancaster
Cacharel	Nina Ricci
Carolina Herrera	Paco Rabanne
Davidoff	Ralph Lauren
Dolce & Gabbana	Salvatore Ferragamo
Givenchy	Shu Uemura
Issey Miyake	Thierry Mugler
Jean Paul Gaultier	

It is in this group that the fight for survival is the most clear-cut. Of these 20 brands, some are growing very fast while others are in decline.

The group of brands with sales below €100 million offers a different pattern. Those that make up this group are many and varied and include Boucheron, Van Cleef, Hermès, Paloma Picasso and Salvador Dali.

The major corporations

This business, despite its creative outlook and its international flavor, is really quite concentrated, with the 10 firms shown in Table 2.7 representing about 50% of the total sector.

Table 2.7: Performance (€ million) of the major luxury perfumes and cosmetics companies (2006)

	Status	Sales	Operating profit	Net Profit	Total Group Sales
Estée Lauder	Autonomous firm (stock market)	4,967	529	317	4,967
L'Oréal Produits de Luxe	A division of L'Oréal (stock market)	3,773	724	580 (E)	15,790
LVMH Perfumes and Cosmetics	A division of LVMH (stock market)	2,519	222	56 (E)	15,306
Procter & Gamble Prestige Products	A division of P & G (stock market)	1,300 (E)	280 (E)	130 (E)	54,000
Chanel	A division of Chanel (Private)	1,300 (E)	N.A.	N.A.	3,600 (E)
Coty Prestige	A part of Coty Beauty and Prestige (Private)	1,280	N.A.	N.A.	2,320
Clarins	Autonomous firm (stock market)	967	127	223	967
YSL Beauté	Part of PPR Gucci (stock market)	626	32	0 (E)	3,568
Shiseido Europe	The European division of Shiseido (stock market)	582	39	17 (E)	4,150
Sisley	Autonomous private firm	450 (E)	85 (E)	50 (E)	450 (E)

Source: Annual reports or authors' estimates. For Shiseido, we have taken the figure reported in its annual report. It includes Beauté Prestige International (Issey Miyake, Jean Paul Gaultier and Narcisse Rodriguez) and Decleor (which also includes Carita). It also includes the luxury distribution of Shiseido in Europe. This figure includes Prestige luxury products sold in Asia and the Americas under the Shiseido brand.

(E) indicates authors' estimates.

luxury **brand** management

Estée Lauder, based in New York, began life as a unique cosmetics firm. Today, it is a very diversified group that has added Clinique, Aramis, Prescriptive, MAC, Donna Karan (under license from LVMH) and Joe Malone, among others, to its brand offerings. In the last few years, it has developed new modern positioning perhaps best illustrated by what it is doing with Origins. It has come with distinctive brands, sold solely through its own stores, rather than through department stores, using "natural" or "active" positioning. The company, still family controlled, is traded on the New York stock market and is very profitable.

L'Oréal, Produits de Luxe, based in Paris, is also a strong operator. It has brands managed from Paris (Lancôme, Armani and Biotherm, for example), but also operates brands from New York (Ralph Lauren and Kiehl's) and Tokyo (Shu Uemura). Its Lancôme brand is very strong in cosmetics, but less so in perfume. Its other perfume lines include Paloma Picasso, Guy Laroche, Cacharel and many others. This division of L'Oréal seems to be very profitable.

The LVMH perfumes and cosmetics division is the third-largest, thanks to Dior, which represents about half of the total. Guerlain is a great brand, but is better known in France than abroad. Though Givenchy has experienced some difficulties in recent years, these appear to have been solved. Kenzo is an interesting growing brand. The fact is that the overall financial performance is not great. It is fair to assume that Dior is quite profitable: this being the case, it is also fair to assume that some of the other brands are probably having difficulties.

The Procter & Gamble Prestige Products division is the result of direct launches (Hugo Boss and Laura Biagiotti), the purchase of the German group Wella (Gucci, Rochas, Montblanc and others) and additional purchases (Lacoste, Patou, Escada and Dolce & Gabbana). In addition to having some of the best brands in the market, it also has less sophisticated brands such as Naomi Campbell and Gabriela Sabatini. The division is based in Geneva and does not publish any figures; sales are included in a very large "beauty division;" which includes, for example, mass-market shampoos.

Coty Prestige, based in New York, but also in Paris and Germany, arose from the merger of the Coty Group, always strong in the United States and Australia, and a group of German perfume brands created 15 years ago by Benckiser as a diversification activity. It has been able to develop or acquire some of the best industry licenses, including Davidoff, Calvin Klein, Lancaster, Jil Sander, Joop and Vera Wang. It has "celebrity perfumes" such as Jennifer Lopez and Sarah Jessica Parker, and has licensed Marc Jacobs, designer of Louis Vuitton ready-to-wear, and Chloé from the Richemont Group. This is a rapidly growing private group that is much more involved in perfumes than in cosmetics.

Chanel, a private company based in Switzerland, does not communicate any sales or profit data. The business is built largely around the Chanel brand, but, in the fashion field, incorporates Holland & Holland and Erès. The group also deals with the Bourjois brand, which is positioned as a middle-market brand in France, but which is higher market abroad.

Clarins was created as a skin-care brand in Paris about 25 years ago. It has become a very strong group that includes Thierry Mugler Perfumes, which it created, and Azzaro, which it purchased. It also has a minority investment in L'Occitane, the figures of which are not consolidated.

YSL Beauty basically produces and sells YSL. It has many small brands, but is in the process of selling, some of the weakest (such as Van Cleef to Inter Parfums). It has started perfume brands such as Alexander McQueen and Stella McCartney from scratch, but with limited success to date.

Shiseido Europe is the group that started the Issey Miyake and Jean Paul Gaultier brands. It purchased Decleor, with which it has done very well, and Carita, which has been much less successful.

Sisley was created by Hubert d'Ornano after he sold the former family firm, Orlane. It is a private family firm that has developed consistently over the last 10 years.

These 10 companies, claiming 50% of the total volume, have very strong brands. Only two groups have taken many new licenses and have created a strong base from almost nowhere 20 years ago: Coty and Procter & Gamble. The French have generally been unable to develop new license deals, with the exception of Inter Parfums (Burberry, Celine, S.T. Dupont and others). However, the company, with sales of €200 million, is still quite small and belongs in the second-tier category.

Is there room for outsiders?

In reviewing the very big groups, questions arise as to whether the barrier to entry is too high and if there is actually room for newcomers.

This really all depends on how consumers react to a new product. If the product gets early consumer interest and acceptance at the outset, it can do very well; and as the margins are very high, it is possible to start the business with a very limited cash investment.

But as the risk of failure is very high, companies with limited funds can only really afford to launch a brand once; if they are not successful, they have great difficulty trying a second time.

There are, of course, brands that were launched independently and with limited funds but that still did very well. These include Bulgari, Lolita Lempicka, Kenzo (before it was purchased by LVMH), and MAC (before it was purchased by Estée Lauder), for example.

Key management issues
Sophisticated marketing

Traditionally, marketing perfumes and cosmetics is different from what happens at the mass-market level. For one thing, a perfume can be "hated" by most people and still be a great success if it is liked very strongly by 3–5% of the target audience worldwide. To be successful, a perfume must be different, and even if it is perceived as unpleasant by many people, it can still do well. In this industry, products that perform well in open tests and in blind tests are not necessarily strong performers in the marketplace. To take an extreme example, it could be said that the fragrance that would perform best in product tests would be Cologne Water: nobody would reject it, even if nobody was very excited about it. Product tests must be conducted to see if a perfume has a strong negative or a special weakness that had not been perceived, but the final product decision should never be based on test results alone.

Another difficulty in market tests is that a very great worldwide success may only have a penetration of 4%: it is very difficult to find users and to interview them. For example, in considering modifications to the packaging of its "Pour un Homme" product, Caron decided it would interview French current users, but these constituted less than 0.5% of the French male population: to interview 200 of them, one would have needed an original sample of 40,000. The company therefore decided to ask a group of perfume stores to take the addresses of those who bought the product and agreed to be interviewed. But, of course, the sample was not really representative of either the total population or of those who used the product.

Unfortunately, because of such limitations target marketing is also quite difficult. Segmentations are difficult to study, to target and to measure.

Selective perfumes marketing is a bit like fashion marketing. Part of it is "top down" in that someone has to decide how the product fits into a given fashion trend at a given time: the shape, the fragrance and even the colors of the packaging are not selected by chance. They often result from an analysis of major long-term fashion trends. Asking today's consumer what tomorrow's product should be would in fact miss the point.

Nevertheless, market research is a very important aspect of the tactical decisions behind such things as shapes, positioning concepts, advertising execution or base-line slogan, for example.

Worldwide advertising and promotion

Contrary to what happens with mass-market products, consumers of luxury perfumes and cosmetics expect to find the same advertising campaign and the same positioning everywhere in the world. In the

luxury **brand** management

mass market, it is possible to adjust positioning and communication to local needs and to local circumstances. In selective perfumes and cosmetics, the same brand platform should apply everywhere.

This does not mean that there should not be specific changes to adjust to one country or another. For example, in Japan, men's fragrance lines include strong hair products (liquids and tonics) because those products are obviously needed there. In the same way, for a cosmetic line, products must be adjusted to meet the specific needs of Asian customers, American customers and European customers. In some markets, people prefer jars; in others, they prefer tubes or dispensing bottles. In some markets the scent should be lighter or almost non-existent: such adjustments must be made locally, but based on a common platform.

In promotional activities in this category, we have identified three different types of countries, leading to large differences. These are as follows:

- Those, including Spain, Italy, Argentina and Brazil, in which small perfumery stores are the most important channel of distribution.
- Those such as France and Germany where dealing is done through large chains of perfumeries that have centralized purchasing systems and only merchandising activities in the local stores.
- Those such as the United States, Japan, Mexico and Australia, where department stores produce more than 50% of the total volume.

In addition, duty-free operations provide a very large part of worldwide purchases (for perfumes, in particular), with major sales recorded in airport duty-free stores and through in-flight outlets.

For each of these, the promotional plan should be different: for department stores countries, "gifts with purchase" or "purchases with purchases" are a very important part of the marketing plan. In countries with large distribution chains, merchandising becomes critical. In duty-free activities, promotional programs must be adjusted as well.

The name of the game is therefore a very strong, generalized marketing platform with specific local adjustments.

Managing distribution networks

Almost everybody uses a mix of fully owned subsidiaries, local distributors and, in some cases, commission agents, and here again marketing programs must be adjusted to these different set-ups. This subject will be covered at length in Chapter 10.

Organizational structures

For perfumes and cosmetics, the organizational structure is very similar to what it would be for mass-market products. Marketing and sales staff are crucial for cosmetics products, making training a high-priority activity both for staff operating counters fully owned by the brand and for multi-brand sales staff who also need to understand the specifics of each of the brand's product and its general brand positioning.

WINES AND SPIRITS

This is the only luxury category in which products are sold in supermarkets (off trade) or in clubs and restaurants (on trade). Duty-free activities are also very important in this category, in some cases accounting for as much as 40% of total volume.

Despite these unusual outlets, this is still a luxury business because of the sophistication of the products and the worldwide market in which it operates. It is also a product category with very strong branding issues, which these will be described later.

The wines and spirits market

As mentioned earlier, this market (excluding fine wines) is estimated to be around €30 billion and is characterized by very different product types: "brown" products (essentially Scotch whiskies and cognacs); "white" products (vodka, gin and rum); and champagne, which is a market on its own.

The "brown" products

This group accounts for approximately €10 billion, split almost equally between the two segments, Scotch and cognac. Though both product categories are fundamentally strong, selling strongly in duty-free outlets and nightclubs, they need to be sold in supermarkets and through wine specialists if they are to build a strong worldwide image.

The cognac market, which continues to do reasonably well in Europe, consists of two distinct strands. The first is the very profitable Asian markets (essentially, Japan and China), where it is a status symbol and where people purchase the most aged products such as XO. Here, though, where cognac used to be the drink of choice with meals, consumers are now turning toward imported wines. The second strand is the large-volume medium-price markets such as the United States where there is demand for lower-priced VS (Very Superior) and VSOP (Very Superior Old Pale) products.

Whisky sales have remained steady and have benefited from producers expanding their range of aged-malt products. But this business is not growing because its development potential is limited in an era when consumers are looking to mix their spirits with, say, cola, but are reluctant to do so with the "brown" products.

The "white" products

Vodka, gin and rum each contribute equally to a sales volume of approximately €10–15 billion, with vodka–the preferred drink of the younger generation and good for mixing–experiencing very strong growth. (Between 1999 and 2003, vodka grew by 40% in volume, at an average of 9% per year.) Gin, on the other hand, is declining slightly, but remains a very strong category nevertheless.

Vodka, gin and rum have another advantage in that there is no aging for such products. In a way they are ideal marketing products and, given that advertising is limited for all alcoholic products, sound positioning is more important than anything else in creating awareness and interest for the product category. Rum, which is famous as a mixer in drinks such as the famous "Cuba Libre," sells almost exclusively in North and Latin America. Table 2.8 gives the breakdown of the major markets for international rum sales.

Table 2.8: Breakdown of international branded rum sales

United States	42%
Spain	10%
Canada	7%
Mexico	7%
United Kingdom	4%
Germany	3%
Italy	3%
Asia	1%
France	1%
All others	22%

Source: Le Figaro, 11 January, 2007
Note: This only takes into account international brands. Local brands, very common in Latin America, are not recorded here.

Champagnes

This is another market of approximately €5 billion. The name "Champagne" applies exclusively to a product that has been made from grapes from a very small territory around the cities of Reims and Epernay in France. Similar products from any other part of the world must be called "sparkling wines." Champagne sales amount to around 320 million bottles per year. Using grapes solely from the Champagne region limits production to a maximum of 360 million bottles. Given this limitation, producers are engaged in a strong movement of trading up and bringing added value to their brands and to their products. As with cognac and whiskey, champagne must be left to age, which allows the possibility of blending different wines from different champagne grapes.

luxury **brand** management

More than half of the world consumption of champagne is within France itself, followed by the United Kingdom and the United States.

Other categories

Other categories, also estimated at about €5 billion, include brandies; liqueurs such as Grand Marnier and Cointreau; specific regional products such as Calvados, Armagnac, Metaxa from Greece, Bols from Holland and so on; and the biggest of all—tequila.

The major operators
The major brands

A study conducted every year by Intangible Business in the United Kingdom defines the "most powerful spirits and wine brands." This is not done simply on volume or sales but through a complex score that includes:

- Share of market: volume-based measure of market share
- Brand growth: projected growth based on 10 years' historical data
- Price positioning: a measure of a brand's ability to command a premium
- Market scope: the number of markets in which the brand has a significant presence
- Brand awareness: a combination of spontaneous and prompted awareness
- Brand relevance: the capacity to relate to the brand and the propensity to purchase
- Brand heritage: a brand's longevity and a measure of how embedded it is in local culture
- Brand perception: loyalty and how close a strong brand image is to a desire of ownership.

What is striking about the results of this survey (see Table 2.9) is that brands such as Jack Daniel's, Tequila Cuervo and Gallo, for example, which are not necessarily known all over the world, still have a very strong clientele and awareness in a given part of the world.

Of this top 20, eight are whiskies, three are brands of vodka and two are brands of rum, underlining the importance of these categories.

Table 2.9: The world's most powerful spirits and wine brands, 2005

		Owner	Country of origin	Sector	Total score
1	Smirnoff	Diageo	Russia	Vodka	90.0%
2	Bacardi	Bacardi Martini	Cuba	Rum	73.2%
3	Johnnie Walker	Diageo	Scotland	Whisky	53.8%
4	Martini	Bacardi Martini	Italy	Light aperitif	47.9%
5	Stolichnaya	Pernod Ricard	Russia	Vodka	47.1%
6	Hennessy	LVMH	France	Cognac	30.8%
7	Jack Daniel's	Brown Forman	USA	Whisky	28.2%
8	Absolut	Vin and Sprit	Sweden	Vodka	27.2%
9	Ballantine's	Pernod Ricard	Scotland	Whisky	23.7%
10	Bailey's	Diageo	Ireland	Flavored spirit	27.8%
11	Chivas Regal	Pernod Ricard	Scotland	Whisky	21.3%
12	Captain Morgan	Diageo	Dominican Republic	Rum	18.1%
13	Dewar's	Bacardi Martini	Scotland	Whisky	17.2%
14	Cuervo	Diageo	Mexico	Tequila	16.5%
15	Gordon's	Diageo	England	Gin	16.1%
16	J&B	Diageo	Scotland	Whisky	15.9%
17	Jim Beam	Fortune Brands	USA	Whisky	15.8%
18	Moët et Chandon	LVMH	France	Champagne	14.8%
19	Seagram	Pernod Ricard	USA	Whisky/gin	13.3%
20	Gallo	Gallo	USA	Still light wine	12.4%

Source: Intangible Business, 2005

luxury **brand** management

Taken purely on volume sold, Smirnoff is the #1 brand (171 million liters), followed by Johnnie Walker. A second vodka, Absolut, follows next, with 117 million liters.

The major corporations

Table 2.10 shows the number of cases (a case generally contains 12 bottles of 75 centiliters) sold by each major group in 2005. This serves to reinforce that this is really a volume business, with some brands selling more than 10 million cases each year. The aggregate number of bottles sold by these 10 major operators each year is around 3.5 billion, which is approximately half of the total world market.

Table 2.10: Volumes sold by different operators		
	Millions of cases	Number of brands in top 100
Diageo (UK)	91	17
Pernod Ricard (France)	77	20
Fortune Brands (USA)	31	9
Bacardi (Bahamas)	31	7
Brown Forman (USA)	15	4
Constellation (USA)	13	1
Vin and Sprit (Sweden)	13	1
Remy Cointreau (France)	11	5
Campari (Italy)	10	5
LVMH (France)	9	6

Source: Intangible Business, 2005

Table 2.11 gives an indication of where these 10 companies stand in terms of size and profitability.

Diageo, with 17 brands among the top 100 and huge sales and profit, is the leader in this field. Its top brands include Smirnoff vodka, Johnnie Walker whiskies, Bailey's, J&B whisky, Captain Morgan rum, Cuervo tequila, Tanqueray and Gordon's Gin. The

Table 2.11: Performance (€ million) of the top 10 operators (2007)

	Sales	Operating profit	Net profit	
Diageo	9,000 (E)	2,500 (E)	1,368 (E)	Assuming Guinness is a €1,536 million business and that profitability is identical across the board
Pernod Ricard	6,443	1,447	833	
Bacardi	3,000 (E)	N.A.	N.A.	Private company not reporting any figures
LVMH	2,994	962	764 (E)	
Constellation	2,177	N.A.	N.A.	Total business including distribution and beer reaches €3,680 million
Fortune Brands	2,000	N.A.	N.A.	Total business reaches €5,650 million
Brown Forman	1,980	424	282	
Vin and Sprit	1,400	N.A.	N.A.	
Campari	810	201	118	
Remy Cointreau	786	154	-23	

Note: (E) indicates authors' estimates, based on discussions with professionals in these fields.

company is public and is the result of the merger between two already big operators in 1997: Guinness and Grand Metropolitan.

Remarkably, for a very powerful group, Diageo has no major cognac or champagne brands of its own. For many years, first Guinness and then Diageo have been associated in distribution joint ventures with LVMH, which means that Diageo products are distributed with Hennessy cognacs and some strong LVMH champagne products.

Pernod Ricard started out selling a local product, Pastis, in France. In 2001, it purchased 38% of Seagram's activities and, in 2005, acquired the majority of the assets of Allied Domecq. To complement its traditional Pastis 51 and Ricard brands, it now has a very large number of others with a lot of growth potential. These

luxury **brand** management

include Chivas Regal, Ballantine's, Campbell, and Jameson whiskies, Havana Club and Malibu rums; Martell cognac; Seagram's and Beefeater gins; Stolichnaya vodka; and Perrier Jouët and Mumm champagnes.

Bacardi is a private group, on which there is very little available data. Headquartered in Bermuda, the company is the offspring of a merger between Bacardi Rum and Martini.

LVMH is a very strong business. It has Hennessy cognac in its stable and is a clear leader in champagne (with Dom Pérignon, Krug, Moët et Chandon, Veuve Clicquot and many others). It has distribution joint ventures with Diageo for a strong worldwide presence. While confining itself largely to the cognac and champagne sectors, in 2005 it acquired Glenmorangie whisky, which may indicate the beginning of a new strategy.

The spirits division of **Constellation Brand** recorded sales of €2.18 billion. Its beer sales (almost €1 billion) are in a different product category. The company is, nevertheless, the leader in wines, with 240 brands and 25% of the U.S. wine market. It is also strong in whiskey, gin and rum, with the Barton brand, in particular.

Brown Forman is a public company created in the U.S. by a pharmacist in Louisville, Kentucky. Its strongest brands are Jack Daniel's, Southern Comfort and Tennessee whiskies; Finlandia vodka; and many Californian, Italian and French wines.

The wines and spirits arm of **Fortune Brands** accounts for €2 billion of the group's overall sales of €6.19 billion, which is spread across many product categories including DIY tools and golf equipment. Its Jim Beam brand is the leading bourbon in the world and, in 2005, it purchased the Courvoisier cognac and Canadian Club Canadian blended whisky brands from Allied Domecq.

Vin and Sprit belongs to the Swedish state and is unique in the industry because it is a mono-brand business. The government has indicated that it would like to sell the Absolut vodka brand, and this is likely to cause considerable interest in a number of groups looking to buy a very clean and probably profitable business.

Campari is an Italian company listed on the Milan stock market, but still controlled by the founding family. Its products include Campari, Cinzano and Cynar and a spirit called Sella & Mosca.

Remy Cointreau is the third French group in this sector. It manufactures Remy Martin cognac, Cointreau liqueur and champagne brands such as Charles Heidsieck and Piper Heidsieck.

All of the groups described above appear to have considerable financial strength. Almost all are the result of a series of mergers, a process that is certainly not finished. In the last 10 years, external growth has been a very large part of everybody's strategy.

Key management issues
Dealing with mass merchandisers
The name of the game is to ensure that the product is available on the shelves of local supermarkets everywhere in the world. It must first be sold to very demanding purchasing managers and then carefully managed in the stores by visiting merchandisers. The fact is, though, that a single product cannot afford the cost of this local merchandising effort, making it an absolute necessity to have a local distribution system that can cover its costs by selling many complementary products. The ideal would be to distribute a brand of whisky, a strong vodka brand, a good cognac and some champagnes simultaneously. This in itself requires associations between the different brands to be present everywhere.

This is also the case for nightclubs and restaurants, which are very important for image but difficult to reach and do not necessarily sell large volumes.

Duty-free outlets are very important for creating and maintaining product availability and a strong image for wines and spirits, as they can sometimes reach 40% of worldwide volumes.

The need for a worldwide structure
Every brand needs to be present and strong everywhere in the world. This often requires joint-venture partnerships such as that between Diageo and LVMH, mentioned earlier. Another such venture, Maxxium, which is now in the process of disappearing,

was created by Remy Cointreau, Jim Beam (Fortune Brands), Absolut Vodka (Vin and Spirits) and Famous Grouse whisky (the Erington group from Scotland). In fact, almost every major operator has, in a given country, one or more of its brands being distributed by a friendly local competitor.

Financing inventories

A difficult part of this business is the need for the "ageing" of the products before they are put for sale. It is considered that the average champagne must wait 44 months before it is sufficiently aged to have an exclusive and strong taste. For cognac, the average is 68 months, or almost six years, and for certain whiskies it can be considerably longer. This has a financial cost, which can reach as high as 40% of the unit cost of the finished product.

As mentioned earlier, this gives "white products" a strong advantage because they do not have to age and therefore have a much better cost structure.

The need for "pull" marketing

When a product is on a supermarket shelf somewhere, it still has to be picked up by the consumer, and this requires that it is known and appreciated. It is the responsibility of the brand to make sure the product does not stay on the shelf. It must be advertised strongly. But the advertising of wines and spirits has two limitations. In many countries, such advertising is not allowed on television and is often limited to magazines and billboards.

A second limitation springs from the fact that all products are quite similar and are perceived to be similar by the consumer. The only differentiating element is the perceived content of the brand. This will be discussed later. But this is without doubt a very difficult marketing and positioning challenge.

Organizational structures

Just as for perfumes and cosmetics, marketing and worldwide sales are the most important activities in this category. Companies require a large international workforce within distribution companies, either directly or in joint ventures around the world. Here country managers, zone managers, duty-free specialists and promoters sell the brand, or a selected number of brands, everywhere in the world.

THE WATCH AND JEWELRY MARKET

In this section, we will first describe the situation of the jewelry market, then deal with the watch business. In fact the two businesses are similar, but they have different customer expectations and different marketing practices.

The market

The jewelry market

Executives in the field generally estimate the jewelry market to be worth €30 billion. Approximately two-thirds of this is accounted for by non-branded business, which incorporates the work of all individual "family" jewelers, who undertake unbranded individual pieces for their customers. Here, products are sold as a function of the weight of gold or silver used in the piece. Precious stones, purchased directly on the open market and valued according to their size, purity and shape, are often brought by the client to a trusted jeweler, who will mount them in a ring or on a special necklace for a reasonable price.

Family jewelers, who may work across several generations of the same family, often manufacture the pieces of jewelry themselves. They may sometimes subcontract the production, but, in every case, they have the trust of their clients and can modify the same piece several times to adapt it to the wishes of different individuals over time.

The branded market is less than half the size (€10 billion) and has a very different set-up. The customer usually does not know anybody inside the store and the trust comes exclusively from the name that appears over the door. Such stores generally sell standard products and would seldom (except, perhaps, for very wealthy clients) recondition an old jewel or add new stones to a piece.

luxury **brand** management

Customer expectations: Given the price of different jewels and the risk of buying a fake or overpriced product, customers rely on someone they can trust. This trust can come from the brand name of a famous jeweler or from individual contact, with the jeweler acting in a role similar to that of a family doctor.

A large part of the business is undertaken for special occasions. Tiffany's, for example, is well known in the United States for its engagement rings. Wedding anniversaries or the birth of a baby, for example, are private, family occasions when people look for something special, visiting several stores before they decide what they want and where to buy it. The sale of a company or a piece of real estate may prompt others into buying an expensive piece of jewelry. In such circumstances, they generally know what they want and are prepared to visit several stores to get it.

As they buy jewelry, for special or standard occasions, customers expect a very high quality of service from people they feel they can trust. They need to be able to feel that the store cares about them and takes as much time as necessary to satisfy their requirements.

Product ranges: Products can vary greatly, from gold to silver and from products with stones to those without them. Precious stones such as diamonds have a set market value, which is known by everybody, everywhere. Producing a diamond ring in the United States to sell in Japan through a local distributor is not that simple, as margins escalate and the final price must still be within a reasonable target. This is why, in fact, gold pieces can be more profitable and provide greater price flexibility.

One jeweler has found a way around this problem: H. Stern, which originated in Brazil, is the specialist in semi-precious stones and brings to the market jewelry pieces with stones such as aquamarine, amethyst and yellow citrine.

Financial aspects: Pricing is a very difficult subject in this business. For precious stones, there is a limited range of possible retail prices. For gold, there is an official measure of the retail price: the cost per gram. It is possible to visit gold markets in many places. Caracas or Bogota, for example, provide a choice of many small retailers and many jewelry pieces, but the retail price is computed by weight and the different pieces are simply placed on a scale together to get the final price.

A simple way to compare the pricing level of the different jewelers would be to list their price in dollars per gram of gold. However, the major brands refuse to do this. They do not see themselves simply as sellers of gold but, rather, of artistic objects, for which the work required varies from one piece to another and that the time and skills involved cannot be compared.

Also, at the brand's headquarters, the difficulty is to ensure that the global margin can be divided between the workshop where the piece is made by specialist craftsmen, the marketing and the promotion, the distributor and the final retailer or department store.

The watch market

The value of this market is considered by professionals in the field to be around €10 billion. It is more heterogeneous than the jewelry market and differs from it in market segments, gender and nationalities.

Combination watches or upscale watches have individual movements and, of course, no quartz batteries. They have a movement that is generally hand-made and can be self-winding. They are called "combination" watches because of the combination of features they offer, such as time, date, situation of the sun and the stars, or the seasons. They often also have a chronograph function. Sometimes, such watches are produced as a single unit or in very limited numbers, commanding prices of up to €200,000.

Jewelry or specialty watches are less sophisticated and are manufactured in larger numbers. In this category, we have put all watches that sell for between €1,000 and €5,000 wholesale. Most are beautifully made objects, sometimes powered by quartz batteries, and are ideal expensive gifts.

Fashion or "mood" watches belong to a third category. Here, we have put those watches that sell at retail from €100 to €1000. These include Tommy Hilfiger, Calvin Klein and Armani watches. The idea in this category is to promote the concept of owning several watches that can match the customer's changing moods.

Men or women?: Watches are one of the few luxury products that men can buy and cherish. Probably 90% of combination watches are purchased by men, many of whom collect old models as they would collect expensive stamps.

Women are important in the second segment as they purchase or are offered expensive watches for special occasions. They are also the largest segment of buyers of fashion and mood watches.

Which nationalities?: Two markets must be singled out. China is a very big market for watches: Chinese men traditionally are buyers of luxury products and expensive watches are taken to be a sign of business and financial success. In Europe, Italians buy more watches than anybody else and have been known to line up outside a Swatch store the night before a limited-edition model goes on sale. They believe that wearing an expensive, well-known watch is the ultimate in elegance and sophistication.

Other important markets are Japan, which is similar to China though to a lesser extent, and the United States, where customers buy both mood watches and more expensive brands, which for many women can become sophisticated "conversation" pieces.

But watches are also a very important part of men's status and dress codes in Latin America, the Middle East and South East Asia. Preferences vary around the world: Europeans generally wear their watches with a leather strap, when in Asia and tropical countries people prefer steel bracelets.

The major operators
The jewelry brands
Table 2.12 shows our estimates of the total sales and of the watch sales of the major operators in the sector. For example, watches account for approximately half of Cartier's total business. For Van Cleef, the figure is 11% of sales, and for Tiffany's only 2%. However, it is not possible to arrive at the jewelry sales by simply subtracting the watch sales from the total, because for Cartier, for

Table 2.12: Estimated sales (incl. watches) of major jewelry operators, 2005/2006

Operators	Countries	Total sales (€ million)	Watch sales (€ million)	Ownership
Cartier	France	2,300 (E)	1,110 (E)	Richemont
Tiffany	USA	1,950	40 (E)	Public
Bulgari	Italy	900	274	Public
David Yurman	USA	550	N.A.	Private
Chopard	Switzerland	500	229	Private
H Stern	Brazil	450 (E)	N.A.	Private
Mikimoto	Japan	300 (E)	N.A.	Private
Lawrence Graf	UK	280 (E)	N.A.	Private
Tous	Spain	200 (E)	N.A.	Private
Harry Winston	USA	153	61	Public
Van Cleef	France	125 (E)	14 (E)	Richemont
Pomellato	Italy	80 (E)	N.A.	Private
Chaumet	France	60 (E)	35 (E)	LVMH
Boucheron	France	40 (E)	13 (E)	PPR Gucci
Buccelati	Italy	30 (E)	N.A.	Private
Mauboussin	France	30 (E)	13 (E)	Private
Dinh Van	France	25 (E)	N.A.	Private
Fred	France	10 (E)	5 (E)	LVMH
Mellerio	France	7.5 (E)	N.A.	Private
Poiray	France	5 (E)	N.A.	Private

Source: Annual reports and discussions with specialists of the sector. We decided not to put Chanel and Dior in this table as our estimates of their sales were too uncertain.

Note: (E) indicates authors' estimates.

example, the total sales include scarves and leather goods, and those of Bulgari also include perfumes. What can also be seen from Table 2.12 is that only 10 operators have a major and meaningful level of activity. Some of the highlights are presented below.

- **Cartier** is the largest brand and an extremely profitable one. It is extremely strong in watches, but has also been able to develop an important jewelry business. It is very strong in Europe and Asia and is an important operator in the United States.

- **Tiffany** is almost as big as Cartier, but not very strong in watches. Its strengths are in the United States, where it is clearly the leader, and in Asia. It is now trying to move into Europe. Tiffany is well known in the United States for its diamond engagement rings, but in the U.S and Asia, in particular, it is also known for such things as ballpoint pens, silver-plated birth spoons and christening medals with low entry prices of less than €75.

- **Bulgari**, based in Rome, is a strong performer that, from its beginnings as a silversmith, has moved slowly into jewelry and watches. It is also quite strong in perfumes, has a very effective collection of ties and scarves, has recently become active in leather goods and is developing its Bulgari hotels.

- **David Yurman**, unknown in Europe and in Asia, is a very strong and much-respected American retailer.

- **Chopard**, a family firm based in Geneva, operates 83 stores around the world and has very impressive performance, primarily as a jeweler but also as a watchmaker. Its "happy diamond" line is well known and well considered.

- **H. Stern** was created in Brazil in 1945 by Hans Stern, who is still running the show. Specializing in semi-precious stones, it now has some 160 stores, mostly in Latin America, but with boutiques in the United States and Paris.

- **Mikimoto** is the leader in cultured pearls, which it develops in Japan. Gradually, though, it has broadened its range to incorporate interesting jewelry collection pieces.

The watch brands

Again, we classify the operators into three different categories, according to their price segments. While industry specialists might object that this segmentation is slightly artificial, it has the advantage of distinguishing between brands that are quite different in style and in size.

Table 2.13 shows the major operators in combination and very expensive watches. In this category, where the total sales of the leading 10 operators are €1.5 billion out of a total market in the region of €2 billion, almost everybody is Swiss. For these very expensive pieces, the business is run from Switzerland even though the consumers are scattered around the world. Some of these brands are still independent, but half of them belong to Richemont or to the Swatch Group.

Table 2.13: Estimated sales of combination/upscale watch operators, 2006

Operators	Nationality	Sales (€ million)	Unit sales	Average wholesale price per unit (€)	Ownership
Patek Philippe	Swiss	390	34,000	11,470	Private
Franck Muller	Swiss	225	45,000	5,000	Private
Audemars Piguet	Swiss	195	28,000	7,000	Private
Piaget	Swiss	186	21,000	8,850	Richemont
Breguet	Swiss	176	21,000	8,400	Swatch
Vacheron Constantin	Swiss	96	17,000	5,650	Richemont
Girard-Perregaux	Swiss	91	17,000	5,350	Private
A. Lange und Söhne	German	86	8,000	10,750	Richemont
Harry Winston	American	61	4,500	13,550	Public
Blancpain	Swiss	60	11,000	5,450	Swatch

Source: Business Montres, 2006

luxury **brand** management

Table 2.14 presents the jewelry and specialty watch operators.

Table 2.14: Estimated sales of jewelry and specialty watch operators, 2006

Operators	Nationality	Sales (€ million)	Unit sales	Average wholesale price per unit (€)	Ownership
Rolex	Swiss	1,890	760,000	2,500	Private
Cartier	Swiss	1,110	710,000	1,600	Richemont
Omega	Swiss	950	850,000	1,100	Swatch
Breitling	Swiss	275	180,000	1,500	Private
Bulgari	Italian/Swiss	274	220,000	1,245	Public
Jaeger-LeCoultre	Swiss	189	52,000	3,600	Richemont
IWC	German	185	48,000	3,850	Richemont
Chanel	French/Swiss	178	58,000	3,050	Private
Hermès	French	105	110,000	950	Public
Baume et Mercier	Swiss	100	90,000	1,100	Richemont
Louis Vuitton	French/Swiss	94	41,000	2,300	LVMH
Montblanc	German	92	98,000	930	Richemont
Dior	French	59	65,000	900	Public

Source: Business Montres, 2006

Table 2.15 presents the last group of watches, which are still "luxury watches" but with an average wholesale price below €900. This category is not particularly homogeneous in that it contains brands such as Tag Heuer and Rado, which could be considered as belonging to the second category, and others such as Calvin Klein and Tommy Hilfiger, which have completely different positioning and retail prices around €100–200.

But the lesson to emerge from this segmentation into three categories is that they are three different businesses: one where

Table 2.15: Estimated sales for fashion and mood watch operators, 2006

Operators	Nationality	Sales (€ million)	Unit sales	Average wholesale price per unit (€)	Ownership
Tag Heuer	Swiss	565	750,000	750	LVMH
Longines	Swiss	245	470,000	520	Richemont
Rado	Swiss	224	350,000	624	Swatch
Gucci	Italian/Swiss	142	270,000	520	PPR Gucci
Raymond Weil	Swiss	125	250,000	500	Private
Calvin Klein	American	87	840,000	105	Swatch
Tommy Hilfiger	American	52	950,000	54	Private
Armani	Italian	38	420,000	90	Private
Burberry	British	37	200,000	180	Public

Source: Business Montres, 2006

units sold are measured in thousands; another where units sold range from 50,000 to almost a million; and a third where figures are measured in their hundreds of thousands.

We said earlier that total sales in the upscale segment were probably below €2 billion. In the jewelry and specialty watches segment, total sales are probably around €6 billion. In the last category, the "fashion" and "mood" segments, even if the unit figures are impressive, the overall sales level—also at around €2 billion—remains limited.

It is also interesting to note that aside from Cartier, Bulgari and Harry Winston, the jewelry brands remain relatively small in the overall watch business. If watches are very important to enable a jewelry brand to develop, to reach break-even in existing stores and to finance new ones, the watch business stands on its own, is almost always Swiss made, and is developing rapidly.

In this business, three groups dominate the market: Swatch

luxury **brand** management

leads, with a 25% market share; Rolex, with 22%, is second, standing on its own brand and with its lower-positioned brand Tudor (with sales of €78 million); and then comes the Richemont Group (20%), which includes Cartier and many other brands. Despite this combined share of 67%, the market is also open to newcomers who can develop a good idea or a special craft skill.

Key management issues
Retail vs. wholesale

While for jewelry a large part of the business is done at the retail level, for watches most of the business is done at wholesale, as the products need visibility and a strong presence at different points of sale.

At one time or another, brands such as Ebel, dealing mainly in watches, have tried to open retail stores, but without much success. Nevertheless, brands like Rolex and Omega have been successful in this. Others have tried to sell their watches only in their own jewelry stores. This was the policy adopted at the outset by Bulgari watches, but the company quickly realized that it had to enlarge the distribution to create interest in the product.

Then, as their wholesale activities flourished, jewelry brands have been tempted to enlarge their distribution with multi-brand stores. However, unless they could come up with a very specific product line, this has not always been effective. Cartier had "Les Must de Cartier" for many years, but while this was probably very useful for building the brand at the beginning, it has now been removed from the catalog. Bulgari has a small jewelry line for multi-brand jewelry stores. Tiffany's has never done it and is unlikely to do so in the near future.

Pricing and product lines

For jewelry, there are different customer segments: those ready to spend up to €5,000 for a small piece; those who are prepared to spend between €5,000 and €50,000; and those who are looking for exclusive pieces selling above that amount.

Different jewelers are often lacking in their offerings in one or other of these segments and are obliged to hire new designers and to develop specific skills to work on overcoming this lack.

For a given brand of watches, on the other hand, there should be only one price range, but this requires a strong commercial and marketing work.

The risk of the major customer

Exclusive brands such as Mauboussin, Asprey or, at one point, Chaumet are heavily reliant on major orders from the likes of the Sultan of Brunei or the King of Morocco if they are to meet their annual sales budgets. When these very big orders arrive, everything is rosy and life is easy. But what would happen if, for one reason or another, the major customer did not place an order for the following year? As in every business, diversification and balance in the client list are very important parts of a healthy business.

Organizational structures

In the jewelry business, the organizational structure is generally limited to a retailing manager and an export manager; a design office and a production workshop; and a comparatively large marketing team to deal with product positioning, brand positioning and public relations.

CONCLUSION

It seems a pity to limit our analysis of luxury sectors to these four categories. It is could be argued that leather goods and accessories are also deserving of mention, as are men's fashion and "art de la table" items. But it is necessary to draw the line somewhere. It would also be interesting to look at the "still wine" market, which we consider to be the biggest product category in the luxury industry. However, this is beyond the scope of this book and would probably require a study on its own.

In the rest of the book, we will give examples taken from different parts of the luxury field, but we will speak of the industry

luxury **brand** management

as a whole, without differentiating the segments. In this chapter, though, we hope we have presented sufficient evidence to convince the reader that there are important differences between each of the categories, but that the luxury business is a separate activity, different from other markets. We hope, too, that we have convinced the reader that these luxury segments, despite their differences, are similar in outlook and in management needs.

chapter **3**

THE POWER OF THE
Luxury
BRAND

So far in this book, we have spoken more readily of brands than of businesses. In fact, the luxury business is above all a business of brands. When customers have a preference for a brand, they are ready to spend a little more on it. Sometimes a brand goes through periods when perhaps the creativity is a bit weak and new products are not as good as they should be, yet it manages to keep its loyal customers. There is always a strong emotional value attached to a strong brand for reasons that are historical and social, as well as emotional.

For luxury goods, brand identity is a very important element of the business. In certain ways, it can also be a constraint: it is not possible to launch a product that is outside of its sphere of legitimacy.

How do we measure the strength of a brand? The first question to ask is: How well known is it? This can be ascertained by asking 500 target consumers: "What are the brands of luxury watches that you know?" Immediate answers—Rolex or Cartier, say—will give what is called the **spontaneous awareness**. But from the same answer, researchers will be able to provide other information. They will record the number of times any one brand is mentioned first, which gives the **top of mind**, an indication of great strength of a given brand for a product category. For example, if we ask a group of consumers to name all the brands of scarves that they know, they are more than likely to mention Hermès first. But recording such information will give the percentage of respondents who put a particular brand first, which allows us to determine any increases or decreases over time. It is also enables us to see any changes in the respective positions of the leading brands in the consumers' top-of-mind responses.

In a second phase, interviewees are presented with a list of brands and asked to say which of them they know. This will give researchers what is known as **aided awareness**, which provides an indication of the closeness of a brand with its customers.

Generally, top brands such as Chanel, Dior and Armani have a spontaneous awareness of between 40% and 60%, depending on the country in which the test is conducted. But they probably have an aided awareness between 80% and 90% in the perfumes or the ladies' luxury ready-to-wear categories. Smaller brands perform less well on spontaneous awareness, and are generally mentioned only by those who have the product at home and use it.

Of course, as we will discuss in Chapter 6, the level of awareness is only a secondary aspect of the total picture. The most important aspect of the brand is its identity; that is to say, the specific contents of the awareness it generates.

In this chapter, we will discuss the value of a brand and how it can be assessed, and then analyze the different ways of looking at the brand and what it represents for the public.

THE VALUE OF A BRAND

In this section, we concentrate on a study conducted every year by the consulting firm Interbrand, the main results of which are published in *BusinessWeek*. Interbrand rates almost every brand in the world, assigning to each an overall value.

The Interbrand methodology

Interbrand relies on a specific brand-value management model that summarizes all of the different elements of a brand as they relate to the customer. This is shown in Figure 3.1.

This model puts the consumer at the center and divides the brand management world into three activities: the evaluation (through research) of brand opportunities; the creative process (brand strategy, verbal identity and brand design); and the management process (culture, implementation and protection).

Figure 3.1: Interbrand brand-value management model

Source: Interbrand

the power of the **luxury** brand

Interbrand's selection criteria for the annual study include:

- The company must be publicly traded.
- It must have at least one-third of its revenues generated outside the country of origin.
- It must be a market-facing brand.
- The economic value added must be positive.
- The brand must not have a purely business-to-business single audience, with no wider public profile and awareness.

The methodology Interbrand uses to assess the value of the different brands is as follows:

- It forecasts the current and future revenues specifically attributable to the branded products.
- It subtracts the cost of doing business (operating costs, taxes) and intangibles such as patents and management strengths to assess what portion of earnings is directly attributable to the brand.

In other words, the idea is to assess the flow of added revenues that come because the product has a given brand, rather than no brand at all. The brand justifies a premium price, which, after subtracting the investment necessary to keep the brand where it is, can be considered the gross profit directly attributable to the brand.

Luxury brands in the total brand universe
Table 3.1 shows how the luxury field fares compared to the other industrial sectors where brands exist. This shows that the luxury sector, with a brand value of nearly €47 billion, ranks only fifth in the 100 most valuable brands. This amount is much smaller than the stock market value of the major luxury groups. For example, the stock market valuation of LVMH alone is around €35 billion. This probably arises from the fact that many profitable brands are not among the top 100 and that private family companies are not taken into account.

luxury **brand** management

Table 3.1: The place of luxury in the global brand picture (2006)

	Number of firms	Number of U.S. firms	Consolidated value (in € million)
Computer hardware, services and software	12	9	175,675
Fast-moving consumer goods. (FMCG) - Food - Personal Care (not always FMCG) - Beverages, including beer	17	12	130,708
Automotive	12	2	91,455
Financial services	9	6	75,900
Luxury & selective wines and spirits	14	1	46,844
Consumer electronics	7	2	34,861
Restaurants	4	4	28,686
Internet services	4	4	21,099
Miscellaneous	21	9	165,995

Source: Interbrand, 2006
Interbrand's figures were expressed in U.S. dollars, but for consistency we have converted these to Euros using an exchange rate of US $1 = €0.7058

It is worth noting that the fast-moving consumer goods sector is three times bigger than that of luxury brands.

Luxury, like the automotive and consumer electronics segments, is a field in which there are few American brands. In fact, there is only one U.S. brand among the group of 14 listed in Table 3.2, which serves to reinforce the comment we made earlier that this is basically a French and Italian field.

As a general comment, it is striking that most brand values are gathered around the computer hardware, software and services and financial services fields.

Table 3.2: Interbrand's top luxury brands (2006)

Overall ranking	Brands	Countries	Value (€ million)
17	Louis Vuitton	France	12,462
46	Gucci	Italy	5,052
61	Chanel	France	3,639
72	Rolex	Switzerland	2,990
81	Hermès	France	2,720
82	Tiffany	United States	2,695
83	Hennessy	France	2,524
86	Cartier	France	2,371
87	Moët & Chandon	France	2,299
93	Smirnoff	United Kingdom	2,140
95	Bulgari	Italy	2,029
96	Prada	Italy	2,028
97	Armani	Italy	2,028
98	Burberry	United Kingdom	1,964

Source: Interbrand, 2006
Interbrand's figures were expressed in *U.S. dollars, but for consistency we have converted these to Euros using an exchange rate of US$1 = €0.7058.

The luxury brands in the top 100

There are several observations arising from this list of luxury brands appearing in Interbrand's top 100 for 2006 as shown in Table 3.2.

First, the estimated brand value of Louis Vuitton is more than double that of second-placed Gucci, and three times that of Chanel. Second, it is significant that 10 out of the 14 brands listed come from France and Italy.

Another peculiarity of this list: for some reason, Interbrand does not seem to have respected its own rules. Contrary to its stated criteria, many of these brands (notably Chanel, Rolex, Prada and Armani) are privately owned. Indeed, if we add the privately owned firms and the companies that are public but still have strong

luxury **brand** management

family control, this accounts for 11 out of the 14 firms. Family control, either total or through a majority shareholding, is almost a peculiarity of these top brands. This probably has something to do with the need for a long-term focus in this business, as mentioned in Chapter 1, which is easier to obtain in family–controlled firms.

How has this position evolved over time? Table 3.3 gives an indication by comparing the Interbrand results for 2001 and 2006.

Table 3.3: Brand value changes between 2001 and 2006 (€ million)			
2001		**2006**	
Louis Vuitton	4,863	Louis Vuitton	12,426
Gucci	3,783	Gucci	5,052
Chanel	3,014	Chanel	3,639
Rolex	2,611	Rolex	2,990
Tiffany	2,455	Hermès	2,720
Bacardi	2,259	Tiffany	2,695
Moët & Chandon	1,826	Hennessy	2,524
Smirnoff	1,715	Cartier	2,371
Polo Ralph Lauren	1,348	Moët & Chandon	2,299
Johnnie Walker	1,165	Smirnoff	2,140
Jack Daniel's	1,115	Bulgari	2,029
Armani	1,052	Prada	2,028
Absolut	974	Armani	1,964
		Burberry	1,964

Source: Interbrand, 2001 and 2006
Interbrand's figures were expressed in U.S. dollars, but for consistency we have converted these to Euros using an exchange rate of US$1 = €0.7058.

Eight brands appear in the results for both 2001 and 2006: two of these have experienced very fast growth (Louis Vuitton, with an annual growth of 30%, and Armani with 14%), while the average for the eight is 8.3%.

There are anomalies in the tables: Hermès, Cartier and Bulgari should have been in the 2001 list. In the same way, Bacardi, which was present in 2001, should not have been omitted from the 2006 list. The fact that this is a private company may explain this, but then again, so are others that appear in the list.

But what lies waiting outside the top 100? A joint effort between Interbrand and the magazine *L'Expansion* gives the opportunity to find some additional values, although this analysis was restricted to the French market. They took all French brands that had a value of over €1 billion, of which they found 23. The luxury brands amongst them are listed in Table 3.4.

Table 3.4: Luxury brands in the 23 top French brands (€ million)

Louis Vuitton	15,630
L'Oréal	5,330
Chanel	4,400
Lancôme	3,450
Hermès	3,100
Hennessy	2,870
Cartier	2,540
Moët & Chandon	2,620
Lacoste	1,310
Remy Martin	1,300
Dior	1,190

Source : *L'Expansion*, June 2006

It is noticeable that the French list includes two brands that are not in the global list: L'Oréal (questions might be raised about whether this is actually a mass-market or middle-market brand) and Lancôme.

Three brands that did not appear in the international list are interesting: Lacoste (which will also appear in the RISC ranking presented in Chapter 4); Remy Martin, the second cognac of the French list; and Dior, which, surprisingly, is valued at a quarter of the value of Chanel, despite the fact that their perfumes and cosmetics businesses are of comparable size. But Dior is probably considered to be less profitable.

luxury **brand** management

Another study conducted by *L'Expansion* in November 2006 asked respondents "Which brands best represent luxury?" The question here was designed to elicit an overall impression of different brands and, in order of importance, respondents mentioned Dior, Chanel, Louis Vuitton, Yves Saint Laurent, Cartier and Hermès. Might this not suggest that while Dior is not necessarily the brand that people want to buy, it is the one they consider most in tune with luxury and its activities?

THE CHARACTERISTICS OF A BRAND

Where does the brand get its power from? A study by Bernard Dubois and Patrick Duquesne[1] found that a brand's value came from the following elements:

- **A mythical value:** this incorporates its reason for being and how representative it is of its time.
- **An exchange value:** this refers to the best value for money, which in itself incorporates the mythical elements mentioned above and the other value components.
- **An emotional value:** this is quite different from the above in that it deals with emotions and impressions.
- **An ethical value:** this is linked to social responsibility and the way the brand reacts in the marketplace.
- **An identity value:** that relates to the way the brand can be used by consumers to convey something about themselves.

We'll begin by looking at the different aspects of the brand, starting with the brand as a contract. We will then look at the time dimension and finish with the role of brands in society.

The brand as a contract

When one company purchases a competitor for an amount above the sum of its net assets, there is a line item called "goodwill" in the consolidated balance sheet following the merger. This term designates the sum total of the intangible, but extremely valuable, positive attitudes of consumers toward the acquired company and its products.

Given the current market uncertainty that prevails at the time of writing, goodwill does not have good press. And yet, though evaluating it can be problematic, it is a genuine added value, built up gradually as consumers become convinced that a certain brand can provide them with a product whose style and quality is above that of its competitors.

When consumers buy a Burberry or an Aquascutum raincoat, they're not simply buying a raincoat; they're buying a fashion product, branded by a reputable name and one which has a strong emotional value.

In the perception of the customer, this capital is embodied above all in a name. At the beginning of the history of luxury brands, this was, as we saw in earlier chapters, generally the name of a skilled designer/craftsman, and was intended to raise the product above an otherwise standardized level, and to emphasize high-quality production criteria. This seems logical enough because if, as we have said, a brand comprises first of all a capital of confidence, then putting his name on a product is, for the vendor, the simplest way of winning that confidence. We are dealing here with a fundamental structure in a great number of human exchanges.

As we will see, the name of a brand, or its logo, is an important, visible part of a more complex reality. It provides the mediation between the essential values of a luxury company—its identity— and the perceptions its customers have of it—its "image."

But note that what the consumer is looking for behind the brand is the guarantee of a specific and superior quality, and a strong exclusivity. That long-term assurance forms the basis of the relationship between the consumer and the producer.

This holds for products and sales policies alike. The Saks Fifth Avenue department-store chain has a rule under which a customer can return any product purchased within the previous six weeks for a refund, with no questions asked. For a long time, the Saks stores had Revillon departments. Every year, certain customers bought

luxury **brand** management

fur coats there on 15th December and returned them at the end of January. The Revillon teams, pointing out that these customers were abusing the return policy to get a free fur coat every winter, tried several times to convince the stores' management to make an exception to the policy. Saks always refused, considering that even if it left them vulnerable to abuse, the return policy was part of the store's ground rules, that it constituted a commitment, and that it was one component of its brand identity.

It's common for managers to speak of the brand as an expression of the company's "genetic program"—a stable structure, rich in potential, which concretizes the company's existence and can win customers' confidence, but which also imposes strict ground rules. While this is an expressive image, it is also a little unclear. We prefer to speak of "semiotic invariants" and of a brand's ethic and aesthetic. As we will see in Chapter 6, the manifestations of a brand can be seen as "meaning facts," and these invariants simply make up a basic grammar, a signature of form and content that allows the brand identity to come into being.

In fact, in ordinary discourse terms, two brands such as Armani and Sonia Rykiel do not express the same values and have distinct brand identities. Giorgio Armani is a very strong proponent of the traditional woman, dressed in a very conservative modern way and with a definite Italian flavor. Sonia Rykiel appeals to a relatively mature and modern woman who is very independent in her choices and who wants to convey a different statement. She is also identified very much with Paris, and particularly with the Left Bank. Products and positioning must take into account these diverse representations with which they are associated in the customer's imagination. As a result, they adopt slightly different strategies in order to be recognized and to win and keep consumers' trust.

A brand is therefore a contract, one that is implicit in nature and that governs the relations between a given company and its customers. This relationship is two-dimensional: it is not only economic in nature, but also, over time, creates emotional ties that are sometimes very intense—with infidelity on both sides, momentary or permanent abandonment and, above all, a capacity for reciprocal influence on the behavior of the two contracting parties.

The competitive dimension of the brand can be included within its contractual dimension. The brand exists only because it differentiates itself from its closest competitors. This is one of the bases of its identity. The consumer chooses a brand for the specific qualities it offers, and, in this sense, the differentiation of the brand is part of the contract between the two parties.

Because it is founded on differentiation, which is the *raison d'être* of any brand, such a contract remains implicit. As such, it cannot be confused with the "standard" regulations of laws governing commerce, which are the same for all. What the brand pertains to is a relationship of another nature, which is exemplified in the automatic-return policy of Saks stores. The brand implies the promise of superior quality and better service; in short, it guarantees added value.

Brands and time

The prolongation of a contract is intrinsic to the notion of guarantee. In order to exist, a brand must not only establish its reputation, but do so durably. Thus the chronological perspective is fundamental to understanding brands.

We will begin with a short historical sketch. In looking at brands as abstract entities, we tend to forget that, behind them, there is nothing more than a vendor who is concerned about his customers keeping him in mind. And this concern is as old as commerce itself. As early as 2700 B.C., artisans were affixing a sign to their creations in order to affirm their originality.[2] In classical Greece and Rome, merchants used generic symbols to designate the business they were in: a ham for butchers, a cow for creameries, and so on. "Individual marks" in the form of seals, identifying a particular merchant, made their appearance circa 300 B.C. More than 6,000 different seals used by Roman potters have been catalogued.

luxury **brand** management

The large-scale explosion of brands—that is, the emergence of the brand phenomenon as we understand it—is largely a result of the Industrial Revolution. Should we view this, then, as a "mercantilization" of the world? It's more a case of a transformation of commerce itself. As exchanges became standardized, it became necessary for producers to establish a relationship of proximity with consumers by other means.

The extension of industrial property to the concept of brand appears in Europe in the second half of the nineteenth century. The U.S. Congress enacted the first federal trademark law in the late 1800s, and between 1850 and 1890, the number of patents granted each year in the major Western nations increased by a factor of 10.

The major brands underwent sustained development between 1900 and 1945, and the development accelerated between 1945 and 1990. On the other hand—and contrary to what their omnipresence in the media might suggest—the trend since 1990 has been toward a concentration and reduction in the largest companies' portfolios of brands.

To understand these recent developments, we must look at things on a smaller scale. These fundamental trends, like the individual fate of a given business sector, can be explained by the differential between, on the one hand, the cost of maintaining and developing a brand, and, on the other, the immediate or longer-term profits to be made from it.

The fashion sector has passed through several phases. It underwent its major explosion, characterized by the emergence of the Italian brands, after the Second World War. Armani, Ferré, Moschino, Trussardi and Versace emerged in the 1970s. During the same period, slightly older brands—Fendi, Salvatore Ferragamo, Gucci—experienced extraordinary growth. Certain provincial brands left Florence or Milan and were soon found everywhere in Italy. They quickly became international, generally with a strong presence in the United States and Japan. But at the same time or slightly later a large number of French brands, such as Phillipe Venet and Per Spook, disappeared and others such as Grès reduced

the power of the **luxury** brand

their activities to a single store in Paris and some license contracts in Japan or South Korea, which brought in royalties to cover the monthly expenses. The Grès store in Paris was recently closed altogether. While the luxury and fashion industry doesn't escape from the concentration of capital, the reduction in the number of brands is less evident there, perhaps because of the versatility of the markets. The novelty effect is a determining factor in consumers' choices. The result is a permanent renewal of the available brands, yet the total number has been significantly reduced. In France, 20 years ago, 24 French firms would present an *haute couture* parade twice a year in Paris. Today they are 10 French brands (Adeline André, Chanel, Christian Dior, Christian Lacroix, Dominique Sirop, Emanuel Ungaro, Franck Sorbier, Givenchy, Jean Paul Gaultier and Jean Louis Scherrer).

And yet an analysis of the effectiveness curves of fashion advertising shows the emergence of what is called a "threshold effect." Such studies show that advertising expenditures on a very broad target of consumers are only effective beyond €500,000 in France, €750,000 in Germany, and probably €3 million in the United States. The costs of advertising and internationalization have clearly changed the rules of the game. Small brands will have to remain local or else disappear.

But history hasn't had the last word yet. There are brands positioned in a specific market that manage, below critical mass, to develop name recognition without advertising. In certain highly federated markets made up of devotees, word of mouth is a powerful force and even more of an advantage than advertising. In the case of fashion, a small, highly innovative brand will sometimes be extremely well received by the press and magazines; fashion writers will adopt it as a favorite discovery; and it will be talked about for its originality. On the other hand, middle-sized and older brands, already "publicized" but with smaller budgets than those of the competition, will have trouble staying in the race.

While it is true that the globalization of the economy, technological progress in communications, and the volume requirements of the traditional production/distribution industries have made brands indispensable, stronger and less numerous, we will show that their evolution also depends on the economic sectors in which the brands operate.

Brands and society

When we think of the presence of brands in today's society, the first idea that comes to mind is not the quality of the products, but the intensity of the messages.

On his desert island, Robinson Crusoe would not have needed his name if Friday hadn't turned up. Brands exist only because we can recognize them. And we recognize them because we perceive the messages they send, their specificities, and a certain constancy over time. We will have occasion to mention these components—communication, differentiation and duration—throughout this book.

The communicative dimension of brands operates in two ways. First, the brand sends its messages to the consumers it targets. This is at first a shotgun type of relationship, where a wide net must be cast to be sure of pulling in the targeted consumers. Second, signs, like money, circulate. Brands, too, display this phenomenon.

Let's imagine the reaction of extraterrestrials who arrive in Times Square in New York, in the Ginza in Tokyo or in the Via Monte Napoleone in Milan. The logos and brand names on the buildings and on the clothing worn by the passersby would probably loom large in their first impressions. They would discover a civilization where brands play an important role in social communication. They would also be discovering, by comparing different places, the multitude of global brands, their systematic presence in the most famous shopping streets, and the apparent homogeneity they impose on lifestyles.

The explosion of brand communication our civilization is now experiencing would never have happened were it not for the crucial social role that brands now play. The three stripes on running shoes, the polo player embroidered on a shirt, the "swoosh" on the cap, or the Kelly bag—not to mention the cars people drive or the restaurants they go to—often say more about the personality of those who wear them than their curriculum vitae.

It shouldn't be surprising, in a society characterized by exponential growth of communication in all its forms and contents, that brands should be at the heart of contemporary life. They guide the purchases we make, influence our judgments about products and people, and force us to position ourselves in relation to the values (or counter-values, or the absence of values) they communicate.

These effects are not limited, of course, to the isolated moment of communication (the glimpsed billboard or spot). The way in which brands circulate, are copied, worn, or co-opted shows the extent and depth to which they affect our society. In fact, they have changed our way of living.

First, by claiming a conspicuous share of commercial and communication territory, they have contributed strongly to the transformation of our urban landscapes.

Further, brands convey values. As we will see in Chapter 6, a brand's identity is made up of invariants that express its vision of the world, the values it believes in and attempts to promote. Nike is the pursuit of excellence in athletic performance; Hermès the aristocratic life; Armani relaxed elegance in the Italian style. Brands oblige us, through their presence in the commercial circuits, to position ourselves in relation to these values. The offering of products and the values associated with them has grown strongly in recent years, giving us a choice our parents could never have dreamed of. We can choose temporary lifestyles as we see fit and reflect our moods in the way we consume.

Finally, brands are at the origin of numerous actions of solidarity. Whether under the influence of consumers or under the leadership of enlightened managers, they have greatly increased their commitments to causes in the general interest. Again, we will return to the mechanisms and the consequences of such commitments. As we will see, they are closely linked to the communicative dimension of the brands. At this early stage in our

luxury **brand** management

examination, we have only touched on these tangible effects on our society.

THE BRAND AND ITS SIGNS

With these initial analyses, we have tried to characterize the broad outlines of a brand's presence. What are the signs through which that presence asserts itself? They are of several orders, in fact, though often closely interlinked. To express itself, the brand uses these different elements, which are not interchangeable but are complementary.

The most important among them, of course, have to do with the name of the brand itself. The logo, now an unavoidable part of our urban landscape, is what immediately comes to mind. However, the name, in its "literal" and onomastic dimension—how it sounds to the ear—is also given a great deal of thought and attention by the brands.

We will consider this literal dimension first, before focusing on the phenomenon of the logo and other mechanisms of recognition.

Brand names

The name remains the first sign of recognition of a brand. It is never neutral. As we have seen, many brands start with the first name and surname of their founders.

For luxury products, the first name, since it identifies the creator, remains an indispensable part of the excellence and creativity of the brand. Saint Laurent never comes to mind without Yves, or Ferragamo without Salvatore. Yet there are exceptions, which have existed in their present form from the brand's origins: Gucci, the name of whose founder—Guccio—would doubtless result in an awkward alliteration; Coco Chanel always preferred to use only her surname.

But when a brand name has taken hold in the collective memory, beware of ill-advised changes. The change of the Marcel Rochas brand to simply "Rochas" was not at all lucky for the business. In the early 1990s, an attempt was made to return to the original by opening a men's clothing store by that name in Paris, but the attempt was soon abandoned.

In the field of brand-name management, one of the most interesting phenomena in recent times has been the progressive disappearance of the "Christian" from Christian Dior. Until 1995, the products and the advertising always bore the complete signature. Then, the forename progressively disappeared. For a long time, it was not shown in full size on the advertising, but on the baseline of the advertising and on the packaging. Today, the brand appears generally without the first name in, for example, the signs of the new stores and in all the advertising material. How should we view this change? Some will think that the company's directors are playing a dangerous game, and are in danger of progressively diminishing the affective component of the brand among traditional European customers and creating a completely new brand, with fewer roots and more appeal to young Asian and American clients. But the brand's excellent results in the last 10 years seem to indicate that this segmentation strategy was a good one.

In the history of brand creation, the name of perfumes under a luxury brand umbrella has given rise to more symbolic names. Attached to the poetics of evocation, perfume makers set the tone in the 1920s, with "Shalimar" from Guerlain in 1925, and "Shocking" from Schiaparelli in 1931.

In conclusion, what needs to be remembered is that there is no ideal name. If there were, it would be the name of a person, easy to remember in all languages, that evokes the qualities of the product or service offered, that suggests the company's philosophy, connotes intelligence and creativity, and begins with the letter "A" or "Z" to stand out in the listings.

The fact remains that the name, in itself, constitutes a vital asset. It is a source of much worry and enormous investment for companies. A good name has two characteristics: it is easy to remember and it has a significant emotional component or rational element. Yet in these two areas, the best is to be found alongside the worst. But such judgments, of course, imply a high degree of subjectivity. For that reason, we won't presume to give examples. But we're reminded of Juliet's lovely speech in Shakespeare:

> "What's in a name? that which we call a rose
> By any other name would smell as sweet."

That may be so for the name of a flower, but certainly not for the name of a brand.

Logos

"Logo" is the abbreviation of "logotype." It contains the Greek *logos* ("speech, discourse") and the suffix "-type," that in this case suggests the process of impression (as in typography).

Originally, for typographers, this word designated a group of signs that were printed all at once and that were all part of the same typographical character. Later, the term began to designate any fixed group of graphical signs representing a brand, a product or a company.

Codification is an essential component of a logo. To be easily recognizable, it must present an invariable visual grammar, where the shape of the characters, the size of the symbol and the colors used are rigorously defined and protected by patent. Also note that the simple fact of codifying the spelling of the name of a brand, even without accompanying visual symbols, already constitutes a logo.

The logo, then, is not the brand, but a particular way of writing the brand. It is the heraldic shield of modern times—a combination of letters or signs, an image, an ideogram, or a group of graphical elements.

The functions of the logo

The logo, a unique and recognizable sign, has always served to mark an object, a work or a building as belonging to a specific category. Logos appear to have always existed. Stone carvers placed their mark on their work, as did the great cabinetmakers. Roman slaves were tattooed with their masters' signs, and aristocrats and armies used escutcheons or standards. The word "brand" originally stood for the mark burned into the hide of cattle with a hot iron.

Communicating via symbols—language, mathematical signs, road signs—is one characteristic of humans. Logos are to modern communication and consumption activities what numbers are to mathematics or words to language: they constitute a new typology of conventional signs. In a way, logos are the new alphabet of an "over-communicating" society, the symbols of our time.

The logo plays a role in social relations for two complementary reasons: on one hand, for the informational content it communicates to the consumer before the purchase; on the other, for the perception it will create of this same consumer after the purchase, when he or she will be associated with the logo.

It's not surprising to see logos occupying such a dominant place in our over-mediatized society. They often fill the need for communicative synthesis pushed to its extreme: a maximum amount of information in a minimum number of signs. The synthetic expressiveness of signs as different from each other as the Nike "swoosh" and the Christian cross is remarkable; independently of their referents, they accomplish an analogous semiotic function. In a few strokes, a maximum number of values or a vision of the world are summed up.

It is difficult to draw a strict typology of logos, since they borrow from a great number of expressive processes. One of the founders of semiotics, the philosopher Charles Sanders Peirce, proposed a classification of signs into three categories: icons, indices and symbols.[3] Each of the three evokes a particular type of relation between the sign and the thing it represents.

The icon, Peirce says, is a representation of a "literal" type, based on the notion of similarity. For example, to represent an apple, we draw the contour of an apple.

Indices correspond to a relationship that is more mental, yet extremely strong, between the sign and the thing. It is a trace, an effect, or an element of the thing, which designates its presence without the slightest ambiguity. For example, if we see smoke on the horizon, it does not literally "draw" fire, but signifies its presence very strongly ("Where there's smoke, there's fire"). In this case the association is based on objective correspondences, in the sense that they are guaranteed by laws that are identical for everyone: in Tokyo as in New York, fire generally makes smoke.

Symbols, finally, correspond to the establishment of an "arbitrary" link between the sign and the thing: for example, a lion for the Republic of Venice. The force of the symbol rests on the establishment of a common culture. There is no graphical similarity between one and the other, nor is there an "objective" link of a physical or logical nature. A foreigner confronted with the symbol would not be able to decode it; on the other hand, for all the members of a given community, its meaning is obvious. We could say that a symbol is a federating element. In Greek, *symbolon* designated the fragments of a clay tablet that had been broken. These pieces were then distributed to the members of a group, who reconstituted the tablet at each of their meetings. When Nike issues a sports advertising spot that it signs only with its "swoosh," without even giving its name or slogan, it is obviously playing on the symbolic and federating dimension of its logo as well as on its fame.

These categories are abstract. In practice, logos are often hybrid, making use of all three at the same time. It might be better, then, to speak of the different functions of the sign. Let's take the example of the original Apple logo, which Jean-Marie Floch has analyzed in detail by comparing it to IBM's logo.[4] It can be called iconic, since it represents an apple; indicial (extrapolating a little), since the hollow in the outline clearly indicates that a bite has been taken out of this apple; and, above all, symbolic—the bitten-into apple is laden with rich suggestions, and the rainbow of the original logo also connotes the cultural blend that is California society.

Nevertheless, the symbolic function is by far the one most called upon. This is not surprising. To say that a logo functions as a symbol for a brand is to describe this notion of consumers' belonging to and having membership in a special and prestigious club. Note that logos that are purely typographical (a very specific way of writing the brand—font, letter size, spacing, and so on) also participate in this symbolic function. In fact, they rely on a set of visual conventions. For example, a serif character[5] will tend to connote Classicism or Neoclassicism, as in the case of Bulgari; a sans-serif font will connote modernity, as illustrated by the Lancel logo.

Ideally, a logo also seeks to take on the indicial function. The brand's dream, of course, is for its logo to represent it in a way that is as elementary as the way smoke signifies fire—even though such an ambition is utopian. Very interesting examples of this indicial function can be found on the boxes of matches given away by cigarette producers in France. Very strict regulations prohibit the display of their name, their brand, their slogan, or any other distinctive sign on the box; but they've still managed to develop very abstract visual grammars, derived from their logos, which still carry meaning. It's a kind of graphical guessing game, and trying to decode them "blind" provides a good indication of a brand's graphical renown.

A few forms of logo

In this rapid overview, we claim neither to be exhaustive nor to propose a coherent typology. We devote the bulk of our efforts to logos that are strongly graphical, in an attempt to suggest the diversity of this universe.

Like the seals of the ancients, most logos consist of an image or of intertwined letters.

In the past, certain logos expressed themselves in three dimensions: Rolls-Royce chose the Winged Victory of Samothrace; Jaguar used the Leaper—a metal statuette of a leaping jaguar—as a hood ornament on its sports cars.

Certain logos have a more iconic function. In the category of images, the most frequent are those of animals. This harks back

luxury **brand** management

to the heraldic tradition, where animals were a prime source of inspiration for the escutcheons of the aristocracy.

Most often, we will find ourselves in the symbolic register, where the animal is an allegory for virtues that are assigned to it by convention. The choice of the brand name "Jaguar," with its stylized but representational logo, is obviously associated with the aspiration to such virtues. And the list is long. There is Ferrari's rearing horse, an expression of indomitable vitality. The emblem was given to Enzo Ferrari by the family of a national hero, the aviator Francesco Baracca, who had it mounted on his plane when he was shot down over Montello during the First World War. For energy and speed, there is the shark of Paul and Shark; the elephant of Hunting World. For perseverance, there is Morabito's tortoise; for toughness and intelligence, the Lacoste crocodile. But many other representative images exist: Hermès's coach, Ralph Lauren's polo player.

Another very widespread category draws more from the history of writing and the signature. These are "monogram" logos, made up of the brand's initials and its derivatives. What comes to mind first are obviously the two intertwined Cs of Chanel and Cartier; Gucci's G; Yves Saint Laurent's YSL and Loewe's "crab," with its L reflected in two axes.

Finally, there are logos of a more abstract nature, where the arbitrariness of the symbol predominates. This is not a new phenomenon. As with the choice of brand names, abstraction has been a trend for some decades. This is so with Tommy Hilfiger, with its red-white-and-blue rectangle, an extrapolation of the American flag, or Bally's red-and-white square.

Regardless of the choices made, a good logo should have the power to express and synthesize the characteristics of the brand, symbolic force, and ease of retention through a certain formal simplicity. Achieving all this is not as simple as it might seem, but success gives a brand a considerable competitive advantage.

Managing logos

Formal fashions change. Those within companies who are responsible for creating graphics are more sensitive than others to such issues and often ask for a logo to be transformed or rejuvenated. They rarely win out. This issue is a manager's nightmare. Many brands prefer to make do with a logo that is seen as somewhat dated rather than take the risk of damaging its fame. The graphical evolutions of logos at major brands extend over entire decades, and each stage of the process is often almost imperceptible.

Examples abound. The British brand Burberry's decided to alter its name to make it more accessible to an international clientele and, in general, to make the brand more competitive by giving it more modern connotations. This involved removing the apostrophe and the possessive "s." (This form is extremely widespread in English in the names of brands and restaurants, but it is less easily perceptible for other cultures.) Thus "Burberry's" became "Burberry." Removing the apostrophe and the "s" implies a change in the lettering as a whole, modernizing the brand, doubtless internationalizing it, but maybe slightly destabilizing part of its Anglo-Saxon clientele. These are not the kind of decisions that can be taken lightly.

Logos are therefore always extremely sensitive to manage. Their creation, their aesthetic evolution and their utilization must be precise and organized to correspond with the general strategy of the brand.

What happens when there is no logo, or at least no graphical emblem? This is the case, for example, with Armani, Tiffany, Ferragamo and Bulgari, among others. Generally, the company looks for one. But, in the case of an established brand with a rich history, this is not easy.

In the early 1990s, Ferragamo wanted to stylize the brand name, to shorten it and make the founder's signature more legible. Also, the founder's baroque logo was very dated and was not used much. The company also wanted to attach a graphical emblem. Numerous trials were undertaken. A design with six horses, recalling the founder's six children, was studied, as was a drawing

luxury **brand** management

of the Feroni Palace, the company's headquarters. But the best intentions are not always successful, and the brand continues to use the Salvatore Ferragamo signature, whose calligraphy and, above all, whose length, contribute to easy recognition.

Certain brands simply have no emblem and get along without one. The name of the brand, with its colors, graphics and sometimes its calligraphy, is still the first point of recognition. The pointed Bulgari "U" has such strength as to make the search for an emblematic logo superfluous.

Logomania

Logos are almost omnipresent. Disseminating these "totems" in all the registers of communication is an easy way of universalizing the representation of the brand. They are visible on products to the point where they have become concrete signs of added value, particularly in the fashion sphere.

Logomania is also cyclical, the last craze dating back to the spring of 2000. By the 2002 Fall-Winter collections, there was a marked decrease in the number of products that were covered with logos. But, starting in 2004, logos are back, it seems. This has implications that have to be faced: fashion changes every season and can make obsolete an element that is strongly attached to the identity of the brand itself.

As for logos of public or private sponsors, they have proliferated in the past few years on posters and billboards for sports and cultural events. Their presence and, very often, their size on the poster are contractually imposed. Graphic artists often complain about this, pointing out that these additional signs, to which they are sometimes required to devote as much as 20% of the total display area, can have a negative impact on the relevance of their communication; and they have a point.

We have said that logos, as symbols, presuppose a cultural community, and taking local specificities into consideration appears to be a determining factor in establishing a threshold of tolerance.

Perceptions vary greatly from one country to another. Logos are much better received in Japan than in the United States or Europe. While a majority of Europeans refuse to wear a necktie printed with the acronym of a brand, Americans have no problem with it, and the very same necktie might well become a genuine fad in Japan.

The majority of brands with global ambitions have the wisdom to take these cultural differences into account and have integrated them. Louis Vuitton, for example, offers its Japanese clientele strongly monogrammed bags; for European consumers, the brand offers a fabric in identical colors, but with a checkerboard pattern, or else Épi or Taïga leather, where the monogram only appears episodically.

And consumers in Paris and Tokyo are very happy with their Vuitton purchases. They've made the effort of acquiring an expensive product and feel that a prestigious logo, one which reflects well on them, is the reward for that effort, provided that it remains below their own particular tolerance threshold. They feel that by carrying the bag in public, they are affirming the values they seek (a certain elegance, perhaps) without the risk of suggesting those they shun (bad taste).

The logo, as the ultimate synthesis of the brand's communication, must appeal to the eye, to the heart and to the intelligence.

A logo is not a necessary and sufficient condition of success. However, not to have an adequate logo is to miss an incredible opportunity to communicate more effectively.

Other signs of recognition

Signs of recognition don't end with the name of the brand or its logo. Certain brands or products have succeeded in appropriating other elements of recognition and differentiation, often by chance or through repeated usage. Yet they manage these additional distinguishing elements closely.

Base lines have become more frequent as they come to complement a logo that is not always sufficiently explicit of the brand nature. Certain advertising slogans, so often heard and repeated in association with the brand, have become extensions operating like synonyms: Nokia's "Connecting people," HP's "Invent," or Sony's "Go create," for example. Faced with the difficulty of finding a logo and a name able to synthesize the brand identity, the addition of a few words often does the trick. Intel's taking advantage of a logo change to add the words "leap forward" provides a recent example of this. In luxury, brands have often used expressions such as "The art of...," which sounds more vintage than trendy, and seem to have abandoned the "creativity" theme to the technology companies.

There are examples of cult products that become emblematic of a brand, such as the Hermès Kelly bag or Gucci moccasins. There are also certain distinctive characteristics such as the matte-metallic feel used in most Porsche design products. Color is another important element: a red sports car has to be a Ferrari. Indeed, Ferrari's monopoly on the color is so strong that it seems a little presumptuous to buy a sports car of another make in the same shade of red. Ducati has done the same with red in the motorcycle sector. Distinctive sound can even be an identifying element: Porsche, Harley-Davidson and Ducati take great pains to maintain a very specific engine noise for their products, which they have even attempted to patent.

Packaging can also be an element of recognition. Tiffany's light-blue box and the Hermès orange box are strong aesthetic elements of their individual identity that travels with the product and are an integral part of the gift.

Labeling, too, is another. It is more important in categories such as ready-to-wear, but it is being discovered, beyond its original informative function, as an important creative element. For instance, the hot Argentine brand La Martina is attaching— inside and out—all sorts of labels to its famous polo shirts, T-shirts and leather accessories, and this has become a strong element of its brand recognition.

Whether through names, logos or other elements, a brand's signs must be identifiable, expressive and easy to remember. They must create a feeling of closeness, familiarity, and even humanity. They must communicate a message of belonging, not only to the brand (at the first level), but also to its universe and its values. This last point is what will distinguish between a brand that projects meaning and one whose significance is vague. Finally, they must stay in their proper place, not be a nuisance, and never give themselves over to semantic inaccuracy, which could complicate decoding. Their primary role is to "speak" the brand and its universe with elegance and conciseness. It is the brand's responsibility to keep a close watch over its signs, their nature and their frequency.

THE LEGAL ASPECTS AND THE DEFENSE OF A BRAND

There are hundreds of very good books on brand protection, written by legal experts. In this book, it would be impossible for us to even summarize what has been said on the subject. Nevertheless, this is so much of a concern for luxury goods—particularly for watches, perfumes and leather goods—that it is necessary here to at least give some indication of the operational methods available for dealing with the subject.

Brand protection
Brand registration

The first step with any new brand is to register it. But this registration must be done by country and by class. Table 3.5 gives a broadly accepted list of brand categories. For registering a fashion brand, categories 25 and 24 are essential, but so is 18 for leather goods, 9 for glasses, and 16 and 34 for writing instruments and lighters. That's a total of six categories. For perfume activities, registering in classes 3 and 5 is essential; and if the ultimate goal is perhaps to come up with promotional articles such as combs or brushes, then it is also advisable to look at class 21. Jewelry and watches have their own class, 14.

The ideal for a new brand would be to register in 10 categories. But this is not cheap. Brand registration in one country could cost anywhere from €1,000 to €2,000 (taking into account the lawyers' fees as well as the tax levied by the national registration authorities). In 100 countries and in 10 classes, this could cost between €1–2 million. This is not easy for a brand which is just starting up.

Table 3.5: Brand registration categories

1	Chemical products
2	Paint, varnishes
3	Perfumes, soaps, cosmetics
4	Oil, candles
5	Pharmaceutical products, disinfectants, cosmetics
6	Metal tools
7	Machine tools
8	Tools, razors
9	Technical instruments, optical products, glasses
10	Medical and veterinary products
14	Jewelry, watches
15	Musical instruments
16	Paper products, writing instruments
17	Plastic products
18	Leather goods
19	Construction materials
20	Furniture
21	Kitchenware, chinaware, combs, brushes
22	Ropes, textile and fabric bags
23	Thread
24	Fabric and textile products
25	Garments, shoes, hats
26	Embroidery
27	Rugs
28	Toys
29	Meat products
30	Food
31	Agricultural products
34	Tobacco, lighters

At the outset, it is not necessary to be registered everywhere in the world; indeed, most European countries that have signed the Madrid Convention require only one registration. But registering in the United States, Japan and China, and in Latin American countries, is essential: not to do so is to leave the way clear for unscrupulous local companies to register the name for counterfeit activities.

Registration renewal

Registration does not remain active forever. It can, depending on the country and the legislation in place, last for either five or 10 years. This means that every year, it is necessary to renew approximately 20% of all registrations at a cost of anywhere between €200,000 and €400,000 for each of the 10 classes mentioned above.

But to renew the registration in a given class, local authorities will request proof of usage. If nobody takes legal action for lack of usage and forfeiture of the original registration, things should be fine. Should such action be taken, however, the courts can be very demanding.

For example, in the 1980s Paco Rabanne was the leader in the field of men's eau de toilette in Brazil. It was heavily advertised and it had a very strong awareness locally. But as customs duties on perfumes were very high, the company's local distributor was smuggling the products into the country. When the court asked for proof of payment of import duties, these could not be presented. The court's judgment was that the brand had never been officially present in Brazil and it enacted forfeiture in classes 3 and 5. The brand was then immediately registered by someone considered by the company to be a counterfeit operator but whom the Brazilian courts continued to consider to be the genuine brand user for many years.

Very well-known brands can fight this situation by pointing to the worldwide awareness of the brand and, in some cases, to the fact that the brand is the patronymic of a given individual, that the local operators knew of the brand's world status when they

luxury **brand** management

registered it and were thus not acting in good faith. Paco Rabanne eventually succeeded in recovering its name in Brazil, thanks to the fact that the brand was the official name of Mr. Paco Rabanne, but it took six or seven years to enforce this judgment.

In their main businesses, luxury companies generally do not have difficulty in protecting and renewing their brands. But in secondary product categories, it is not that simple. For example, to protect itself against actions for non-usage under classes 24 and 25, Cartier has developed a range of scarves. Very famous brands that do not have a perfume business are well advised to make a standard perfume every three to five years and to invoice it to their overseas subsidiaries or distributors to ensure that there is minimum proof of usage, in the form of receipts for payment of customs duties, in most parts of the world.

The potential dangers of not protecting registration rights are evident in another case involving Cartier. In Mexico, an individual registered the brand before Cartier itself, opened a Cartier store and traded in Cartier watches before the company could manage to regain its full registration rights. For many years, Lacoste had problems in Hong Kong and China with a locally registered brand, "Crocodile," which had a similar logo. The brands finally came to an agreement that the Chinese company would modify its logo in such a way that it would not be confused with the Lacoste crocodile.

While registration for any brand can be difficult, costly and tedious, it is absolutely necessary, and is even more so for perfume houses. Dior, for example, has to register both its brand and each of its individual products—Poison, Dolce Vita, J'adore, Fahrenheit, L'Eau Sauvage, Capture and many others.

The original registration

It is not easy to register a new brand, not least because for perfumes with suggested names such as Romance, Romantique or Romantic it is likely that the name has been registered and is already in use somewhere in the world. Generally, brand names are generated through creative group discussions or creative sessions, at the end of which maybe 50 names have come up for consideration. A first run on the Internet will probably eliminate most, if not all, of these: the names are already in use or may have sufficient legally acceptable "proofs of usage" to discourage their adoption. Sometimes a registered letter to a company indicating a desire to start a legal action for lack of usage and forfeiture of its early brand registration may give rise to an opportunity to buy that registration. Where there is no real proof of usage, this may be done for €10,000–20,000. Where there are strong worldwide registrations and convincing proof of usage, this may rise to anywhere between €200,000 and €500,000. This is not a very easy subject.

When Paco Rabanne launched its La Nuit perfume, it was possible to sell it everywhere in the world except Venezuela. Caron had tried and failed to get permission to sell its own "Nocturne" fragrance because a local manufacturer had an eau de Cologne registered under the same name. Caron had tried to purchase the name or to negotiate a coexistence agreement with the local manufacturer, but to no avail. So Caron's Nocturne was sold under a special label– "La Nuit"–in Venezuela. However, it was willing to free the La Nuit name if Paco Rabanne could obtain a coexistence agreement from the local manufacturer enabling Caron to sell its Nocturne fragrance under that name. Paco Rabanne tried and never succeeded, and its La Nuit perfume has never been sold in Venezuela.

Fighting counterfeit activities

Some activities are considered legal in one part of the world and illegal in others. We examine some of these first, look at the specific case of China, and then move on to what we call the "lenient" countries.

Knock-offs and tables of correspondence

In the United States, supermarkets sell cheap perfumes with labels that proclaim: "If you liked Youth Dew by Estée Lauder, you will love our No.36," or "If you liked Chanel No.5, you will love our

luxury **brand** management

No.17." In most countries, such products—known as "knock-offs"—would be prohibited because they exist only by feeding off the awareness of and preference for established brands. Elsewhere they would be seen as unfair competition or, to put it more accurately, "commercial parasites," but in the United States consumer advocates take the view that such products provide fair value to the customer and reduce selective luxury perfume houses to what they really are—providers of a given scent that can be copied. Each country has its own system and its own specific characteristics.

Tables of correspondence are the German equivalent of knock-offs. Here, perfumes are sold with a designated number that corresponds with the customer's usual, more expensive, brand of choice. To openly link any known named brand with a cheaper corresponding numbered brand is prohibited by law as unfair competition. But German firms have found a way around this: as long as they and their sales staff don't make such links, in writing or orally, products can be sold in this way. Again, consumer advocates are very much in favor of these products and this approach, and such sales are strong.

What can brands do about this? The answer is, with both knock-offs and tables of correspondence, absolutely nothing. In other countries, such practices would be fought very strongly.

This is not unlike the Thai T-shirts with the name Chanel, Dior or Prada embroidered on the front. Such products are clearly counterfeits and are clearly perceived as such. In a way, they are the unwanted outcome of brands' success. Whether such things should be fought against is debatable, since the consumers who buy these products are well aware that they are not buying the real thing.

Chinese and Korean counterfeits

Tourists walking around in Seoul or Shanghai will be stopped quite frequently by people offering "fake watches, shoes or handbags." If they show some interest, they are led to a store down a back street somewhere and are then presented with as many copies of luxury watches as they could hope for. It seems that every single brand of watch is on offer, along with any number of handbags. While the watches sometimes never work more than two or three minutes, the handbags are more or less "no risk," even if the product finishes are not in line with those of the genuine products.

Again, some might say that it is not necessary to fight such counterfeit activities, because those purchasing know that the products are fake and they would never have bought the genuine article. This is to put the genuine branded product and the fake into two different market segments. A Japanese or other Asian tourist would not be interested in a fake product: they value the legitimacy of the authentic goods too highly for that. Americans, too, are not interested in anything other than the genuine article. The only ones who are really interested are the Europeans, who believe they are smart and they can get a good deal and nobody would know the difference anyway. Which is almost never true.

The fight against the counterfeiters is never a simple task. It requires both the will and the means tackle the whole distribution chain, from those offering the fakes in the streets, to the back-street shops, to the wholesaler and on to the manufacturer. Even if the manufacturer is located and sued, the machinery and equipment is simply moved to another location or sold to another company, and the cycle will start all over again.

Though it may seem an endless fight, it is nevertheless a necessary one if the development of such counterfeiting trades is to be curbed and their volumes curtailed.

The "lenient" countries

In some countries, the authorities are not particularly interested in curbing an activity that provides local jobs and brings in hard foreign currency. Morocco is a case in point. There it is possible to buy copies of every type of branded leather goods, a trade that obviously provides jobs for local leather-goods specialists.

Italy provides another example of where perhaps the authorities may sometimes turn a blind eye where counterfeiting is concerned.

luxury **brand** management

In Rome or Vintimille, for example, you can find copies of every single French luxury brand–Chanel, Louis Vuitton, Dior. Strangely, though, it's much more difficult to get Gucci or Ferragamo copies. Here again the Italian government and police could be more active and more effective. We can only hope that the European Union can bring the necessary pressure to bear to counter such activities more effectively than simple bilateral discussions have been able to achieve to date.

What makes counterfeiting such an interesting activity is the fact that the margins of luxury goods are very high. The higher the power of the brand, the more interesting it is to move into the field. Counterfeit goods are, in their own way, a clear indication of the desirability and power of the original brand.

Endnotes

[1] *Des Brevets et des marques, une histoire de la propriété industrielle* (Patents and Trademarks: A History of Industrial Property), INPI (French Patent Office), Fayard 2001.

[2] Austria-Hungary, France, German States, Great Britain, and United States. Source: S. Lapointe, for Leger Robic Richard.

[3] C. Harsborne and P. Weiss (eds), The Collected Papers of Charles Sanders Peirce, vol 1-6, Cambridge: Harvard University Press, 1931-35.

[4] Jean-Marie Floch, *Identités visuelles*, Paris: PUF, 1995.

[5] A serif is the horizontal line that serves as the base of the letter in certain typefaces. Fonts of more recent invention tend not to have serifs (and are referred to as "sans serif").

chapter **4**

BRAND
Lifecycle

Brands are a part of our most intimate history. Their history is not quite one and the same as that of the company that brought them into existence: they have an independent life and, having become part of our imagination, sometimes survive there long after the company has disappeared.

A brand's history comprises phases of strong expansion alternating with phases of relative stagnation, and perhaps rapid decline. This situation is not really different from what is termed the "lifecycle" of a product or a company. As shown in Figure 4.1, the life of a brand can be represented on a graph, with time mapped against an estimate of the brand's "strength" based on a given convention.

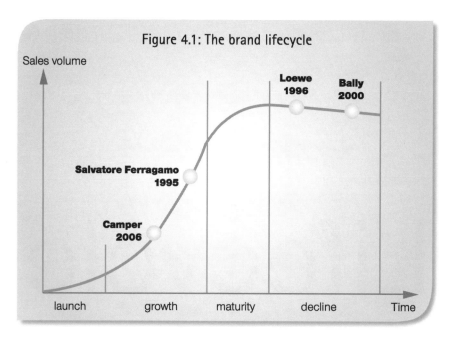
Figure 4.1: The brand lifecycle

The graph follows the same phases—launch, growth, maturity, decline, re-launch and disappearance—that characterize the lifecycle of a product. At each of these stages, the problems faced by the luxury brand's director are posed in specific terms.

The fashion and luxury sector is particularly concerned with the re-launching phase, which can become a real problem for brands that have reached maturity or decline. The most spectacular example of successive re-launchings is that of Gucci, as illustrated in Figure 4.2. The brand's first major re-launch took place in 1995/96. Its results for 2002 were affected by 9/11, as well as the struggle between the LVMH and PPR groups for control of the brand. Even after the departure of Messrs. Ford and de Sole, who were, respectively, the creative director and the chairman, 2004 and 2005 produced very strong performances despite the fact that they had been perceived as the only possible developers of the brand. The curve looks a bit like a roller coaster, but it reflects the brand's strength and ability to rebound.

luxury **brand** management

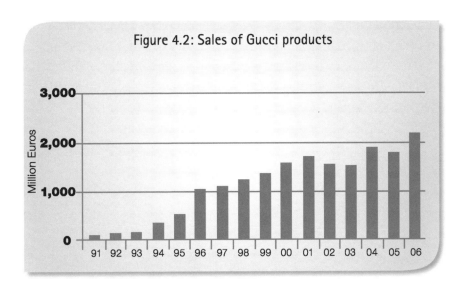

Figure 4.2: Sales of Gucci products

Re-launching can create a new lifecycle for the brand, though re-launches are rarely as successful as this. The first jump in 1995/96 illustrates what we refer to later in this chapter as "the great leap" and involves a drastic repositioning of the brand, its identity, and, in this case, its target consumers. It's like giving the brand a new lease on life through new values (which are, of course, compatible with the earlier values).

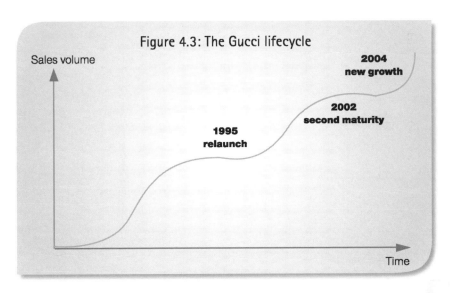

Figure 4.3: The Gucci lifecycle

brand **lifecycle**

Another luxury brand that has been the object of a major re-launch is Burberry. Under Rose Marie Bravo's wise leadership, the brand is clearly in the growth phase of the new lifecycle, following a major jump in 2000/01 when its operations in Spain went from license fees to full revenue.

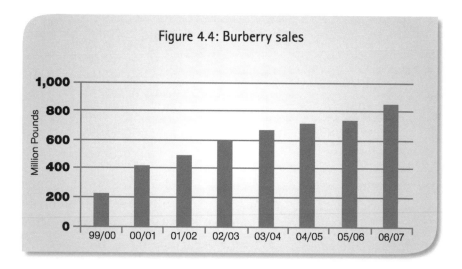

Figure 4.4: Burberry sales

Other brands in the luxury industries sector are at different stages of their respective lifecycles. Bulgari, for example, enjoyed a

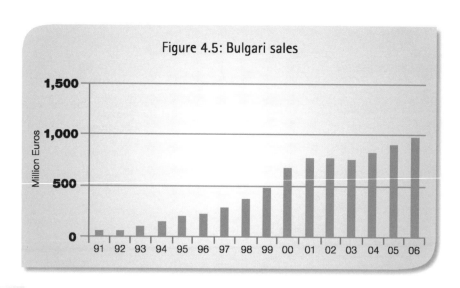

Figure 4.5: Bulgari sales

luxury **brand** management

strong growth phase from 1993 until 2001. Then, like many others, it suffered the effects of 9/11. Now, it is probably nearing its maturity.

Hermès, a brand that is over a century old, has had relatively constant growth since the early 1990s. It seems little affected by the different economic slumps, as if the attraction of authentic luxury were continuing its evolution independently of economic crises. As with Bulgari, there was a decline in 2003, but the growth has since returned to the pace of the 1990s. The aristocratic French brand has yet to reach its maturity.

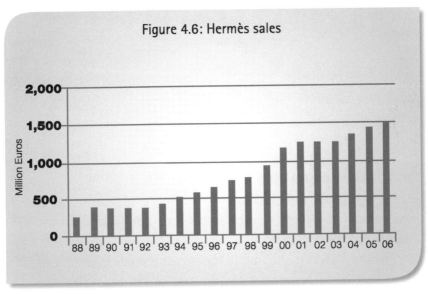

Figure 4.6: Hermès sales

Ferragamo, on the other hand, seems to have passed into its maturity phase. The discontinuity of the year 2000 corresponds with the consolidation of sales that followed the purchase of its Japanese retailing subsidiary. The curve for comparative yearly business volume is, in fact, very close to the theoretical profile of the lifecycle. New competitive dimensions will have to be activated if the brand is to recover its growth rate of the 1990s, even though 2006 results are encouraging.

The ambiguities of this last example are a good illustration of the fact that business volume does not provide a very homogeneous measurement of the strength of a brand, which is, in fact, very

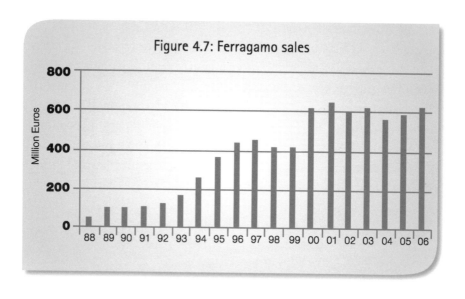

Figure 4.7: Ferragamo sales

difficult to quantify. However, as we shall see, approximations are still possible.

MEASURING A BRAND'S STRENGTH

Business volume is the most easily accessible measurement. But its homogeneity has to be ensured by converting all sales to retailers and license royalties into a retail value.

Where business volume is the measurement used, the brand's lifecycle will correspond with the sum of the lifecycles of all its products. But such an estimate doesn't quantify such notions as name recognition or desirability. Also, it only partially represents the result of the brand's economic operations because it doesn't show profits and financial flows.

This approach can be completed without difficulty using other indicators that are superimposed on business volume. Obviously, profits and cash flows should achieve their maximum at the start of maturity and reach their lowest ebb after a few years of decline. As for stock prices, they can be seen as a measurement of the brand's strength as investors see it—in terms of its ability to generate financial flows in the future.

luxury **brand** management

THE BIRTH OF A BRAND

How are brands born? We are talking here of strong brands, ones destined to make their mark on their time. One thing is sure: fame can't be guaranteed. This is as true of brands as it is of individuals. Certain measures and resources can aid their ascent, but success is never certain.

Analysis after the fact inevitably reveals that a strong brand has its origins in an ambitious project supported by the faith of a talented individual. This will often be the founder of the company, whose confidence in the underlying vision and ability to make it a reality are determining advantages. Boldness, vision and determination are indispensable qualities.

Innovation is the second essential factor. Creative genius consists in reading the mood of the times and offering products that respond to it in novel ways, be it at the level of style, technology or in the identification of a new need.

In the category of stylistic innovation, we find all the great names of *haute couture* and accessories: Coco Chanel, Christian Dior, Yves Saint Laurent, Salvatore Ferragamo, Giorgio Armani, and so on. These creators were able to express new ideas that captured the interest of sufficient numbers of people to justify the launch of a durable economic activity.

In the area of technological innovation, there are all the great pioneers of the automobile industry: Ford, Ransom Olds, Bugatti, Panhard, Renault. And, of course, the likes of Thomas Edison, William Hewlett, Dave Packard, Bill Gates and Steve Jobs also belong on this list, as does Walt Disney.

The innovation we are speaking of is rarely synonymous with invention because it is integrated into the conditions of distribution of the product—its production on a mass scale, for example. It often operates through appropriation or extrapolation of techniques already worked out on the theoretical level, to which it gives concrete industrial reality. It is true, for example, that Bill Gates is not an "inventor" of software; but it is also true that this visionary businessman understood, before most people, the potential of the microcomputer and was able to turn it to his advantage.

Consequently, there any many dimensions of innovation. They can be in the development of a specific production tool that makes the mass production of a new product possible. Innovation can also consist in revolutionizing the production or distribution of an existing product, or the way in which a business or its associated services are organized and conducted. Aside from the fact that the company knit in white yarn and dyed to suit demand, Benetton was born of an innovative system of distribution. Zara's success arose out of logistical organization and an exceptional capacity to read the needs of the markets. These assets make it possible for the brand to supply products to the places where they are required within 10 days. Ray Kroc founded McDonald's in 1955 and invented fast food. Prada began to make a name for itself through the use of nylon in the manufacture of its bags.

Communication has also become an important innovative dimension. Take, for example, the lingerie brand Lise Charmelle, which suddenly became famous in Spain in 2002 following a billboard campaign that captured people's attention. In the fashion milieu, illustrious personalities like Louis Vuitton, Carl-Franz Bally, Enrique Loewe and Guccio Gucci were not creators in the stylistic or technological sense of the term, but artisans who developed their industrial and commercial vision beginning in the mid-nineteenth century.

But at what exact point does a brand become a brand? The question is somewhat rhetorical, but a few commonly used indices can be mentioned here:

- when the brand's creator dies and it continues to prosper
- when advertising is no longer needed to sell the products
- when a €35 million sales volume is reached
- when new categories of products can be developed successfully
- when more than 50% of the general public in a given country are familiar with the product/company's existence

luxury **brand** management

- when the product/company has established a presence in Europe, the United States and Asia.

We feel, in fact, that any economic activity has within it the seed of a brand which will develop if conditions are favorable. How many brands started with the activities of small-scale artisans or merchants? Many brands that are not international and have low name recognition continue to prosper.

GROWTH OF A BRAND

In a growth phase, a brand will implement a strategy of expansion, both quantitative and qualitative. Most brands that are successful today are in this phase of development, and are characterized by two-figure growth rates.

On the quantitative level, the brand will try to establish itself in new geographical markets, while extending its presence in its existing markets. The logic of volume is more evident in this phase: more has to be sold in order to absorb fixed costs more easily. But since communication is generally managed in terms of a percentage of sales, the greater the sales, the more the brand can communicate.

On the qualitative level, the brand will optimize its production and distribution tools; possibly improve its product; and use its growing reputation to move into new areas. Such extensions through launching new categories of products are, of course, a growth factor, but they also increase awareness of the brand by making it more accessible, thanks to multiple and/or wider distribution channels. They plant the seeds of future legitimacy in new sectors. The budget for communication and strengthening the brand's identity then serves as an umbrella for several categories of products and becomes profitable more easily.

The fact that there are multiple axes of development—sectoral growth, geographical expansion, the introduction of new product categories, the optimization of internal processes, and repositioning the brand—explains why this phase can last several decades. With the exception of sectoral growth, these are all ways in which a brand can take market share away from its most significant competitors.

Sectoral growth

The most recent case of rapid sectoral expansion is the explosion in the market for cellular telephones. Between 1996 and 2000, Nokia and Ericsson experienced growth rates of 252% and 120%, respectively.

But this single axis cannot ensure stable growth in a market that is volatile or is rapidly reaching saturation. This is what happened to Ericsson, whose sales dropped by 57% between 2000 and 2003 only to rebound by 51% between 2003 and 2006. Ericsson seems to have enjoyed a major re-launch of its brand.

Meanwhile, Nokia reached a peak in 2001 and was down by 6% in 2004, only to rebound in 2005 and 2006. It is definitely reaching maturity, unless a new socio-technological breakthrough hits the mobile telephone market.

Again the curves are very close to the theoretical lifecycle model.

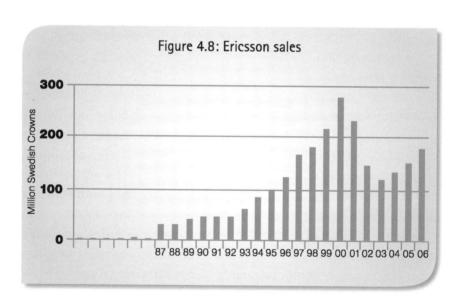

Figure 4.8: Ericsson sales

luxury **brand** management

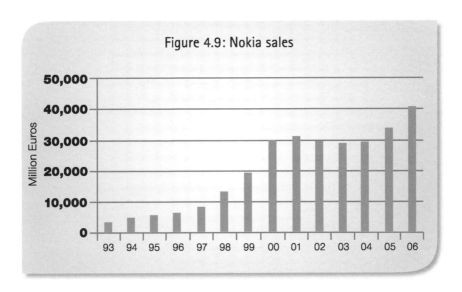

Figure 4.9: Nokia sales

Geographical expansion

As soon as a product is successful in one country, it is logical to think that it should sell well in other countries. Attempts to put this into practice are varied and take on a great diversity of forms.

In some cases, especially in the mass markets, the same product, with the same communication strategy, can succeed. This is the worldwide strategy of Coca-Cola and Pepsi Cola, for example. We are not strong advocates of universal communication, which we feel is now applied increasingly less, and even in the cases of these products, which rely on target populations that are federated by transnational values (youth, dynamism, a relaxed attitude toward adults), there is room for adjusting to local conditions. In the case of certain big advertisers, the central marketing teams send out a complete, flexible kit that, for example, utilizes the same strategy but with different approaches. Thus, each national team can choose the particular campaign that will be most applicable to its environment.

This is also what is done with all fashion and perfume brands, a large percentage of whose sales are to overseas consumers. The advertising will generally be identical. In certain cases, however, it may have to be modified slightly; for example, for the Persian Gulf countries.

In the cosmetics industry, the product will be identical, but the communication will vary depending on the country. In one country the product may not serve quite the same function as in another. In the United States, for example, a Yamaha 125cc motorcycle is a leisure product; in Taiwan, it's a means of transportation. In such cases, the advertising will be different.

There are also cases where the product is different while the communication remains more or less identical. For example, in the Asian markets, certain cognac producers propose sweeter versions of their products. While the name remains the same and the advertising is similar, the formula might be adapted to meet the needs of local taste.

There are cases—in the detergent business, for example—where both the product and the communication differ, but they are generally outside the luxury categories and therefore not within the purview of this study.

This diversity of situations is a good illustration of the many difficulties that can be involved in exporting a brand. Cases of failed geographical expansion are legion. Leaving aside organizational dysfunctions related to a poor understanding of local conditions and requirements, a brand, or its product, can sometimes prove to be simply not exportable.

There are products that have a cult following in a given country, but whose potential outside the national borders is limited. Pastis 51 and Suze, typically French products that are heavily consumed in France, are difficult to export. Italy's Martini is used as an aperitif in the United States, but is unlikely to become an international product consumed habitually and at high volume.

Another type of brand that is very strong in its own country but difficult to export is the department store—witness Marks & Spencer's recent failure in Continental Europe. The French might wonder why the Galeries Lafayette stores have not succeeded in locating elsewhere—in New York, Singapore, Bangkok or Berlin. The explanation is simple. The success of the Galeries Lafayette in France is linked to a certain French lifestyle, represented by a group of French brands that are known and liked by French consumers. In Berlin or New York, those French consumers are not present, and brands thought of as representing French chic are not necessarily available to the store: if they are very strong brands, they already have a presence in the target market, often through exclusivity agreements with other local department stores or with their own boutiques. The challenge is that of creating a French lifestyle abroad, without French customers and without the leading French brands. It's hard to build a strong case for the existence of such a store. The only cases of the successful export of department stores are Japanese stores such as Sogo and Daimaru in Southeast Asia. But they benefit locally from the support of numerous Japanese residents and tourists. The French Le Printemps store in Tokyo, unable to stock any of the major French brands, reinvented a "French style" aimed at very young girls. It offers new brands, unknown in Japan and sometimes even in France, or created especially for the store.

Zara is a special case. The company's growth during the 1990s happened without advertising and was based on the opening of new single-brand stores outside Spain, relying on its skill in reading trends and its rapid logistical responsiveness. In 20 years, Amancio Ortega created the Inditex group, the owner of the Zara brand, which has 3,131 stores in 64 countries around the world with sales of €8.2 billion in 2006.

In conclusion, while geographical expansion would seem to be the most natural dimension of development, it is also complex, and requires time and heavy investments. In addition, the results are often unpredictable—as the French chain Séphora, which early in 2002 closed the stores it had just opened in Japan and in the United States has learned. For these reasons, the process of development on the international level makes for a more wide open game, but a more difficult one.

New product categories

It's natural to want to amortize communication efforts on a larger number of products. That is why the development of new categories has always been a favorite area for brands.

One of the keys to success is a correct reading of the lines of relatedness between the original product and the area of diversification.

The Michelin Guide (1900) and roadmaps (1910) are an interesting historical example of this type of diversification. The promotion of automobile tourism by a tire manufacturer showed a concern for innovation, but also fit perfectly into the context of an industry that was in its infancy. At the time, the automobile remained a leisure item for the privileged classes rather than a generalized means of transportation.

If diversification seems natural in the fashion and luxury milieu, it's because couturiers became aware very early on of the importance of their labels. The famous No. 5 fragrance, launched by Coco Chanel in 1921 and now the world's largest-selling perfume, is still one of the great successes.

During the past decade, this trend has reached feverish proportions, with the launch of new products that are sometimes quite removed from the legitimacy of the original products.

The couture brands, without venturing too far from the original matrix, first moved into secondary lines: Rive Gauche for Yves Saint Laurent; Ungaro's Ivoire and Emanuel; Versus by Versace; "Emporio Armani"; D&G for Dolce & Gabbana; Donna Karan's DKNY; and so on. Then, during the 1990s, they developed lines of accessories (luggage, shoes, silk articles, eyewear...), a sector with higher margins and rates of growth and also an effective vector of communication.

Ungaro, after being taken over by the Ferragamo family in 1996, launched a line of accessories. Louis Vuitton began offering shoes. Loewe did the same, only to discover that you don't become a shoemaker overnight, and that to succeed with a new category of products, you have to be able to get across to the consumer a message of seriousness, competitiveness not only in terms of product quality, wealth of the offering, and service at the point of sale, but also, above all, coherence with the brand's values.

Going in the opposite direction, the accessories brands (Ferragamo, Gucci, Bally, Prada, Loewe also and others) diversified into ready-to-wear. They developed (generally through licensing) a line of eyewear, perfumes and, often, watches. Bulgari began as a jeweler and then developed accessories and perfumes. Jewelry and watch-making took on importance in the mid-1990s. It now looks as if "intimate feminine apparel" will be the New Frontier: Christian Dior and Burberry, for example, are developing strongly their activity in this area.

Finally, the hospitality business is attracting the luxury brands. In 1987, Maruccia Mandelli (Krizia) opened its K Club hotel in Barbados. The Ferragamo family began investing in it in the mid-1990s, but without associating the brand with it. Armani, in the wake of the launch of its Armani Casa products and stores, invested in hotels in Sardinia. But Bulgari has associated its brand most openly with the industry in a joint venture with Marriott International Luxury Group to create Bulgari Hotel & Resorts, in which Bulgari is in charge of decoration and Marriott handles management. There is also Versace, who opened the Palazzo Versace in Brisbane in 2000, and intends to develop in this sector. After all, creating a living space—if well done and compatible with the brand's values—should be an effective way of moving toward achieving the coveted status of "lifestyle brand." Camper's only diversification away from shoes has been in the hotel and restaurant area.

Other types of companies have also taken an interest in the potential offered by diversification. Marlboro launched a line of clothing in keeping with the mythology of the wide open spaces of the West on which it has based its advertising for decades. Coca-Cola has opened single-brand stores to sell a whole series of gift and souvenir items, from T-shirts to coffee mugs, and including such items as trays decorated with advertisements from the 1930s. Disney, Warner Brothers, and even soccer clubs (Manchester United,

Juventus of Turin, Real Madrid) have successfully developed this diversification toward "gift and souvenir" products.

Most automotive and motorcycle brands have started offering clothing and accessories more or less associated with the use of their basic products. The Pirelli brand was one of the first to move into shoes, watches and clothing. However, the most extraordinary products and customer-segments extension has been made by one of the most luxurious of brands: Ferrari. In 2001, it embarked on a major development of gifts, souvenirs, books, games, T-shirts and so on through licensing and co-branding, and opening flagship stores (20 in 2005, with an objective of 50 for 2010) and boutiques around the world—activities that, in 2006, generated almost €600 million. The company is also looking to open a theme park in Abu Dhabi in 2009. Ducati is following in the same strategic direction, showing 42 licensees on its website in 2006.

For certain brands, such incursions can be regarded as being merely speculative, with no real development ambitions and far removed from the core products and the brand identity. Such is clearly the case with "brand restaurants," which have met with varying degrees of success (Lustucru, Eurosport, Nescafé in Paris). And one may also wonder what future there is in Harley-Davidson fragrances. Others, on the other hand, have succeeded over the years in developing new territories of legitimacy that have made them stronger. Time is the essential factor here.

In his determination to reduce the number of brands in his group, Edwin Artz, the former CEO of Procter & Gamble, would urge his people to: "Find the way, the unique selling proposition or the reason for being, which will enable you to sell several products under the same brand."

The second key to the success of a strategy of product diversification is the brand's degree of conceptualization. The more the values expressed by the brand are conceptual in nature, the easier it becomes to adapt to different and seemingly unrelated product categories. This has led to the current vogue for the "lifestyle brand," the natural culmination of the principle of diversification.

The concept is a strong one. It aims at all objects and services people use every day—what they wear, eat, drink and smoke—but also their sedentary or traveling environment—furniture, bedding, wallpaper, decorator items, draperies, floor tiles, paint, tableware, luggage and so on. The lifestyle is carried through to the hotel they stay in. Having a single umbrella-brand is a way of guaranteeing the profitability of all the investments made on the promotion of this all-encompassing identity.

For brands whose identity was originally founded on a lifestyle, product diversification is often easy. Such is the case of Ralph Lauren, who promotes the traditional New England "WASP" lifestyle. All the products, which incorporate tableware and entertainment as well as paint for customers' apartments, are very well presented in the stores, particularly in the flagship on Madison Avenue in New York, where the lifestyle offered is very clear.

Other brands, whose identity is strongly linked to a product or to specific signs, have more difficulty or are more prudent. Missoni, which established its identity on a specific type of fabric and a specific chromatic palette, does not venture far from the domain of clothing and a few accessories.

Besides, the most original initiatives are not necessarily crowned with success. They may result in a temporary gain in fame for the brand, but without paying back the investment they represented. Consumers are always there to remind us that the further products depart from the domain of established legitimacy, the more difficult it is to score a quick success.

Diversification, then, is an area that can be profitable if a general principle—intelligent relatedness—is adhered to. But this is not always in evidence. When the new "Tambour" watch was launched in May 2002, did any fashion writers or customers remember the watch launched (and subsequently withdrawn) by Louis Vuitton in the early 1990s? And we might question the significance and the future of the Louis Vuitton nail polish launched in 2003. Is this a prelude to the development of a complete line of cosmetics, or just a diversion?

It's important to take every precaution, to be skilled in piloting the evolution of the brand or the characteristics of the products over time, and, above all, to treat time and the limits of evolution of the brand's identity with respect.

Optimization of internal processes
This is an area of development that is too often neglected because it is too difficult to deal with. It's easier to design and open new points of sale than to reduce the development time of a product. Yet optimizing internal processes is what often succeeds in taking market share away from direct competitors.

In the fashion sector, receiving the products from the new collections promptly means increased sales and, above all, significant increases in margin. Reducing the development time for new products (that is, the "time to market," the time that elapses between the initial concept and the availability of the product for sale) can be the decisive competitive weapon in numerous sectors, including automotive, food products, telecommunications, clothing and accessories.

An effective reading of market signals, product design oriented toward surpassing the competition and satisfying the target customers, production that adheres to quality standards, and flawless logistics that supply distribution networks at the proper time all have a positive impact on brand performance.

Brand repositioning
In fact, the term that should be used here is "adjustment." By repositioning, we generally mean "the great leap," which takes place where a brand exchanges its existing clientele for another one that strategists are more comfortable with. This operation is fraught with risk and obviously would not be undertaken by a brand in its growth phase. As we will see, it is a radical remedy, more appropriate in phases of decline.

In our case, therefore, the action is more subtle. It aims at making the brand more attractive without alienating the existing

luxury **brand** management

customers. On the contrary, the brand can try to entertain them a little, while taking advantage of the circumstances to try to draw new ones in.

When Marc Jacobs was recruited by Louis Vuitton in 1997 to develop a ready-to-wear collection, many people were skeptical. The first show got a cool reception from the press and the brand's hard-core fans. They had trouble seeing the connection with the "art of travel" or the "conservative spirit" that had come to be associated with the brand's identity.

However, fashion, which had seemed incompatible with the brand at first, proved to be an unexpected source of dynamism. The fashion shows and the opening of the "global stores" in Paris, London and Tokyo extended its media coverage, and the choices made for the collections proved to be a *tour de force* in rejuvenating the brand's identity without alienating the existing customers. The sales volume of the fashion and leather-goods branch of LVMH—where Louis Vuitton represents the majority—increased from €3.6 billion in 2001 to €5.2 billion in 2006.

This success is the result of a profound understanding of the brand's identity and of the way it is perceived. Louis Vuitton was able to find in its historical identity the elements of a "fashion discourse." The values of tradition associated with his luggage connote not so much conservatism as excellence and distinction—the nostalgic evocation of a time when travel was still an adventure and the domain of a small circle of privileged individuals. "Nostalgic exoticism" is the stock-in-trade in the fashion magazines today, but style counts less than fantasy. The brand has made extensive use of this imaginative capital. In a time of mass activities and the homogenization of leisure, where the trend is toward the search for originality and refinement, such distinctive signs have an undeniable seductive power. Louis Vuitton itself perpetuates this tradition by publishing books that are appropriate to its brand territory. In 1994, the collection *Voyager avec...* (Travels with...) offered authors' travel accounts. The *Carnets de Voyage* (Travel Notebooks) presented the world's great cities in the form of colorful illustrations. The recent *Louis Vuitton City Guide—European Cities* aims to become a guide for high-end tourists.

What we call the "turbo effect" of fashion is also at work in the case of Coach, an American luggage brand with hand-crafted origins founded in 1941. The designer Reed Krakoff was recruited from Tommy Hilfiger in 1996 to give Coach—known until then for its sturdy leather bags—a fashion aspect and, in the words of its CEO, Lew Frankfurt, to "invent the classics of tomorrow." The brand has also introduced new categories of products (shoes, eyewear, watches) and the talent brought to bear has reaped success.

The latest example of the turbo effect is the success the team led by Rose Marie Bravo at Burberry has been experiencing for four years now. Superb ad campaigns blending modernity and British tradition, a product offering with appropriate prices, the systematic use of the brand's famous tartan—all these strategic choices have paid off. Burberry's results positioned the brand ideally for the float launched in 2002 and have continued growing since then, as shown in Figure 4.4.

In these three examples, the turbo effect works because it is based on an intelligent transposition of the brand's identity values—its invariants—to the stylistic grammar of fashion. Far from being an obstacle, the "traditional" connotations of Louis Vuitton or Burberry become in themselves the sign of a certain world of imagination that can be reinvented, extended to other products and adapted to the taste of the times. These successful adjustments show an accurate assessment of the brand's identity and of how it is perceived by the markets. Such strategies, when they meet with success, lead to substantial increases in growth rates.

Conclusion

The lessons to be learned from the examples we have looked at include the following:

- The less the values expressed by the brand's identity are conceptualized, the more difficult it is to adapt to new product categories.

- Time alone lends legitimacy to brands that penetrate new product sectors, but only to the extent that these new products fit within the brand's pre-existing ethic and aesthetic (or cause it to evolve while respecting a certain continuity) and where the brand shows tenacity, authenticity and determination with its new offering.
- It is wise to approach any drastic change in brand identity with great circumspection in a growth phase. When the "great leap" is made, it is never clear whether the new clientele will more than compensate for the one that may be alienated. It's a risky exercise that is best applied to brands in decline.
- All growth areas have their limits. Maturity lies in wait for brands, as it does for men and women.

A BRAND'S MATURITY

This is the time of optimum *cash flow*, but also the time to wake up.

Generally, the rate of growth has been in single figures for several years; decline is approaching.

In ordinary language, we would say that a "new lease on life" needs to be found, and that is what brand managers of mass-consumption products work at. They try endlessly to improve the technical performances of their product. But they also introduce novelty in the form of extensions—say, a lavender or a lemon-lime version of a fabric softener or a room deodorizer. This diversity, of course, entails additional production and storage costs and, above all, a business volume that is averaged downward by the lower-selling products. This sometimes requires reworking the existing sizes to make sure that the diversity of packaging is matched by the performance of each of the new varieties.

The period of maturity, then, is a period of broadening and diversification of the product offering. One product may specialize in a single form and function while another product is launched to cover another application—but care must be taken to avoid excess. When Pampers, for example, launched its disposable diaper differentiated for girls and boys, it seemed like a very creative idea;

but what did mothers think of it? This is perhaps best gauged by the fact that the experiment was quickly abandoned.

Managing the maturity of luxury brands is even more delicate because the possibilities for introducing extensions or complementary products are limited. Of course, a new and slightly different clientele can always be aimed at. Fendi did just that by launching a line of ready-to-wear and accessories targeting young people, under the brand name Fendissimo; Charles Jourdan did the same with its CJ Bis line of shoes in a slightly lower price range. But the difficulty then, if the experiment works, is to find ways to bring the new clientele back toward the principal brand.

Chanel, which has been facing the challenges posed by maturity for several years, reacted by broadening its product offering and launching—with much effort and impressive results—a leather-goods line, then a line of watches, and finally a line of luxury jewelry. But what can come next? Products for men, perhaps? But would the brand's essentially feminine positioning allow that?

In this maturity phase, the same possible growth vectors exist as in the preceding phase. The sole difference lies in the fact that certain brands are capable of anticipating their maturity and their decline while still experiencing strong development, while others can only resign themselves to their fate.

DECLINE, RE-LAUNCH AND DEATH

Decline is announced by a progressive loss of market share and decreasing sales volumes.

At this point, there are only three possible developments: continuing decline over a more or less long period, followed by the death of the brand, or its re-launch.

Continuing decline

This period can last as long as financial resources permit. Such is the relatively common case of brands that have been trying for several years to curb a decline that is not yet under control. Examples are numerous.

Bally's business volume has been decreasing since the early 1990s, and in that time 12 top management teams and two shareholders have strenuously attempted to turn the tide. Losses have been accumulating: the "turbo effect" of fashion doesn't work for everyone.

Dunhill, Kodak and many other brands have been attempting for many years to engineer an upturn, often without visible results.

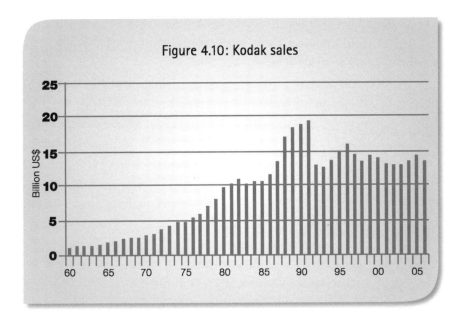

Figure 4.10: Kodak sales

The curve of Eastman Kodak's business volume since the early 1960s, again close to the theoretical curve of brand lifecycles, is typical of a brand in decline. In this particular case, the reasons have to do essentially with technological evolution and strategic choices. The strategy pursued in the past few years—aimed at positioning Kodak as an "imaging technology" brand providing digital and film imaging, health imaging and information, graphic communication and display and components—generated some renewed growth in recent years, only to suffer a lapse in 2006.

The death of a brand

Death comes from a lack of financial resources, from the erosion of demand, or as a result of a management decision. Management can condemn a brand to extinction at the time of its acquisition. When the Spanish department-store chain Corte Ingles bought out its competitor Galerias Preciados from Venezuelan financiers, it kept the best sales outlets and got rid of the others, but put all the stores under the single Corte Ingles name. Overnight, the Galerias Preciados name disappeared—as also happened in France with the Nouvelles Galeries after their purchase by Galeries Lafayette. The stronger, more evocative name won out.

This is a frequent scenario in acquisitions. But the launch of a new product can prove to be the death knell of a product of inferior quality. When Gillette launched its Mach 3 razor with three pivoting flexible blades, it spelled the end of its former "top of the line" products, Gillette Contour and Trac II. Of course Gillette will have to continue manufacturing and distributing Contour blades for the many owners of this type of razor, but, little by little, they'll be won over by the new product and move to it.

Many companies in the mass market have sacrificed brands on the altar of expansion or survival. We've already mentioned the process of drastic reduction Procter & Gamble has undertaken. The La Roche Aux Fées brand, created in 1926 in France, disappeared in 1988 when the owner company merged with Chambourcy. The latter, created in 1948, was closed out in 1996 by Nestlé.

These decisions, motivated by economic interests, are not without risk. Particularly in the case of prestige products such as automobiles or watches, whose added value is high and very apparent, disappointing loyal customers can expose a brand to harsh penalties. This was made very clear in the Peugeot group's tampering with the Simca brand in France. Simca represented a brand in its own right, with a network of energetic, efficient dealers who were proud to sell the cars and serve customers who were devoted to the brand. Simca was more than a name on the hoods of cars; it was a federating universe. Thus, replacing the

luxury **brand** management

name with Talbot models from a certain date was bound to upset many customers. What, for example, of the customer who had just bought a new Simca, and who was happy to drive the car and project himself into the brand's values? The least that might have been done—and wasn't—was to allow dealers to change the brands on the hood, steering wheel, and trunk lid, in the guarantee booklet and manuals of their model, and so on, to reflect change of name. Should that have been done for all owners of Simcas, even 10-year-old models? Probably; and again, it probably wouldn't have been enough.

The directors of Peugeot thought it would be enough to repaint the dealerships and launch billboard campaigns announcing the changeover for consumers to accept the transition. But consumers don't react rationally. They subscribe to the values of a brand and make them their own. For example, each time a driver is in a line of cars behind the same make or model as his own, he experiences a slight feeling of satisfaction. How will he react when he loses this type of reference point?

While companies sometimes sacrifice their brand, its fame may survive indefinitely nevertheless. Makes such as Panhard or Hispano-Suiza are still alive in the imagination of several generations, though the plants that produced the cars have long since disappeared. Such resilience can, in the case of most prestigious brands, also lead to their resurrection (as, for example, with Westinghouse). There is the case of the famous Orient Express, now a registered brand, the property of the American group of the same name; or Solex motorbikes, now produced under license since 2000 following an agreement between the brand's owner, Magneti Marelli, and the manufacturer Impex Hungaria. These examples show how the concept of the brand is also associated with ideal values, different from the economic realities faced by companies in their day-to-day operation.

The service sector is not exempt from resounding disappearances. The case of Arthur Andersen, for example, is considered at the end of this chapter. In November 2002, the UBS bank announced the disappearance of the prestigious financial names Warburg and Paine Webber. Their activities will be continued under the parent company's name, UBS.

Re-launch

The last means for a brand to achieve growth is through what we call the "great leap," which, to date, few brands have succeeded in making. The term generally refers to a repositioning of the brand to encompass a programmed change of clientele. It applies to companies in decline that have already undergone heavy restructuring and improvements to their internal processes but without managing to reverse the trend.

The decline of a brand is always visible in an erosion of its relevance to consumers. The brand and its products are no longer interesting; or, rather, they are less interesting than those of competitors. The evolution of the brand's identity that results from a successful re-launching plan is a synthesis of the brand's response to this problem.

One of the most stunning cases of a successful re-launch is that of Gucci. The business volume of Gucci N.V. went from around €140 million in 1992 to €1.594 billion in 2001. The Gucci products division, the only one existing in 1992, made it possible to purchase other brands and itself achieved sales of €1.055 billion. After the preparatory work done by Maurizio Gucci and Dawn Mello, creative director Tom Ford and CEO Domenico de Sole conducted the largest operation of wealth creation in a minimum amount of time, starting with a brand in the fashion sector. This is an exceptional case that can probably never happen again.

The brand of today bears little resemblance to what it was when Tom Ford took over as creative director in 1992. His action transformed Gucci's identity. The brand's traditional values—quality craftsmanship, the Italian jet set of the Cinecittà years—were replaced by the universe of the Hollywood "swingles." Seduction is now central to all of the brand's discourse, and the new designer has truly made it his own. The clientele, entirely renewed, has more than

luxury **brand** management

compensated for that which was disappearing in the late 1980s.

Brand re-launchings are always difficult exercises. Growth has natural limits, and it seems doubtful that a successful brand can be re-launched indefinitely. Gucci understands this and is now developing as a multi-brand group. In the past four years, it has acquired Balenciaga, Sergio Rossi, Bottega Veneta, Boucheron, Alexander McQueen, Stella McCartney and Yves Saint Laurent.

Puma is another example of a successful re-launch. After seven years of losses, the company appointed Jochen Zeitz to lead it. During the initial years, he concentrated on returning to profitability by improving internal processes (particularly through rationalizing production facilities). In 1998, the brand repositioned itself from the playing field to the street. Expenditures for communication doubled. Sales followed suit, doubling between 1998 and 2001, while Nike's results were stagnating and Adidas's grew by only 20%. "We want to make Puma the most desirable brand for young people, representative of their lifestyle," Zeitz told the French daily *Le Monde* in February 2001. Consolidated sales went from €279 million in 1997 to €2.4 billion in 2005, and the share price went from €26.9 in December 1997 to €285.5 in December 2006. It was then purchased by the PPR Group in 2007.

GLOBAL BRANDS, LOCAL BRANDS

The opposition between the local and global dimensions of brands is most visible in the urban milieu. Brands which naturally follow their markets contribute to this breakdown of cities into heterogeneous segments. The global brands occupy the most prestigious shopping streets; minor and local brands are in the adjacent streets, the periphery, and the malls.

Conditions and advantages of a global strategy

We have seen the advantages of geographic extension as a principal area of growth: amortization of the costs of managing the brand's identity (creation, research and communication); growth of reputation; and the implementation of volume strategies (economies of scale) that are still prevalent in many industries.

The degree of globalization possible depends on the degree of universality inherent in the brand's offerings, but also on its ability to offer its products or services everywhere at competitive prices.

The chances of globalization of a brand as a function of the potential for universalization of its identity can be illustrated as shown in Figure 4.11.

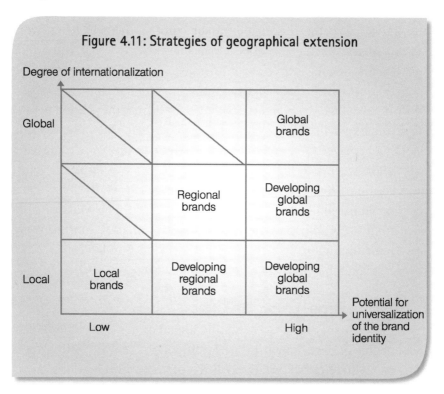

Figure 4.11: Strategies of geographical extension

We can see that, except for certain constraints that prevent the exportation of a product, the essential ingredient of successful globalization remains the potential of universalization of the brand's identity. There's no point in hoping to locate abroad if the values expressed by your brand don't interest the Japanese, the French or the Chinese.

That doesn't mean you have to produce Model T Fords for the whole world. As we've seen, perceptions of a brand in different markets generally form a heterogeneous ensemble. An intelligent

luxury **brand** management

global approach will try to fit into local markets while maintaining, as much as possible, the invariants that make up the brand's identity.

A truly global product is rarer than it might seem. Aside from the financial services, aeronautics, consumer electronics, perfumery and, perhaps, fashion sectors, there are few in which products and communication are identical across all markets.

The major global brands aim, at the very least, for regional integration around the three major zones: the United States, Europe–Middle East–Africa, and Asia.

Possibilities for local strategy

There are certain types of activity that cannot be globalized. These include:

- Activities linked to a specific place: a restaurant with a view of the Golden Gate Bridge or the Eiffel Tower, a hotel overlooking the Monte Cervino or Mount Rushmore, and so on. In this category can be included all products (cement, for example) that won't travel because of the costs of transport and the nearly universal availability of the raw materials.
- Basic products such as milk, rice, bread, and so on—although the recent vogue for "organic" and quality foods has resulted in a few timid initiatives.
- Brands with local appeal, which are tied to a specific local taste—for example, dark-tobacco cigarettes (Gauloises in France or Ducados in Spain), or Welch's Concord grape juice.

Between such brands with local appeal and the "major globals," there is an entire range of aspirants at various stages of their evolution toward achieving the status of a global brand. All brands begin locally. If you can't be competitive in your own territory, what can you do in the rest of the world? This argument is surely the best proof that there are such things as local strategies for success.

Once competitiveness has been achieved in the local market, global development then requires only the presence of entrepreneurs and capital ready to be mobilized based on projected returns and an understanding of the risks inherent in the project. The difficulty lies in evaluating the potential for universality of the brand's identity.

Local cultural characteristics are often the guarantee of clear differentiation from competitors in the sector and a determining factor of success. Exoticism works in all directions. Any culture with a strong identity is a candidate for offering products with universal appeal. And directors of local or regional brands have a more profound knowledge of the sensibilities of local consumers. The success of Korean films, television and songs in the past few years is a good illustration of how a successful regional strategy can be put in place without giving up the peculiar character of a local culture.

For 10 years or more, hip-hop, which originated in the African-American ghettos, has dominated Korean pop music. It was introduced by Koreans born in the U.S., but minus the sex, guns, money and drugs that characterize the music of the likes of Eminem or Puff Daddy in the United States. In their place are substituted themes questioning the authority of parents or teachers and revolt against the strictures of traditional Korean society. As a result, the music finds regional echoes with young people in Southeast Asia, who lean toward rebellion, but not to the point where they identify with American "gangsta rap." In Korea today, music sales for such local groups represent 70% of total sales.

The same phenomenon is at work for television and film. The shows broadcast are relatively conservative and borrow from Confucianist values. Families made up of three generations are shown living under the same roof. The Chinese market is the principal importer, as a result of the cultural similarities and the quality of the productions.

One result of this affirmation of a cultural specificity is that Seoul is becoming a fashionable destination for regional tourism. That effect was greatly increased by the 2002 Soccer World Cup

luxury **brand** management

held in Korea and Japan, where the Korean team caused a surprise by making it to the semi-final.

The vulnerability of global brands

Paradoxically, any strategy of globalization represents both a strength and a weakness for a brand, as Naomi Klein has pointed out: the more globalized the brand, the more vulnerable it is to consumer actions.

As their internationalization progresses, the worldwide giants prove to be increasingly sensitive to whatever can affect the way in which their identity is perceived. The combination of immediate global dissemination of information and a rigid production and logistical apparatus that handles considerable volumes of business makes them particularly vulnerable to consumers' reactions.

The example of Coca-Cola "Classic," which was reintroduced less than three months after the launch of the new formula, and the discovery of traces of benzene that threatened Perrier are well known. The sweatshop scandal, which threatened producers of sporting goods like Nike and Adidas, has been well documented. And very recently, the implosion of Arthur Andersen is a good illustration of the vulnerability of the global brands.

Among the "Big Five" auditing firms, Arthur Andersen–deployed in 80 countries–was the best integrated internationally, both in the coordination of its human resources and its methodological expertise. In an extremely fragmented sector, it had succeeded in creating a model company and an authentically global brand. But that very strength is what might well have contributed to its disintegration. The bankruptcy scandal surrounding the American energy giant Enron, for which Arthur Andersen was auditor, landed the American directors in court in late 2001, accused of having destroyed sensitive documents. The result was an immediate disaffection of the clientele, which was not limited to the United States.

Most local branches merged with competitors to avoid professional fallout. The Arthur Andersen brand identity has been marred to the very core of its *raison d'être*: the confidence of consumers in its ability to maintain the same professional standards of independence and professionalism. If the brand survives in some regional offices, it will be insignificant compared to what it once was.

chapter **5**

THE
Luxury
CLIENT

In earlier chapters, we speak repeatedly about the consumer. This is, in fact, something of a misnomer. A consumer, as the name implies, consumes the products he or she purchases. We have already seen in Chapter 1 that in luxury there are no products, only special objects that clients want to acquire and keep. Someone purchasing a Rolex watch or a Hermès handbag is not going to "consume" the product and then go back to the store to acquire a new one.

The client purchases iconic objects on special occasions and does so with a special mood or spirit. Even repeat purchases of objects such as a bottle of perfume or of champagne are exceptional events, charged with emotional and social content.

In this chapter we will first ask who the luxury clients are. We will then study how such clients behave, before looking at differences in national behavior.

WHO ARE THE LUXURY CLIENTS?

Luxury clients are in fact the very rich, and, also... everybody. We will begin by looking at some quantitative analysis that has been done, mainly in the United States, to see who those clients buying a bottle of champagne or an expensive watch really are.

The rich, the very rich, or everybody?

There have been several studies analyzing the very rich. According to one, conducted by EuroRSCG in 2002,[1] there were 7.2 million people in the world with net assets exceeding US$1 million. Of these, one-third lived in the United States. Countries such as France, the U.K. and, strangely enough, China each had approximately 300,000 millionaires.

A United Nations report published in 2006 said that 1% of the world's population (that is, some 66 million people) had assets of over €500,000. While the currencies used in each are different, the two studies are complementary.

Obviously, having a million dollars in China is not exactly the same thing as having that amount in the United States, where the cost of living is very different and where the disposable income is also quite different. But purchasing a Tiffany ring for €10,000 is somehow a similar step.

Every year, *Forbes Magazine* publishes a list of the world's wealthiest individuals, with a special section on the richest Chinese men. In the United States, there are said to be 170 billionaires. The Swiss magazine *Bilan*, for its part, reports that there are 286 people living in Switzerland who have assets of above a €1 billion euros. But do you need to be a billionaire to buy a Chanel handbag? Any middle-management executive from a DINK (double income, no kids) household can afford one.

Researchers have tried to move from the very rich to those

luxury **brand** management

who could purchase some or many luxury objects. Don Ziccardi[2] identifies four consumer segments:

Millennium money: Into this category who made a fortune around the turn of the century come all celebrities and sport stars, as well as those who became rich through the Internet business.

Old money: This is the traditional category of those who have inherited their wealth and don't really work, or who manage a business they have inherited, or who perhaps have a professional life with a standard of living that is not related to their salary.

New money: This category incorporates those who have made a fortune themselves. Unlike the millennium-money category, they are not necessarily young and they did not come by their money easily. These individuals have worked hard and are still working hard. They are careful about money and seem to know its value.

Middle money: This is the category of the upper-middle class, which is careful about money. Their main revenues are through salaries or professional income and they are reasonable spenders.

When the economy is going well, all of these groups buy luxury goods. When the economy is in recession, the majority do not have to cope with major drops in their income and their disposable income does not really vary. But their assets, made up in large part of real estate and financial investments, drop in value: they feel less inclined to spend their money and are careful and restrained. Of course, while the middle-money category reacts more than the others in this regard, this is a general phenomenon that can be observed across the board.

So, then, are millionaires or members of these four categories the only luxury clients? Obviously not. We noted earlier the total luxury business amounted to around €190 billion, including some at wholesale or export prices. If the millionaires were the only clients, they would each purchase goods to the value of more than €25,000 a year. While this segmentation of the very rich may be a useful outlet for high-value jewelry pieces or a high-performance Porsche or Ferrari, it is not a true reflection of luxury clients as a whole.

When asked "Have you bought a luxury product in the last 24 months?" 63% of respondents in developed countries answered "Yes."[3] This is actually the real group of luxury clients: more than half of the general population in developed countries. And the rapid growth rate of this industry (an annual average of 8%) results from the fact that every year a new group of "middle class" consumers from developed or developing countries can, for the first time, afford to buy a bottle of champagne, a €1,000 handbag or a €1,500 watch. With the increased accessibility of such goods, luxury is, for 63% of people in developed countries at least, becoming part of their everyday experience.

This is, of course, still a very far cry from the 4,000 women in the world who can afford an *haute couture* dress; or even from the 7.2 million who can afford an expensive piece of jewelry. The luxury client is almost everybody. But he or she purchases a luxury object very rarely.

THE EXCURSIONISTS

The term "excursionist" was coined in 1999 by Bernard Dubois and Gilles Laurent[4] and arose from their observations from an early study by the Paris-based research company Risc Consumers in developed countries. These findings are presented in Table 5.1.

Table 5.1: Breakdown of luxury clients in developed countries	
Have not purchased a luxury product in the last 24 months	37%
Have purchased a luxury product in the last 24 months	63%
Have purchased more than five pieces	12% (i.e. 20% of purchasers)
Average number of purchases	2

Source: Dubois and Laurent

luxury **brand** management

Their findings showed that, apart from the "happy few" (12%) who had bought more than five items in the previous two years and who obviously represented a very large volume of the total market, the largest group (51% of the population) had bought between one and five items. What immediately leaps to mind here is the lower middle-class group, who are very careful about their general spending and who look for special promotions in the supermarket, but who decide to buy a Cartier watch for their son's graduation or a small Tiffany engagement ring for their future daughter-in-law. Dubois and Laurent used the word "excursion" to describe how this group approached the purchase of luxury items. Entering a Cartier or Tiffany store was, for such consumers, a bit like taking a boat ride or visiting a museum. The interesting question Dubois and Laurent asked themselves was what these "excursionists" were expecting from their "ride" to a luxury store. So they investigated further, asking the question: "What were you looking for?"The answers they received from the "excursionists" were as follows:

- They expect the product to be of outstanding **quality**, in both the materials used and in the service. This is not like visiting a supermarket: it is a very special experience and must be rewarding for them.
- They expect the product to be **expensive**. For the function it satisfies, the luxury product should clearly belong to another price range: the purchase is not a "natural" or "matter of fact" activity and the price should reflect this.
- They want to be sure that the object they acquire is **scarce and difficult to obtain**, open only to **a very few individuals**.
- They expect the shopping experience to provide a **multi-sensuous** moment: when they walk into the store, across the thick wall-to-wall carpet, they want to be surrounded by sophisticated music, to see beautiful objects and to know that what they are about to do will be worth it. And, of course, they expect sales staff to treat them as people who are doing something exceptional.

- They expect to come to a world that has its **roots in the past**. They want to make a purchase that is **timeless**. They want their act to become part of an environment that has always existed and will always exist.
- They know that their purchase does not make too much economic sense and they are happy with that. They accept the fact that what they are doing is **slightly futile or unnecessary**. They speak of jewelry or perfumes in the way, for example, others may speak of a Jaguar: they are not concerned with its engine or its technical characteristics, but they speak about the luxury of the passenger space.

The "excursion" must be something memorable and different. This is why in-store service is so important in the luxury field. But having described the "excursionist" model, it is important to remember that this is part of a larger movement that analyzes the marketing and consumer process, that not in terms of the segmentation of individuals, but in terms of different situations in life and explaining the different purchasing behaviors.

THE NEW CONSUMER
New clients will evaluate products and buy them as a function of their individual situation. For example, a woman may in the course of one day buy Zara jeans, a Celine jacket and Wolford leggings. She may then end her day shopping at Carrefour and buying coffee because of a cut-price promotion. This apparently changing behavior is what specialists have tried to understand: customers today have new expectations and new patterns of behavior.[5]

New customer expectations
Customers are not rational when they purchase a luxury object. They don't claim to be rational. More than anything else, they value the affective and aesthetic contents of their purchase and they perceive the different product offerings along such lines.

They are **affective** because they consider their own pleasure

luxury **brand** management

to be more important than any other rational criteria. To judge a product on rational criteria would reduce their shopping pleasure. As they compare different product offerings, they value intangible elements like the sophistication of the atmosphere in the store, or the opportunity to go to an area of the town where they can meet people or, even better, famous people. Even the type of music they hear in a given store can condition the way they perceive products from a particular brand and, ultimately, the way they buy.[6]

This affective component of the consumer information process is used in advertising, as we will see in Chapter 8. Luxury advertising is not only based on information. It is based on the fact that it should surprise, attract and communicate a specific mood.

A second expectation relates to **a need for beauty**, the belief that a product should be evaluated by its shape, its special feel in the hand, the types of "fashion models" used by the brand, or the aesthetic value of its new advertising.

This is one of the reasons why the aesthetic elements of a brand are so important in its development. People associate different aesthetic values with different brands. Gucci and Yves Saint Laurent belong to completely different universes. This should be reflected in the shape of the lady's perfume bottles, the concept of the ready-to-wear stores and the shopping bags clients are given when they purchase something.

New customer behaviors

Customers are **eclectic**. They want to be different from the crowd and they want to indicate to everybody that they know what they are doing. Patrick Hetzel speaks of a "toolbox" where they can define what is best for their given mood or their specific style.[7] They do not want to rely on a single brand: the "total look" (all Chanel or all Versace) is seen to be completely out of fashion today—it does not show who you are and what you have decided for yourself. But a creative mix between Givenchy and Zara shows that you are creative and that you have taste.

Now, though, eclecticism has some limits. Customers still want to belong to a group and are rewarded by this group for the choice they have made. While 15 years ago people wanted to be identical to their group of references or their close friends (at school, students wanted to carry the same brand), this is no longer so today. Today they want to be similar to a very small number of individuals that they have selected as part of their mini "tribal" group. The social norm still exists and is still very strong, but its base is scattered between a myriad subgroups that are organized along different types of activities or behaviors.

Consumers are also looking for **hedonistic** values. They price their own pleasure more than anything else. Here again, they do not look only for the functional elements of a product's attributes, but to the imaginary world that they have created themselves and that becomes their own world, leading to their own vision of luxury in general and individual luxury brands in particular.

This brings us back to the cultural dimension described at the beginning of Chapter 1. Each customer's individual vision of a given brand integrates aesthetic and cultural values, often of a specific national atmosphere and of what this brand can and cannot do.

Consumers can be fragmented in their expectations and in their behavior and can change rapidly over time.

The result for luxury brand management is quite clear: sales trends are changing rapidly and brands that are successful are those that are able to give an added cultural, aesthetic and hedonistic value to their overall identity.

ARE CLIENTS FROM DIFFERENT NATIONALITIES SIMILAR?

The question now is to know if there is such a thing as a worldwide client, if people from different nationalities behave in the same way.

Pierre Rainero, Manager of Market Research and Communication for Cartier, has a view on this:

luxury **brand** management

"The Italians like watches that are slightly flashy and insist on a mechanical movement. They collect them and may change their watches several times per day. The Germans prefer quartz watches with a very simple design: rigor and effectiveness. The French have a strong preference for the 'Engineer's' watch: sporty and full of several chronometer dials."[8]

"Different European nationalities also have different ways of wearing a piece of jewelry."

"In Germany, women who have a management job purchase their jewelry pieces themselves and wear them in a triumphant way. In the style, they look for the purity of the raw materials and they like the stone to be set up in a very natural way. The Italians are looking for movement so they like "baroque" pieces. They are interested in the curves of the jewel and the way gold is set up. Ring shapes are moving like a piece of fabric. In Japan, but also in France or in Spain, group pressure is stronger than individual taste. The French, afraid of social critics, are looking for 'reasonable' jewels, which must be 'balanced' and appear 'in good taste.'"[9]

So, even within the European continent, there are large differences. Extend this to the world at large and the differences become even more pronounced.

Differences in consumption patterns between nationalities
Global Refunds is a Scandinavian firm specializing in the handling of value-added-tax returns for tourists. When tourists make a purchase in a luxury store, the store completes a form and sends it to Global Refunds, which, in turn, adds up all of the tax-free purchases and sends the appropriate tax refund to each tourist after each has left the territory. Global Refunds is therefore in the best position to assess what tourists from different nationalities purchase in France. Table 5.2 sets out its findings (based on an average duty-free purchase of €675).

Some differences are striking: Japanese purchase three times more leather goods than Americans. Americans have a more diversified mix of purchases but they buy significantly more jewelry and department-store products (including, probably, perfumes). Japanese tourists concentrate 59% of their purchases in ladies wear and leather accessories.

Table 5.2: Breakdown of purchases of American and Japanese clients in Paris

Japanese purchases		American purchases	
Ladies' wear	34%	Ladies' wear	22%
Leather and fur	25%	Watches and jewelry	16%
Men's wear	14%	Men's wear	12%
Watches and jewelry	10%	Department stores	11%
Department stores	6%	Leather and fur	8%
Others	11%	Souvenirs	5%
		China and glass	5%
		Hi-fi/electronics	1%
		Others	20%
Total	100%	Total	100%

Source: Global Refunds Newsletter, 2001

Before continuing with the analysis, it is useful to take a look at the different product categories.

Ready-to-wear and accessories

The ready-to-wear category is, in a way, the specialty of the Japanese. Japanese purchases generally represent 30–40% of the worldwide volume of French and Italian upscale fashion brands, making the Japanese market the leading market in the world, well ahead of the United States, which represents only 10–15%.

This is why Japan is a key market for fashion brands and for leather goods, in which it probably represents an even higher percentage than that indicated above.

luxury **brand** management

The Japanese fashion interest extends to Southeast Asia, partly because it is often an important duty-free zone for Japanese tourists and also because the citizens of Hong Kong, Singapore, Taiwan and Thailand, who generally have less financial means than the Japanese, are very interested in this product category.

The situation in China is slightly different. In 2006, China contributed less than 3% of worldwide volume of the ready-to-wear and accessories category. Like the Japanese, the Chinese are very interested in fashion brands, and even if the business is growing by approximately 30–50% a year, it still remains relatively small. At the present rate of growth, China will probably represent around 10% of worldwide purchases in 2010—still three or four times smaller than Japan.

Also, products sold in China are quite different from those sold in Japan. In Japan, women purchase goods themselves. In China, men are the main purchasers. This is why men's brands are generally doing very well there and much better than women's brands. Now, when men purchase fashion items for their wives or their friends, they buy much less ready-to-wear and generally confine themselves to buying simple tops or jackets, for example. They also buy a larger percentage of accessories and handbags, with a strong preference for "iconic" products that appear in advertising and that they know will be the ideal gift.

European markets are strong in fashion, with a large part of the purchases being made by executive women. This is where brands like Armani and Jil Sander have a strong following.

Perfumes and cosmetics

Unlike ready-to-wear, perfumes are not very important in Japan, with sales representing just 1% of worldwide consumption. In Japan, perfumes are often viewed as products to cover up and hide the natural smell of the body, or as unnecessary. They are sometimes perceived as an intrusion, something that a woman imposes on her environment. In many companies, there is an official or informal rule prohibiting the use of perfumes in the workplace, and they are also not well received in the subway or in other public places. Teenagers wear perfumes as a way to express themselves, but many lose the habit when they start work. In some areas of Japan the rumor persists that perfumes are unhealthy for young babies, causing many mothers to stop using perfumes altogether.

Perfume brands in Japan try to develop usage by promoting the sophistication of the products and as a means of self-expression at parties or special events.

The United States and the American continent at large are strong perfume markets, with approximately 30% of worldwide consumption. The Middle East is also an area where perfumes are much appreciated and consumed in large quantities.

Cosmetics are a different matter and Japan is a very strong market. The Chinese market, too, although still small, is both a perfume and a cosmetic market.

The perfume market is also very segmented geographically, and very few fragrances are able to obtain a worldwide appreciation. Women in the Latin countries tend to like fresh and floral notes— citrus and lavender fragrances that are not much liked elsewhere. Anglo-Saxon women prefer heavy perfumes, with a very strong heart and a strong presence. Asian women are divided. Japanese women like very light perfumes, so that a product like Tartine et Chocolat, designed for babies and very young girls, is a top seller among mature women.

The challenge in launching a new perfume with global ambitions is to find a note that is light enough to please Japanese women, strong enough to satisfy American or German women, and fresh and floral enough to satisfy Latin women. Products that are globally successful are those that find a way to cut across these preferences and come up with a completely new note. This is not easy.

Wines and spirits

In consolidated terms, the wines and spirits market is more or less balanced equally, with approximately one-third of the total business done in each of the three major markets: the Americas,

luxury **brand** management

Europe and Asia. But as we saw in Chapter 2, there are considerable differences in the types of products favored in each.

Rum is mostly consumed in the Americas, while gin is essentially a British and American drink. About 60% of the worldwide volume of champagne is consumed in France, with a very strong additional volume in other European countries. In contrast, whiskies and vodka are sold everywhere in the world and are thus relatively balanced.

Cognac is a product that is also sold everywhere in the world, but with clear differences in types of product consumed in different locations.

What is clear at this stage is that consumer behavior differs from one part of the world to another.

Differences in attitude between nationalities

In this section, we describe and discuss the results of a study conducted in 1996 by Bernard Dubois and Gilles Laurent,[10] for which they interviewed 86 consumers in 12 countries: Germany, the United States, Norway, Austria, Denmark, Poland, Australia, the Netherlands, Spain, Belgium, Hong Kong and France. The questionnaire was presented in English to business students and they were asked to answer items such as "I almost never purchase luxury products," or "Luxury is pleasant," and so on. (Although there were 34 such items, Table 5.3 reports on 13 of the major statements.)

Despite the fact that questions were put to students, who are not necessarily the best or most appropriate people to ask about luxury goods, four different groups—quite homogenous and quite different in their responses—emerged:

- *The Elitists: traditional luxury.* In this category, people are clearly favorable to luxury (only 4% say it does not interest them, while 88% say it is pleasant). They believe luxury is useful and they like it.

Table 5.3: Different typologies of consumer perceptions to luxury (% of respondents agreeing)

	Elitism	Democratization	Aversion	Detachment
Attitudes toward luxury				
Luxury is pleasant	88	88	7	68
Overall, I like luxury products	84	66	4	27
Luxury is actually unnecessary	7	4	71	20
Luxury does not interest me	4	4	77	30
Vision of luxury				
Few people own luxury products	66	6	51	59
A real luxury product cannot be sold in supermarkets	83	8	43	76
Luxury products are necessarily very expensive	80	43	26	80
Real luxury products cannot be mass manufactured	81	36	34	66
You must be quite a snob to buy luxury products	37	7	74	47
Behavior				
I almost never buy luxury products	17	20	58	56
I don't know much about luxury products	11	9	53	43
Luxury products improve life	78	54	24	33
Luxury is too expensive for what it is	39	29	22	71

Source: Dubois and Laurent

luxury **brand** management

As consumers, they are also very favorable. They consider that luxury products improve life and 83% of them claim they purchase luxury goods (only 17% say they almost never do). In attitude and behavior, they are clearly in favor of this activity and perceive themselves as consumers or would-be consumers. Dubois and Laurent label this group as "classical" and "elitist" because these people consider that luxury is in fact targeted at a very small group of individuals—the "happy few"—in which, naturally, they include themselves. They say for example that "few people own luxury products" and that "a real luxury product cannot be sold in a supermarket." In saying this, of course, they conveniently forget that they can buy a good champagne—a luxury product—in a supermarket.

- *The Democrats: open luxury.* In this second group, the attitudes and behavior revealed in Table 5.3 are almost identical to those of the first group: only 4% say they are not interested in luxury and only 20% say they "never buy luxury products."

Where this group differs, though, is in its "vision" of luxury. They believe luxury is for everybody (only 6% say "few people really own luxury products") and only 8% of them believe that "a real luxury product cannot be sold in supermarkets." In fact, while the "Elitists" have a "Hermès Kelly bag" or a "Van Cleef diamond necklace" view of luxury, the "Democrats" think about a bottle of perfume or of Dom Pérignon. For the "Democrats," luxury can be mass produced, and this is obviously the case for perfumes, cosmetics and wines. Among the "Elitists," the concept of craftsmanship mentioned in Chapter 1 would probably figure large in their thinking.

- *The "anti": opposed to luxury.* In this category, people are very much against luxury: only 7% say that "luxury is pleasant." (What then of the other 93%? What do they find unpleasant, and why?) Only 4% say they like luxury products and their behavior is in line with this: 58% state that they "almost never buy luxury products."

In its vision of luxury, this group has a very strange position. Relatively few (26%) consider that "luxury products are necessarily very expensive," and half consider that "luxury products are owned by almost everybody." But, on the other hand, 74% consider that "you must be quite a snob to buy luxury products." So, in fact, they know luxury products are available, can be sold in a supermarket and bought by almost everybody, but their rejection of the category is so strong that it encompasses all those who use such products. It is more of an ideological position than anything else.

- *The detached: "luxury far away."* In this group, people are not strongly opposed to luxury as in the previous group. In fact, 68% consider that "luxury is pleasant," and they know that most people buy luxury products. They have nothing against the category (only 20% say they are not interested), but such products are not for them.

  When 71% of them state that "luxury is too expensive for what it is," what they're saying, in fact, is: "This is great; it is not unnecessary, but personally I don't need it." As with the previous group, a majority of them say they almost never buy luxury products.

These groups are quite interesting because they provide a typology of attitudes and behavior that can be used to analyze any group of consumers: these four positions are underlying patterns that can be found in many different groups, even within the same country.

But the aim of the study by Dubois and Laurent was to find differences in perceptions amongst different national groups. Table 5.4 summarizes their findings.

luxury **brand** management

Table 5.4: Frequency of typologies by country (%)

	Democrats	Elitists	Detached	Against
Denmark	84	8	8	0
The Netherlands	68	20	12	0
United States	53	27	20	0
Norway	68	7	24	1
Austria	38	33	29	0
France	14	56	26	4
Germany	32	33	34	1
Poland	17	56	26	1
Hungary	8	47	45	0
Belgium	31	21	45	2
Spain	12	36	48	4
Australia	0	1	2	97

Source: Dubois and Laurent

The most striking finding is just how different Australia is from all the others. It is clear that Australians have a very specific culture and they seem to have a strong negative attitude toward luxury products in general and toward the concept of luxury in particular. The luxury world is a world quite different from the normal Australian way of life. This does not, of course, prevent Australian executives from wearing Hermès ties or Rolex watches, no matter how ill-at-ease this may cause them to feel.

There is a group of four or five countries, including Denmark and Austria, which have favorable attitudes toward luxury. While, on average, 20% are detached, nobody is opposed to it. In this group, luxury is perceived as positive, but also open and democratic. It is there for everybody to enjoy. In Denmark and Norway, very few belong to the Elitist group. In the United States, people are quite favorable to luxury but divided by a ratio of almost 2:1 between the "democratic" group and the "elitist" group. In a way, in the United States, as well as in Austria and Germany, two clear visions of luxury cohabit within the same population. In other words, this is a market that is very segmented and where different groups must listen to a slightly different story if they are to be convinced. But probably in those markets, when asked about luxury, some immediately think of a diamond necklace and others think of a perfume.

In the second group, as shown in Table 5.4, it is clear that we have countries with a relatively strong "detached" group of people, who have a positive attitude but who generally consider themselves non-users. But the fact is that there is a group of countries, including France, where luxury is perceived as an elitist market: the preserve of the happy few. Spain has a lot of "detached" people, which is consistent with its relatively small number of luxury brands. If Italy were in the sample, it would probably be quite similar. Belgium, like Germany and Austria, has a pattern where two groups coexist for and against the elitism in luxury, but in Belgium's case there is also a strong "detached" segment.

Thus, to the question "Do people from different nationalities behave the same way and do they have similar attitudes?" The answer is clearly "No." One of the weaknesses of this study is that it does not include two very strong luxury markets: the Italians and the Japanese, not to mention the Chinese and the British. Nevertheless, it is very useful in that it highlights major differences from one culture to another.

THE RISC STUDY

RISC International is a consulting firm specializing in consumer research and brand marketing, and a pioneer of research into attitudes to luxury in different countries.

RISC conducts studies every year in three major zones: the United States, Japan, and five European countries (France, Germany, Italy, England and Spain). It conducts additional studies in China, Korea and India. These studies are not public, but we

luxury **brand** management

have had access to the 2003 results, which were based on 18,500 questionnaires (men and women).

The advantage of RISC studies is that they provide a detailed analysis of attitudes toward luxury in general, and then go one step further to gather information on awareness, penetration and "dream" ("If you were to receive a beautiful gift overnight, which brand would you want it to be from?") on a list of 40 brands.

They also record purchases in the previous three years in the following product categories:

- Watches (with a retail price of more than €550)
- Jewelry (more than €400)
- High-fashion clothes (more than €2,000)
- Clothes for men and women (more than €500)
- Shoes (more than €250)
- Bags (more than €550)
- Leather accessories (more than €250)
- Other accessories (more than €200)
- Underwear (more than €100)
- Perfumes (more than €40)
- Sunglasses (more than €120)
- Writing instruments (more than €175).

So, with the exception of wines and spirits, most of the product categories are represented here.

Of the 40 brands, Armani, Burberry, Cartier, Chanel, Dior, Gucci, Hermès, Hugo Boss, Kenzo, Lacoste, Louis Vuitton, Ralph Lauren, Rolex, Yves Saint Laurent, Calvin Klein, Bulgari, Prada, Dolce & Gabbana and Cacharel are studied in the seven countries comprising the three major zones. Other brands are adapted to different market situations, with, for example, Loewe for Spain and Japan, Max Mara for Italy and Japan, and Moschino for Italy, Spain and Japan.

The overall brand interest ("the dream") is summarized in Table 5.5.

Table 5.5: Top luxury "dream" brands (% of mentions received)

Japan		United States		Europe	
Rolex	40.9%	Rolex	39.3%	Armani	21.6%
Hermès	31.1%	Tiffany	32.6%	Chanel	20.1%
Bulgari	30.2%	Calvin Klein	27.3%	Calvin Klein	18.1%
Gucci	29.1%	Gucci	25.7%	Hugo Boss	16.5%
Louis Vuitton	28.5%	Armani	25.5%	Dior	14.8%
Tiffany	27.6%	Tommy Hilfiger	25.1%	Rolex	12%
		Ralph Lauren	24.7%	Cartier	10%
		Cartier	24.4%	Gucci	10%

Source: RISC International, 2003
Note: Respondents were asked to name just five brands of their choice.

From this we can see that only two brands—Rolex and Gucci—are common to all three zones. Very few of the others—Tiffany, Armani, Calvin Klein and Cartier—are in more than one zone. Here again we can see the differences in perception and in brand status.

In Japan, there is a strong concentration on a few iconic brands, with very high percentages. Also, of the six top brands, only Gucci is really a fashion brand; all the others are high-status jewelry, watch or leather-goods brands.

In the United States, Rolex records a performance very similar to that in Japan, but the other results are quite mixed. American brands account for half of those mentioned, with two Italian brands—Gucci and Armani— and one French brand—Cartier—making up the rest. There is a mix of casual brands such as Tommy Hilfiger and, in a way, Ralph Lauren, and only one sophisticated high-end fashion

luxury **brand** management

brand: Gucci, which is probably known in the United States for its penny loafers, its scarves and its handbags.

In Europe, the situation is even more complex, as brands have much smaller scores and the situation is quite scattered. To understand this, it is necessary to look at specific performances for each country, as shown in Table 5.6.

Table 5.6: Top luxury "dream" brands (% of mentions)

France		United Kingdom		Germany		Spain		Italy	
Yves Saint Laurent	31%	Calvin Klein	29%	Hugo Boss	26%	Adolfo Dominguez	27%	Armani	38%
Chanel	28%	Armani	26%	Joop	17%	Armani	22%	Valentino	23%
Dior	25%	Chanel	23%	Chanel	17%	Chanel	19%	Dolce & Gabbana	22%
Lacoste	21%	Gucci	20%	Calvin Klein	17%	Lacoste	19%	Versace	18%
Hugo Boss	19%	Yves Saint Laurent	20%	Armani	14%	Dior	17%	Calvin Klein	16%
JP Gaultier	19%	Burberry	16%	Jil Sander	12%	Hugo Boss	15%	Rolex	16%
Cacharel	18%	Hugo Boss	16%	-	-	Calvin Klein	13%	Chanel	15%
Kenzo	14%	Ralph Lauren	13%	-	-	Cacharel	11%	Lacoste	12%
Calvin Klein	14%	-	-	-	-	-	-	Prada	12%

Source: RISC International, 2003

What is striking here is the strong national bias. In France, no Italian brands seem to get people dreaming, and, with the exceptions of the institutional brands of Chanel, Calvin Klein and Rolex, Italy has an otherwise all-Italian brand scorecard.

In the United Kingdom, Calvin Klein heads a table in which the British Burberry brand and another U.S. brand, Ralph Lauren, also appear amidst French and Italian brands. Yves Saint Laurent has maintained a very strong image, as in France, despite its low sales and is hoping product merchandising and sales will follow.

In Germany, a trilogy of German brands—Boss, Joop and Sander—performed well, along with Chanel, Calvin Klein and Armani.

In Spain, there is a relatively open market, with a Spanish brand, Adolfo Dominguez, coming out on top. Four French brands, including Dior, appear in the list.

Another approach to the European market is presented in Table 5.7, which compares the results to the same survey conducted in 1996 and 2003.

Table 5.7: European trends in top luxury "dream" brands (% of mentions)			
1996		**2003**	
Chanel	22.4%	Armani	21.6%
Armani	21.4%	Chanel	20.1%
Rolex	21.4%	Calvin Klein	18.1%
Dior	20.9%	Hugo Boss	16.5%
Cartier	20.8%	Dior	14.8%
Lacoste	17%	Rolex	12%
Calvin Klein	12%	Lacoste	12%
Hugo Boss	10%	Cartier	10%
Gucci	8%	Gucci	10%
Ralph Lauren	4%	Dolce & Gabbana	9%
Louis Vuitton	4%	Cacharel	7%
Dolce & Gabbana	4%	Ralph Lauren	6%

Source: RISC International, 2003

Many comments can be made here:
- With the exception of Lacoste, the "accessible luxury" brands—Calvin Klein, Hugo Boss, Cacharel and Ralph Lauren—have all improved their status. They open stores, they advertise,

luxury **brand** management

they generally have several lines with different price positionings; and it works. While this is an interesting price strategy, results are strongly dependent on how men respond. Luxury is more normally associated with women, who are responsible for more than two-thirds of luxury purchases. As the RISC study was based on an equal sample of women and men, the responses are skewed in favor of men's brands or brands that men like and should not, therefore, be considered as an indication of potential market when it comes to men's and women's brands.

- The French "institutions," in particular, Dior (20.9% to 14.8%) and Cartier (20.8% to 10%) have lost attractiveness. This may have something to do with their positioning and their advertising concepts. Only one French brand has maintained a strong performance: Chanel, which is placed in the top three in four of the five European countries.

- The brands that have been overly product-oriented, such as Rolex (21.4% to 12%) and Cartier (20.8% to 10%), have stopped providing dreams and aspirations for their customers, or may not have taken into account that consumers have changed.

- The general trend has been to go from "institutional brands" with strong codes to more relaxed, international brands with no strongly affirmed country of origin.

But the RISC studies go well beyond presenting brand performances and can explain major shifts in those performances. They can also compare social and cultural trends and the differences in each zone between purchasers and non-purchasers of luxury products, as illustrated in Table 5.8. Here, the responses of the users of luxury products are recorded and measured against an index of 100 that is used to indicate the level of interest of the average consumer. If we take, for example, the first figure of 148, this indicates that where Japanese respondents indicate an average interest in fashion of 100, those who are luxury-product users register 48% higher than the average consumer.

Table 5.8: Values specific to luxury-product users (index of 100 for average consumers)

	Japan	United States	Europe
Interest for fashion	148	181	156
Self-performance	154	141	158
Multiple identity	134	137	142
Gender identity	173	173	140
Seeking challenge	142	158	140
Cultural mobility	138	169	139
Personalization	138	141	139
Body enhancement	142	139	137
Personal impression	136	148	137
Fame and fortune	142	122	134

Source: RISC International, 2003

There are few differences between the three zones. While at first sight it might appear that the Americans have a higher interest in fashion than other nationalities, in fact "luxury product users" are less numerous in percentage terms in the United States than, for example, in Japan. They simply stand out from the crowd more than in Japan, where the interest for luxury is more general.

From these results it appears that luxury purchasers all want:

- To be individuals. They seek self-development, individual freedom, personal creativity and autonomy.
- To mix styles. They play with codes and integrate foreign ways of life.
- To be "winners." They have a strong social presence, they seek challenges and they like to experiment.

luxury **brand** management

- To be distinctive. They want to be different from others and to assert their individuality. They are fashion trend-setters, using their appearance to express their difference, their modernity and their creativity and to achieve their social ambitions.
- To look and perform better. They care about their body, looking on it as a source of sensations and pleasure, as a partner to their success.
- To keep their vitality—physical, mental and emotional.

This profile of the user of luxury products could be very useful to define the type of positioning and advertising platform that is most effective today.

At this stage we have moved very far from the **classic, conventional** and **institutional** idea according to which a luxury product is rare and expensive.

We are in a very different ball game. We are in the realm of the *avant garde* and the **trendy**. The brand and product environment must deal with **emotions**, with **sensuality** and **physicality**, with **escape, success, performance, optimism** and the **ephemeral**. It is no longer the product that is rare and expensive: it is the **individual**.

On this platform, it is possible to come up with positioning and communication objectives that make a lot of sense, as we will see in Chapter 8.

To finish with the RISC findings, it is possible to derive a comparison between American and European types of luxury brands, as shown in Table 5.9.

From this table it is clear that American brands are very much in phase with socially active American consumers. They are in fact "marketing brands" in that they are clearly "customer driven." On the basis of American consumer needs, they have defined an accessible, open, relaxed and casual style.

European brands are clearly creativity driven, in the sense that the creator seems to be given full authority over the content and personality of the brand. They value aesthetics and things that appeal to the senses. For them, function is secondary to the emotion created. They want to maintain a strong distance between

Table 5.9: Differences between American and European luxury

United States	Europe
Social motivations	**Individual motivations**
Realization of social dreams	Realization of personal dreams
Ambition: what would I like to be?	Realization of emotional desires
Perfume: social accessory, brand name	Perfume: me, my identity, my sense
Relationship	**Emotional relationship**
Practicality, utility, functionality	Aesthetics, sensoriality, style
Wearable clothes, always comfortable	Futility
Customer-driven brands	**Creativity-driven brands**
User friendly, easygoing brands	Eccentricity, no real sense of utility, no limits
All needs, all circumstances	Distance
Service	Keeping the dream alive, fantasy
Exclusivity: prices and rarity	**Elitism**
High prices are the best luxury sign	Prices
Giving value to the buyer	Cultural codes (Hermès)
Lifestyles	**Intellectual concepts**
"Old England"	**Ways of being**
Casual	**French brands**

Source: RISC International, 2003

the brand's cultural values and the consumer: those values should be something in which consumers aspire to participate, to join the "happy few." They buy the products in the hope of one day becoming part of this elite group.

The trend today seems to favor the customer-driven American brands, but this may change in the future.

From everything that we have seen in this chapter, it is clear that creating a brand that satisfies every customer in the world

luxury **brand** management

is a real challenge. This is where market research is absolutely necessary, but market research that is based on consumer attitudes and expectations. We will look more closely at this in the next chapter, when we investigate brand identity.

As we finish our review of the luxury client, it must have become obvious that in this very strong marketing environment, where emotional values have an overriding impact on the acceptability and on the desirability of a product, market research, undertaken in different parts of the world, is an essential tool for success.

In the next chapter, we look at other analytical and management tools that enable us to master one of the most valuable elements of luxury brands: their brand identity.

Endnotes
[1]Euro RSCG, Living a good life, 2002.
[2]Don Ziccardi, *Influencing the affluent: Marketing to the individual luxury customer in a volatile economy*, MFJ Books, 2001.
[3]RISC, The luxury market, 2003.
[4]Bernard Dubois and Gilles Laurent: "Les excursionnistes de luxe." Hommes et Commerce, No.271, MW 1999.
[5]See Patrick Hetzel, "Les entreprises face aux nouvelles formes de consummation." Revue Française de Gestion, September/October 1996.
[6]P. Siberil, *Influence de la musique sur les comportements des acheteurs en grande surface de vente*, thesis, University of Rennes, 1994.
[7]Patrick Hetgel, *Marketing Experientiel et Nouveaux Univers de Consommation*, Editions d'Organisation, Paris, 2002.
[8]Corinne Tissier: "Divided colors of Cartier," *Le Nouvel Economiste*, 10 January 1995.
[9]Ibid.
[10]Bernard Dubois and Gilles Laurent: "Le luxe par delà les frontières: une étude exploratoire dans douze pays," *Decisions Marketing*, September–December, 1996.

chapter **6**

BRAND
Identity

What is the identity of a brand? Our first answer might be that it is what the brand "says" to consumers—making a distinction between what it says and how they understand it. The notion of identity is still too little used by managers, and that's a shame, because to our way of thinking it offers some very useful and concrete glimpses into the essence of the brand phenomenon itself. It constitutes the foundation and the federating element of all the activities we have designated as being manifestations of the brand.

We sometimes have a tendency to confine brand identity to the intuitive, affective sphere, which the company's concrete and methodical processes cannot influence. Yet tools for analysis do exist, originating in the field of semiology, with which this area can be at least partially rationalized and provide very concrete lessons about managing a brand. During our careers, we have had occasion to use them "in the field" from the pragmatic point of view of managers, and with tangible results.

In this chapter we want to describe the operational importance of the notion of brand identity in light of our personal experience, and present a few simple tools for formalizing it. Of course, like any phenomenon that produces meaning, a brand represents multiple values, which can give rise to infinite interpretations. Yet it is in this latent set of values that the real source of its past and future reputation lies. If certain brands are "richer" than others, and that should be the case for luxury brands, it's because their evocative potential is greater and more easily mobilized. To manage a luxury brand well, therefore, we have to begin by understanding what it consists of, and separate its essence from the variable perceptions it engenders among consumers.

A STILL-TOO-UNFAMILIAR CONCEPT

While the term "brand identity" is encountered frequently in professional jargon, it is nevertheless a fairly new one. It is probable that an in-depth and systematic consideration has been undertaken of the identity of few brands today. To formalize this concept a little more, we might refer you to Merriam-Webster's *Collegiate Dictionary*, tenth edition, which gives the following definition of "identity":

1. a: sameness of essential or generic character in different instances; b: sameness in all that constitutes the objective reality of a thing: ONENESS
2. a: the distinguishing character or personality of an individual: INDIVIDUALITY; b: the relation established by psychological identification
3. the condition of being the same with something described or asserted.

What we call the brand identity corresponds to an extension of the definition above, with a strong human dimension. But the term suits our purposes because two necessary (though not sufficient)

luxury **brand** management

elements are present in it: on the one hand, differentiation; on the other, permanence—or, if you will, "durability."

We may attempt a more precise initial definition of brand identity: the capacity of a brand to be recognized as unique, over time, without confusion, thanks to the elements that individualize it.

One might think that an attachment to these criteria of individuality is somehow spontaneous with managers, but the history of brands is full of examples to the contrary, as a result of either ignorance or else a voluntary disregard for the virtues of reflection on the identity of brands.

Take the case of Givenchy. The house of Hubert James Taffin de Givenchy dressed elegant, refined women, with a sophistication that was quintessentially Parisian. Audrey Hepburn, who was the creator's muse for 40 years, typified all its values. In 1996 Hubert de Givenchy retired. John Galliano succeeded him—for one season only, before moving to Christian Dior. Then came Alexander McQueen, a 26-year-old Scottish designer. In 2001 a young Welshman, Julian Macdonald, replaced him. And in 2005, another change: Riccardo Tisci was appointed creative director.

This revolving door for designers would not have been so harmful had there been, at least, a concern for respecting the values that were at the origin of the brand's prestige. We don't mean to call into question the great individual talent of these creators, but it must be recognized that such was not the case. Consequently, the "message" of Givenchy was clouded, its identity dispersed by uncoordinated stylistic daring. The priceless capital the brand's reputation represented, instead of being preserved and prolonged by the innovations of these young talents, now has to be rebuilt. It is certainly possible to express elegance, femininity and sophistication, and still be modern (Ungaro used to do it very well)—even if these three values are not sufficient to define an identity.

Another counter-example, which we have encountered in the banking sector, is a good illustration of the absence of consideration of brand identity in such important undertakings as the definition of a new graphical identity. Banco Sabadell is a bank of Catalan origin, extremely dynamic, which was successfully introduced on the Madrid stock exchange a few years ago. In 1998 the bank decided to transform its "corporate image," notably by adopting a new graphic identity. It called in Mario Eskenazi, an Argentinian architect based in Spain, the winner of numerous awards and the creator of several logos for major Spanish companies. He was put in charge of designing a new graphics charter, with a new logo to be used on all communication media, and also of redecorating the bank's agencies. Once the job was done, the designer gave an interview, which the bank itself published. Here is an excerpt:

What does the new image of Banco Sabadell try to get across?

That's a very difficult question to answer without falling into excessively pompous phraseology. I think that, when you create a new image for a company, it's very rare that you start by considering what you are trying to communicate. It's very difficult for a corporate image, in and of itself, to transmit something. Its role is to facilitate clear identification of the company. In this sense, the new image of Banco Sabadell is not trying to get anything across.[1]

This may have been provocation on the part of the designer; it may have been his way of asserting the primacy of his "intuitive" creativity over the careful calculations of the communicators. Or maybe it was a way of discreetly expressing his disdain for the idea that a commercial brand can actually "produce meaning." Whatever the case, a statement like this one does a disservice to the extensive collaborative and deliberative effort that must be inherent in any renovation of a corporate identity. It shows that the notion of brand identity is not sufficiently widespread in the corporate world and in corporate communication. Otherwise such a statement, made in the name of the bank itself, would be unthinkable.

luxury **brand** management

We recognize that the logo created by Mario Eskenazi is very original (a white B within a blue circle and a bigger black S separated on the right), graphically much more modern than the one it replaced (a blue S enlaced in a blue B encircled by a blue circle, with white background) and more easily recognizable—qualities that many brands might envy. But what a loss of an opportunity to reflect on the specific and unique characteristics of the Catalan bank and create a corporate image that produces meaning!

The case of the French bank Crédit du Nord, on the other hand, is a good example of careful reflection on the identity of a brand. In 1984 Crédit du Nord, the fifth-ranking French banking group at the time, introduced a new image, involving redesign of the logo, the graphics of the name, the architecture of the branches, and advertising and public relations campaigns. The image was entirely founded on the concept of clarity. For 10 years the bank had suffered from an indistinct image as an old, serious, provincial bank. Its merger with the Banque de l'Union Parisienne, a business bank active in high finance, had not helped clarify the situation.

The detailed history of the development of a new logo and all the elements of communication, starting with the concept of light or clarity, has been recounted in a book by the semiotician Jean-Marie Floch.[2] In it he explains how the communication agency Creative Business, with whom he collaborated, developed, using semiological tools, all the elements of the new communication—beginning with the blue star, which replaced the orange cube as the brand's logo.

The concept of light, in the banking field, was analyzed as the choice of a certain type of relationship between the banker and the client. This relationship was based on the recognition of the competence and sovereignty of the client. The idea of light thus crystallized a value involved with the very essence of what any relationship with a bank should be: confidence. This concept led first of all to the choice of a code; that is, a style: a brand aesthetic resolutely classicist in nature, wherein the logo had to contribute to conveying frankness and personalized attention. The star was chosen because it represents a visible element in open space; it is also a navigational reference point with rich symbolic connotations.

In these last two examples, two approaches to graphical identity are in confrontation: the intuition of the creator alone, as opposed to the intuition of that creator contained within the framework of an understandable discourse on the part of the brand.

To avoid formalizing the values that are to be expressed is to have blind faith in the graphic designer. And in no way should it be assumed that the latter is happy with such a situation. What such an attitude shows above all is a lack of real reflection on the brand's identity. Graphic designers and communication consultants know this and shy away from the unwieldy freedom left to them in such cases. They are the first to complain of the lack of substance in the briefs they're given—*if* they are given any, that is.[3] Too often, they say, clients express extremely imprecise intentions ("Our logo will be young and pleasant"), or provide purely technical specifications ("Our logo is to be six centimeters high and should reflect our values"). Instructions like these tell design professionals very little about the nature of the values to be communicated.

The creative function, like all other functions necessary to a brand's operation, must be part of an overall strategy. The brand's identity is a major resource and a frame of reference for the development of that strategy. It influences not only creation and communication, but also logistics, production, distribution, human resources management, information processing, and so on. At all levels of its activity, a brand aspires to become what it truly is. And in fact, concrete tools exist for apprehending and managing that individuality.

Tools for analyzing brand identity

We will present some of these tools here. Our intention is in no way to cover exhaustively all the existing tools for analyzing a brand's identity. The tools we will present have been used effectively by the authors at various points in their careers, and we would simply

luxury **brand** management

like to share them with our readers. Analyzing a brand's identity is a fairly new approach, one whose history is related to that of the concept of brand identity itself.

Naomi Klein[4] rightly refers to the work of Bruce Barton—who was, incidentally, the creator of Betty Crocker and the second B of the BBDO advertising agency. In the 1920s, this advertiser began to seek out the "corporate soul." Awareness of the fact that a brand can have meaning beyond the products themselves and beyond the advertising slowly developed, and the vocabulary was enriched with concepts such as the "essence," "*raison d'être*," "consciousness," "soul," and "genetic code" of a brand. But it was not until the 1970s that the word "identity" made its appearance in the specialized literature, generally linked to the concept of "corporate identity."[5]

The use of "brand identity" appeared in the early 1980s and spread quickly among professionals in advertising agencies.[6] Originally, the term designated, in a limited sense, everything that can identify the brand by linking it to the content of the advertising material. It soon evolved toward a real personification of brands. The use of the words "personality," "individuality," and "identity" became common. The French advertiser Jacques Séguéla speaks of the perception of brands through the intermediary of their physicality, their character and their style. In 1980, he developed this new methodology under the name "brand person," which later became known as the "star strategy." The concept of identity began, in an indistinct way, to be joined with that of image.

In 1984 David Bernstein, in his book *Company Image and Reality*, devoted a chapter to brand identity.[7] Little by little, the specialized literature began to study this area. David Aaker attempts a classification, still quite heterogeneous, of "brand equity." This includes brand loyalty, name awareness, perceived quality, brand image and, finally, other assets.[8] The term "personality" appears briefly in the book, which also proposes the diagram shown in Figure 6.1, which was one of the first tools for analyzing a brand's identity.

This model, however, maintains a certain confusion between the concept of brand image and that of brand identity. This confusion remains common today. It is important to point out that, in our view, these two concepts do not coincide. The images (rather than "the image") correspond to the perceptions induced in the different consumers who make up the market segments. They are receptive in nature. The identity is the substance of the brand, expressed via all the methods of communication used by the brand. It is emissive in nature.

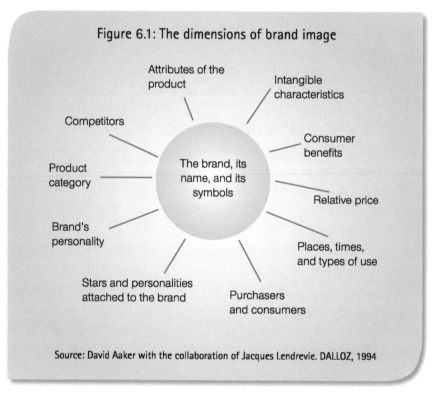

Figure 6.1: The dimensions of brand image

Source: David Aaker with the collaboration of Jacques Lendrevie. DALLOZ, 1994

There is a difference between these two concepts. Imagine, for example, that you ask someone about his or her work. This person has a highly specialized profession or trade, about which you know nothing. He or she tries to explain it to you simply, but either because of a poor choice of words, or because you yourself are not paying attention, you "get it wrong." Or, more precisely, never having seen this person at work, you form an image of the job he or she does that is more or less removed from reality, an image that

luxury **brand** management

does not correspond exactly to this person's professional identity. After all, it's not easy to describe that identity in "purely objective" terms. In any case, there is a palpable difference between what the person wanted to get across and what you actually understood.

To avoid misunderstanding, we avoid using the word "image." For us, the expression "brand identity," as we have just said, refers to a "substance." We will see what this substance, which can be expressed in terms of ethical and aesthetic invariants, encompasses. On the other hand, when we want to refer to the representations induced by the markets, we will speak not of image but of perception of the brand's identity.

We can see the progress made by respected authors like Aaker in tackling the inherent complexity of brands' identities by comparing his early approach to the model he developed in 2000, as illustrated in Figure 6.2.

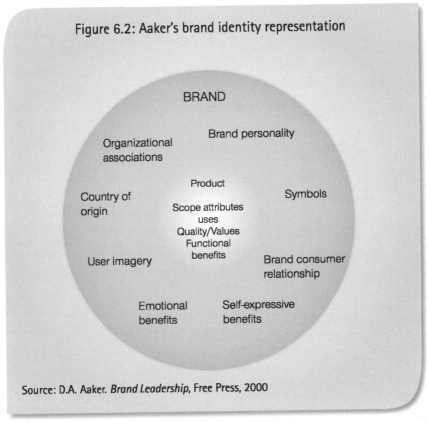

Figure 6.2: Aaker's brand identity representation

BRAND

Organizational associations

Brand personality

Country of origin

Product

Scope attributes uses

Quality/Values

Functional benefits

Symbols

User imagery

Brand consumer relationship

Emotional benefits

Self-expressive benefits

Source: D.A. Aaker. *Brand Leadership*, Free Press, 2000

Let's return to our historical perspective. Jean-Noël Kapferer, in 1992, introduced the first fairly sophisticated analytical tool for dealing with the difficult area of brand identity: the identity prism.[9]

The identity prism

Advertising and creative agencies used and still use the graphics charter or "copy strategy" in developing campaigns or collections, but these tools have never really been able to identify a brand's ethical and aesthetic constants. Kapferer's prism, on the other hand, allows a much more detailed approach to the problem. Its introduction represented a major step forward.

Here is how the interpretative diagram works. Six dimensions are positioned around a prism (see Figure 6.3). Let's look at the different elements of identity.

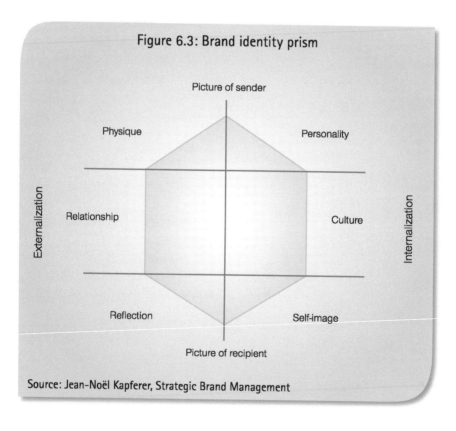

Figure 6.3: Brand identity prism

Picture of sender

Physique   Personality

Externalization

Relationship   Culture

Internalization

Reflection   Self-image

Picture of recipient

Source: Jean-Noël Kapferer, Strategic Brand Management

luxury **brand** management

The "physique" of the brand relates to the concrete element that comes immediately to mind when the name of the brand is mentioned. It is a set of sensory and objective characteristics, exemplified by the following:

- Aubade: women's lingerie.
- Hermès: a "Kelly" crocodile handbag and a silk "carré."
- Levi's: a pair of blue jeans, with a distinctive label.
- Toblerone: a chocolate bar with a triangular section, in a yellow and red package.
- Bally: a pair of shoes.
- Tod's: moccasins.
- Ferrari: a red automobile.
- Ducati: a red motorcycle with a tubular trestle frame.
- Missoni: knitted fabrics or materials colored in a specific way.
- Opinel: a pocketknife with a wooden handle, fitted with a safety catch.

Brand "personality" is apprehended by means of questions such as: If it were a man, what kind of character would he have? Professional, aesthete, performance-oriented? Original, like Audi? Colorless and odorless, like Opel? This is what is behind the intensive use of famous personalities who have acted as lasting incarnations of the brand's values in recent years: Kate Moss for Calvin Klein, Inès Sastre for Lancôme after Isabella Rossellini was dropped, and so on. These constitute easy short-cuts for giving a semblance of personality to brands that may be a bit too weak or too opaque in their specific values. Fashion brands like Armani and Paul Smith, who have their creators to fill this role, don't encounter such problems.

The brand's "culture" is linked to the original values of its creators—often, the culture of the country, the region or the city where the brand developed: Madrid for Loewe; Sicily for Dolce & Gabbana; Majorca for Majorica; Japan for Shiseido; and so on. But the geographical dimension is not the only one expressed. Hewlett Packard, for example, puts forward the "garage spirit," its two gifted pioneers and the spirit of an American company.

"Relationship" is involved with the social communication of the brand. A brand with identity influences relations between individuals, first through signs of belonging to a group, and then well beyond. What do people think when they see me stepping out of my Maserati or wearing the latest Christian Dior swimsuit? Gucci strongly suggests seduction; Diesel, provocation; banks, confidence in general.

The brand's "reflection" describes the typical customer the market associates with the brand (the customer it imagines for it). This is not to be confused with the target customer: Kapferer is referring here to the market's perception.

The brand's "self-image" corresponds to the image consumers have of themselves when using the product. When a man lights up a Marlboro, climbs into a Porsche, or puts on an Armani suit, how does he perceive himself?

Figures 6.4 and 6.5 are examples of use of the identity prism on two prestigious French luxury brands.

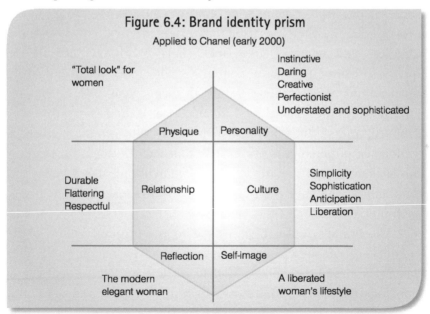

Figure 6.4: Brand identity prism

Applied to Chanel (early 2000)

"Total look" for women

Instinctive
Daring
Creative
Perfectionist
Understated and sophisticated

Physique | Personality

Durable
Flattering
Respectful

Relationship | Culture

Simplicity
Sophistication
Anticipation
Liberation

Reflection | Self-image

The modern elegant woman

A liberated woman's lifestyle

luxury **brand** management

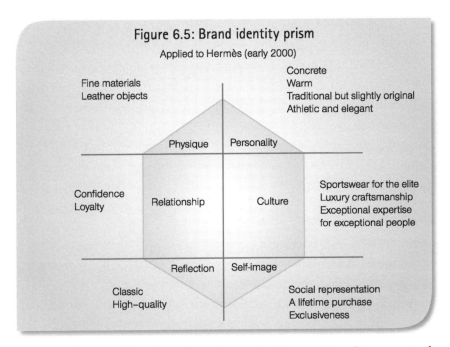

Figure 6.5: Brand identity prism

Applied to Hermès (early 2000)

Fine materials
Leather objects

Concrete
Warm
Traditional but slightly original
Athletic and elegant

Physique | Personality

Confidence
Loyalty

Relationship | Culture

Sportswear for the elite
Luxury craftsmanship
Exceptional expertise
for exceptional people

Reflection | Self-image

Classic
High–quality

Social representation
A lifetime purchase
Exclusiveness

Kapferer's prism introduced a major innovation. It was a tool that, for the first time, made systematic study possible while showing the complexity of any approach to brand identity. Nevertheless, it does have limitations. Self-image and reflection—the "two sides of the mirror" as Kapferer calls them—are receptive in nature: they have more to do with the perception of the brand's identity than the identity itself. As for the "relationship" dimension, it belongs more to the cultural domain. Personality and culture overlap. After having used it ourselves numerous times, our judgment is that the prism is a useful tool but tricky to use, in particular because of the lack of homogeneity in its categories.

The most enlightening parts of the prism are still "physique" and "personality." These two concepts were studied in greater detail with the semiotic approach of Jean-Marie Floch. In the late 1980s, the semio-linguistics research group directed by A. J. Greimas (at the École des Hautes Études en Sciences Sociales in Paris) was the hotbed where Jean-Marie Floch, then director of the seminar on visual semiotics, developed a number of tools derived directly from the methods of structural semantics, intended for analyzing the conditions under which meaning can be produced and perceived. In parallel, François Schwebel, founder of the Creative Business consulting firm, was also a pioneer in launching the "global communication" concept. He maintains that everything is in communication, and that coherence among all these messages is provided by a federating concept, called "personality" at the time. One of the authors had the privilege of working with Jean-Marie Floch and François Schwebel on formalizing the identities of Ferragamo, Loewe, Bally and some other minor brands.

Brand ethics and aesthetics

Of all the tools available today, semiology is, in our opinion and based on our experience, the discipline best suited to aiding a manager in defining, prolonging and defending the identity of a luxury brand. From our perspective as non–specialists but convinced users, we would like to take a moment to discuss this discipline.

First of all, what is semiology? Imagine two "No Smoking" signs, one of which gets its message across better than the other. Is it possible to describe exactly what makes one more effective than the other, without the discussion becoming simply a matter of subjective tastes? And is it possible to describe it in general terms, to aid us in, say, designing another type of sign (for example, a "No Parking" sign)? In broad terms, that is the project of semiology. Its aim (according to Greimas) is to describe, as objectively as possible, the process of production of meaning, and generally of all the practices of signification that make up cultures. But it can be extended, Jean-Marie Floch adds, to a certain disposition of the mind, curious about anything that has (or could have) meaning.

If we accept the validity of applying semiotics to the study of brand identities, we are making the following basic premise: brands are systems that produce meaning. The tools we present require a certain degree of formalization, so we should assure the reader at the outset of their operational viability. We have used them ourselves "in the field," and while they can't, of course, solve all problems, we feel that their usefulness is undeniable.

The hinge

The first of these semiotic tools is the "hinge," a simple framework developed by Jean-Marie Floch to bring out the different levels of analysis or definition of a brand universe. To clarify the discussion, we should briefly recall a few basic principles. First, semiology studies any and all "discourse" or signal capable of being interpreted; that is, of producing meaning: text, music, film, photography. The concepts, then, are not limited to a particular area of expression.

Second, in order to attempt to understand the processes through which we manage to interpret a signal (text, sound, image), semiologists, following Ferdinand de Saussure, have introduced a distinction between the "signifier" and the "signified." The signifier is the material part of a sign; the signified is the representation with which that material part is associated. For example, for the Egyptian hieroglyph that resembles a wavy line, the signifier is simply a zigzag; the signified is a simple sound, the consonant "N." What is true of hieroglyphics is also true of our own writing and of all signs. The succession of letters "T_R_E_E" written on a blackboard corresponds to the mental image a reader of those letters produces—that of a tree, a woody plant having a trunk, and so on.[10]

However, these two dimensions are the two sides of a single coin or, as Saussure put it, a single sheet of paper: one side cannot be separated from the other. A poet choosing one word rather than another (which might be an almost perfect synonym) to signify the same idea is playing on sound, transforming the beauty but also the meaning of the line. And no one can pretend to translate a book of poetry armed only with a good catalog of correspondences between signifier and signified (in other words, a dictionary). A sign is an indivisible whole, even if its twofold dimension is evident.

All signs, then, are articulated at a hinge between the signifier (or level of expression) and the signified (or level of content). The same is true, by extension, of groups of signs—and thus of the creation and physical manifestations of brands. This articulation also extends to criteria of invariance and variation. For example, as regards expression, the "pool" of the vocabulary, the principles of rhyme are the same for many writers, but the style of the poet is unique; as regards content, the poet's favorite themes–which remain the same from one poem to another–are not necessarily sufficient to describe the particular subject of a given poem.

The advantage of this methodological approach is twofold. First, it brings out the two fundamental levels of a brand's discourse, clearly separating content and container. Then it places the accent on the invariant elements of the brand. These invariants are precisely what make it possible for the brand to be recognized as itself over time. They constitute the very foundation of its identity.

Figure 6.6 shows the hinge principle applied to a brand universe. Looking at this diagram, one thing becomes clear: ethic and aesthetic are the invariants on which the brand's identity is founded.

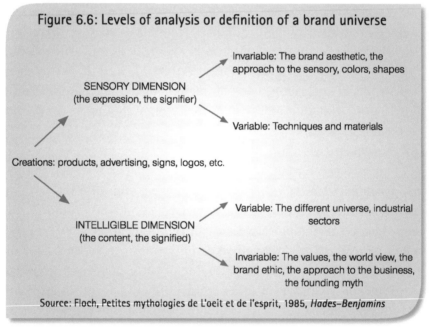

Figure 6.6: Levels of analysis or definition of a brand universe

Invariable: The brand aesthetic, the approach to the sensory, colors, shapes

SENSORY DIMENSION
(the expression, the signifier)

Variable: Techniques and materials

Creations: products, advertising, signs, logos, etc.

Variable: The different universe, industrial sectors

INTELLIGIBLE DIMENSION
(the content, the signified)

Invariable: The values, the world view, the brand ethic, the approach to the business, the founding myth

Source: Floch, Petites mythologies de L'oeit et de l'esprit, 1985, *Hades–Benjamins*

The use of the hinge is relatively simple. It aims at characterizing the brand's identity through its expression and its content–that is, at giving a formal definition of its aesthetic and of its ethic. The aesthetic study is fairly easy to put into practice, especially if the

luxury **brand** management

brand in question is a very "typed" one, where the colors, shapes and materials are resolutely baroque or classical. In this domain, the contribution of Jean-Marie Floch, who updated the work of Heinrich Wölfflin, has been essential.

Note that generally, the Northern European brands—Jil Sander, Ikea, Helmut Lang, BMW—and North American brands—Calvin Klein, Donna Karan, Coach—have an aesthetic of the classical type, characterized pictorially by:

- clearly defined lines and contours, emphasizing individually recognizable elements
- space divided into easily identifiable zones, each with its own autonomy
- closed shapes, visible in their entirety: planes
- impressions of stability: symmetries
- saturated colors.

On the other hand, Mediterranean brands—Loewe, Ferragamo, Dolce & Gabbana, Rubelli, Majorica, Lamborghini, Versace, Roberto Cavalli—have a tendency toward the baroque, characterized pictorially by:

- lines delineated by shadow effects: curves and criss-crosses
- open forms, which can appear accidental
- each part losing its autonomy and taking on meaning only in association with the rest of the work
- movement treated in depth: volumes
- chiaroscuro and deep colors.

The study conducted on Loewe in 1996 by one of the authors, who was its president at the time, in collaboration with Creative Business and Jean-Marie Floch, led to the development and the communication of the concept of a "minimalist baroque" aesthetic. These apparently contradictory terms met with much success with the press. In the late 1990s, this Spanish fashion brand—a century-

and-a-half old and often referred to by the French as the "Iberian Hermès"—had good name recognition, associated with quality and a strong presence in Spain and Japan, but was still weak in the other markets. Struggling to achieve international status, and also suffering from the absence of a charismatic founder in its history—unlike Chanel, for example—Loewe had the appearance of a slightly "tired" brand. The characterization of the brand's aesthetic effectively transmitted the message of a brand that was faithful to its roots (the baroque) and with a strong desire for modernity (minimalism, which at the time was still in vogue). That message was coherent with the recruiting of designer Narciso Rodriguez, who was himself a blend of modernity and respect for tradition.

The study of the brand ethic, on the other hand, is considerably more difficult, above all for brands that were not founded by a creator with a strong personality, or that have squandered their heritage. Certain brands are so clearly positioned that the task is easier. Take Nike, for example. Since the appearance of its initial slogan—"Just do it"—Nike has cultivated the universal values associated with sports and the Olympic movement: surpassing oneself, determination, competition, accomplishment. Nike, remember, is the goddess of victory. This is where the brand's ethic, its vision of the world, and what it believes are situated; "what it stands for," to use Jean-Marie Floch's expression.

The launch of the controversial Mecca-Cola in France in November 2002 is a very significant example of a brand that directly communicates the values underlying the ethic of its brand identity. Its bottles and the opening page of its website say: "No more drinking stupid, drink with commitment!" and "10% of our net profits, for Palestinian Childhood. 10% for [local] charity—an NGO." This is clear to everyone, without the need for a semiotician to translate.

Another recently successful brand is Camper. The Spanish shoe manufacturer expresses very clearly which brand ethic it wants to promote through its slogan "Walk don't run": a whole philosophy of life.

luxury **brand** management

In certain cases, setting about finding the permanent values the brand has expressed since its inception is a frustrating process. It sometimes leads—as was the case with Loewe—to a recognition of the non-existence of a brand ethic. Such a situation has an advantage in that it leaves open a very broad field for the choice of values, but it also shows that the brand has had no obvious permanent values over time, and therefore has been perceived in a very imprecise way.

Using a semiologist who is experienced in the study of the corpus of brands is an absolute necessity in this type of research. The role of the semiologist consists not only in finding possible meanings beyond the signs, but also in determining precisely the objective procedures to be used in constructing that meaning. By describing in detail the nature of a brand's identity and the means of its expression, the semiologist will help the manager perpetuate that identity and prolong its life.

Figure 6.7 is an example of the use of the hinge approach. Taurus is a fictitious name for a real brand—in existence in Europe for over a century, designing, manufacturing, and retailing luxury products—whose real name contractual considerations forbid us to reveal. The brand's state in 1997 is represented on the hinge.

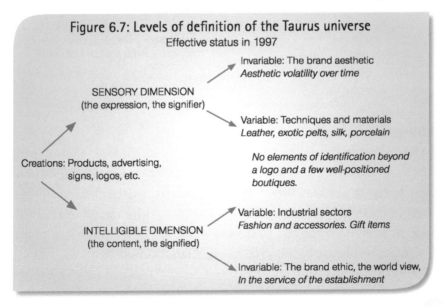

Figure 6.7: Levels of definition of the Taurus universe
Effective status in 1997

Invariable: The brand aesthetic
Aesthetic volatility over time

SENSORY DIMENSION
(the expression, the signifier)

Variable: Techniques and materials
Leather, exotic pelts, silk, porcelain

Creations: Products, advertising, signs, logos, etc.

No elements of identification beyond a logo and a few well-positioned boutiques.

Variable: Industrial sectors
Fashion and accessories. Gift items

INTELLIGIBLE DIMENSION
(the content, the signified)

Invariable: The brand ethic, the world view,
In the service of the establishment

brand identity

The recommendations that came out of the above assessment and the competitive conditions of the sectors where the brand was active are presented in Figure 6.8. As can be seen, these recommendations are expressed in concrete, precise terms, on the level of both aesthetic and ethic. Real choices are made, ones that clearly define values to be cultivated and others to be shunned. The brand's identity is anything but a melting pot of fashionable values. On the contrary, it is structured by differentiation. These recommendations were the starting point for a series of briefs dealing with all aspects of the company's communication and creation.

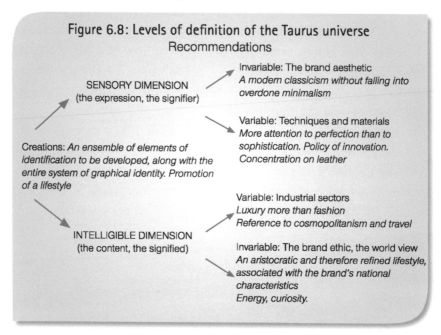

Figure 6.8: Levels of definition of the Taurus universe
Recommendations

SENSORY DIMENSION
(the expression, the signifier)

Invariable: The brand aesthetic
A modern classicism without falling into overdone minimalism

Variable: Techniques and materials
More attention to perfection than to sophistication. Policy of innovation. Concentration on leather

Creations: An ensemble of elements of identification to be developed, along with the entire system of graphical identity. Promotion of a lifestyle

Variable: Industrial sectors
Luxury more than fashion
Reference to cosmopolitanism and travel

INTELLIGIBLE DIMENSION
(the content, the signified)

Invariable: The brand ethic, the world view
An aristocratic and therefore refined lifestyle, associated with the brand's national characteristics
Energy, curiosity.

The semiotic square

After the signifier/signified hinge, a second semiotic tool can be used to make a more profound analysis of a brand's identities: the semiotic square. When Jean-Marie Floch used it in studying Ferragamo's brand identity in 1992, he was really the pioneer in the use of semiotics applied to luxury brands.[11] The square has since come into wide use by advertisers, specialists in brand management, and trend agencies.

This diagram aims at describing a situation not in terms of static objects, specific events and the like, but in terms of dynamic relations. To provide an analogy: in describing a boxing match, a commentator can concentrate on the actions, the physique and the personality of each boxer, but can also choose to concentrate on the "flux" of punches exchanged (contacts, acceleration, deceleration), since the dynamics of the bout are what occupy our attention more than the identity or the presumed motivations of the fighters. Even if we know very little about the latter, this approach can still be used to describe the fight. In the same way, the power of the semiotic square lies in its ability to organize an abstract universe coherently, in spite of the fact that it is not recognized as being rational itself. It can point out meanings that are present, from a logical point of view, but latent, not yet active. It can also describe the way in which new meanings will appear.

This approach begins with Saussure's assertion (in 1916) that any system of meaning is a system of relations and not only a system of signs. These relations are established between "semantic poles" (a thing and its opposite form two poles united by a relation of opposition) to constitute semantic categories and axes of dynamic significance. For example, the category "gender" exists only to the extent that "gender" is articulated as a relation between masculine and feminine. Relations are considered as taking precedence over their terms, which are only the intersections of those relations.

Putting the accent on the dynamics of meaning effects is a help in finding the latent meanings of a discourse. Take the sentence "I am not a traitor." If a man utters it to an interrogator who demands that he betray his accomplices, he is making a strong assertion, a courageous refusal. But if, later, the man utters the same sentence to his accomplices whereas no one has accused him of anything, he might give his comrades the impression that its opposite may well be true. The simple fact that he mentions betrayal (even to deny it) makes him suspect. What he is denying will be taken into account more than what he is saying. In this extreme example, the relation of opposition in itself imposes another meaning, independently of the logical sense of the utterance.

For similar reasons, no advertiser would ever dare use the slogan "We are not crooks," as a certain U.S. president once did. But there are other, more subtle meaning effects than those shown in these examples, and the control of latent meanings is a primordial issue in the management of a brand. And the semiotic square, developed over time by Greimas (1979), Courtes (1979) and Floch (1983), has proven its usefulness.

The most significant example of a square, one that is the starting point for numerous analyses, is the one relating to the axiology of consumption, as illustrated in Figure 6.9. This square dealing with consumption values is still much used because it gets at the primary mechanisms of all planned human action.

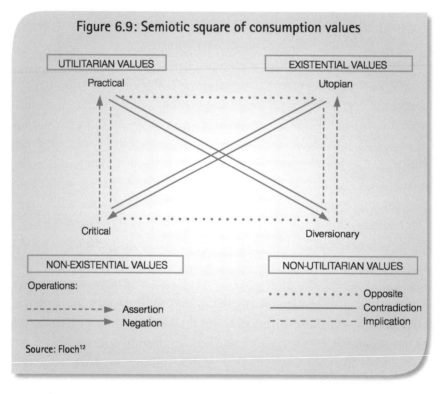

Figure 6.9: Semiotic square of consumption values

The two principal typologies presented on the square (utilitarian values/existential values) are taken from narrative semiotics, which distinguishes, in a narration, life values (existential, utopian

luxury **brand** management

or mythic) and practical (or utilitarian) values. In any story—and especially in mythic and folkloric narratives, which are the starting point of this discipline—the life values that give meaning to the hero's quest can be identified. These are generally values of an existential nature, corresponding to a vision of the world, a moral system, and so on. They are sufficiently universal and profound to motivate the hero's actions: good, beauty, glory, sacrifice, love, freedom and the like. These values are the initial justification of the narrative.

The practical values, on the other hand, are secondary and instrumental. They represent the means necessary to the hero for attaining his underlying objective, expressed in terms of existential values. An example is the hero's search for a sword made of a magical alloy (a practical value) with which to kill the dragon and free his people (a life value).

It should be noted that this type of analysis was posited for structured stories, ones that are self-contained in a certain way. To apply the semiotic square to the analysis of brands, we must accept the presupposition that a brand can represent a micro-universe of meaning. Once this semantic axis, consisting of two opposites (practical—or convenience—and utopian), which applies ideally to the mechanisms of consumption, is in place, the semiotic square can be used to develop all its nuances.

Each of the contrary terms can be seen in relation to another term, differentiated by the absence of the characteristics of the first. The practical corresponds to the non-practical; that is, the diversionary, the playful, the aesthetic. The utopian corresponds to the non-utopian: the critical, the utilitarian, the practical. On the left-hand side of the square, vertically, are two propositions where the term critical or non-utopian implies what is practical and utilitarian.

Placing the accent on mechanisms of meaning is by no means superfluous where brands are concerned because the problem here is that of defining the communication on which they base a large part of their relations with consumers. We present below a few examples of use of the square in the study of the identity, the creation, or the communication of a few brands.

The first study concerned Salvatore Ferragamo (1992) (see Figure 6.10). It was conducted by Jean-Marie Floch and François Schwebel, who were then working with Creative Business, at a time when Ferragamo was developing its ambition to become a global brand.

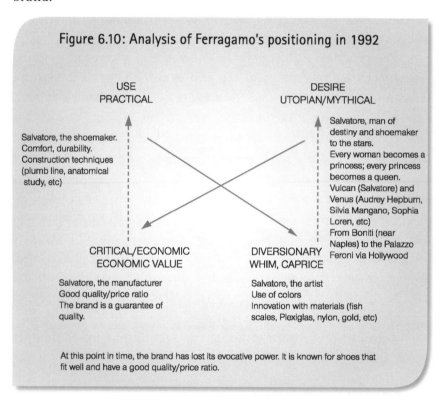

Figure 6.10: Analysis of Ferragamo's positioning in 1992

USE
PRACTICAL

DESIRE
UTOPIAN/MYTHICAL

Salvatore, the shoemaker. Comfort, durability. Construction techniques (plumb line, anatomical study, etc)

Salvatore, man of destiny and shoemaker to the stars. Every woman becomes a princess; every princess becomes a queen. Vulcan (Salvatore) and Venus (Audrey Hepburn, Silvia Mangano, Sophia Loren, etc) From Boniti (near Naples) to the Palazzo Feroni via Hollywood

CRITICAL/ECONOMIC
ECONOMIC VALUE

DIVERSIONARY
WHIM, CAPRICE

Salvatore, the manufacturer Good quality/price ratio The brand is a guarantee of quality.

Salvatore, the artist Use of colors Innovation with materials (fish scales, Plexiglas, nylon, gold, etc)

At this point in time, the brand has lost its evocative power. It is known for shoes that fit well and have a good quality/price ratio.

The figure gives a very general and structured picture of the evolution of the brand's positioning. It gave rise to a plan of action for products and communication. The choice made was to stress the right side of the square—the non-practical dimension of the brand. Note than the launch of the first Ferragamo perfume, with its heavy advertising, was meant to contribute to strengthening that mythic and aesthetic dimension.

We won't deny ourselves the enjoyment of presenting two quick

luxury **brand** management

sketches by Jean-Marie Floch. The first concerns a study he conducted to define a packaging system for eggs. The square was developed, still using the practical/existential semantic axis (see Figure 6.11).

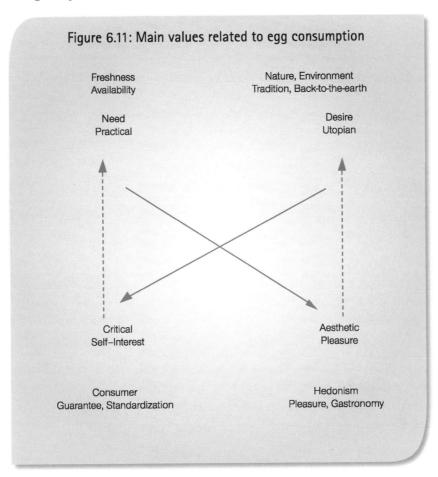

Figure 6.11: Main values related to egg consumption

Freshness
Availability

Nature, Environment
Tradition, Back-to-the-earth

Need
Practical

Desire
Utopian

Critical
Self–Interest

Aesthetic
Pleasure

Consumer
Guarantee, Standardization

Hedonism
Pleasure, Gastronomy

The second study concerned an analysis of the communication for Calvin Klein perfumes, at the time of the launch of CK One (see Figure 6.12). It was presented by Jean-Marie Floch to the students of the Luxury MBA at the ESSEC Business School. The most significant semantic axis proved to be culture/nature, where the four Calvin Klein perfumes existing at the time were in natural concurrence.

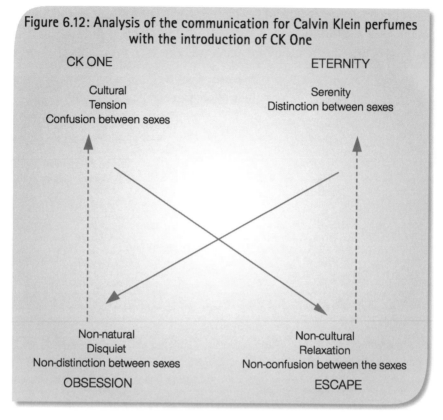

Figure 6.12: Analysis of the communication for Calvin Klein perfumes with the introduction of CK One

CK ONE

Cultural
Tension
Confusion between sexes

ETERNITY

Serenity
Distinction between sexes

Non-natural
Disquiet
Non-distinction between sexes

OBSESSION

Non-cultural
Relaxation
Non-confusion between the sexes

ESCAPE

Jean-Marie Floch's thesis was that CK One could already be anticipated with the launch of Eternity, which is its semantic opposite. His argument is based on the analysis, using the square, of the advertising for the brand's four perfumes:

- Eternity: photo of Christy Turlington smiling and holding a young child in her arms. "Kennedy family" atmosphere. Open, natural people. Several generations. A fecund woman and an active father.

- Obsession: photo of a prone Kate Moss, naked on a divan. The complement of CK One. Closed, contrasted spaces. Sculptural bodies and the brutality of desire.

- Escape: photo of a couple embracing on a deserted beach among the rocks, with a surfboard next to them. The least clearly defined. Baroque white background that encroaches on the rest of the photo.

- CK One: photo of a group of teenagers of both sexes. Attitudes of intense discussion. More homogeneous white background. A single generation. Lack of distinction between the sexes. Tension and discontinuity.

These examples illustrate, if that were necessary, the power and versatility of an instrument that can also be applied, depending on the semantic axis chosen, to a brand's strategic positioning in relation to luxury, to fashion and to its competitors.

The existential/practical semantic axis has been used extensively, but it is far from providing answers to all the questions relative to brand identity. Another axis introduced by Jean-Marie Floch proved highly useful in the case of Loewe and Bally. This axis could be called "authenticity/superficiality," that of perpetuating signs as opposed to producing meaning (see Figure 6.13).

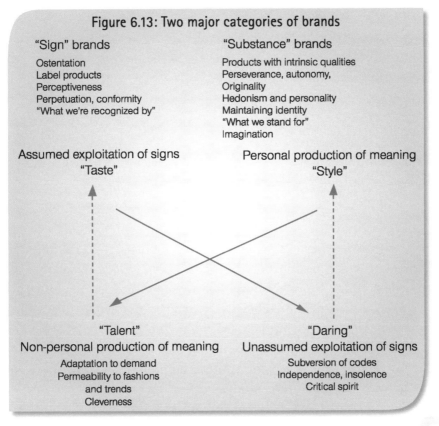

Figure 6.13: Two major categories of brands

"Sign" brands

Ostentation
Label products
Perceptiveness
Perpetuation, conformity
"What we're recognized by"

"Substance" brands

Products with intrinsic qualities
Perseverance, autonomy,
Originality
Hedonism and personality
Maintaining identity
"What we stand for"
Imagination

Assumed exploitation of signs
"Taste"

Personal production of meaning
"Style"

"Talent"
Non-personal production of meaning

Adaptation to demand
Permeability to fashions
and trends
Cleverness

"Daring"
Unassumed exploitation of signs

Subversion of codes
Independence, insolence
Critical spirit

Floch proposed a classification of luxury brands into two major categories: those that produce their own meaning (the "substance" brands) and those that exploit signs (the "sign" brands). As Figure 6.14 shows, the semiotic square quickly breaks down this basic distinction and provides a very detailed analysis of the respective positioning of all the luxury brands. Since then, many brands that desire to be seen as authentic have sought to position themselves on the upper-right corner of the square.

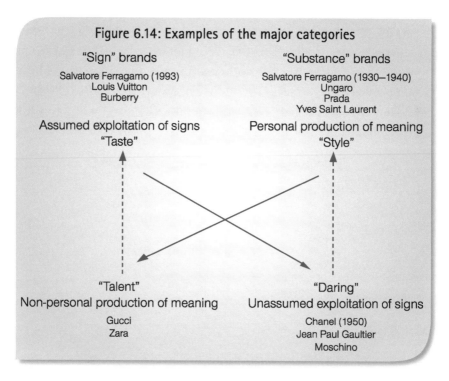

Figure 6.14: Examples of the major categories

"Sign" brands

Salvatore Ferragamo (1993)
Louis Vuitton
Burberry

Assumed exploitation of signs
"Taste"

"Substance" brands

Salvatore Ferragamo (1930–1940)
Ungaro
Prada
Yves Saint Laurent

Personal production of meaning
"Style"

"Talent"
Non-personal production of meaning

Gucci
Zara

"Daring"
Unassumed exploitation of signs

Chanel (1950)
Jean Paul Gaultier
Moschino

The same formalization can also be used to position the brands in a sector, and thus to find a brand's place in relation to its competitors. However, note that any classification of this type involves a good deal of subjectivity, that brands evolve over time, and that they are all present, with varying intensity, at the four corners of the square. The classification of a few brands presented below each type is solely the authors' opinion; it appeared to us to be valid at the time of the study.

Late in 1999, one of the authors was in the position of re-launching the Swiss brand Bally, famous around the world since the middle of the nineteenth century for its shoes. The brand, very "tired," needed a profound restructuring and a drastic repositioning. The choice was made to take a position on the upper-right corner of the square and to promote Bally as a luxury brand in the field of shoes, accessories and clothing, representative of values that connote Switzerland and modernity. Beginning with the phrase "a Swiss lifestyle luxury brand," all the Swiss values of creativity, security, solidity and respect for nature were mobilized to inspire the creative and communicative activities. A Northern European brand aesthetic of the "classical" type was imposed, leading to the development, *inter alia,* of a logo that was square, red, with two white dots superimposed to represent a letter "B."

At the same time, the airline Swissair was going bankrupt. A company called Crossair, under another form, became Swiss and took over the former airline's international activities. The directorial team did an extraordinary job, both rapid and in depth, with the identity of the new brand. It communicated its conclusions very effectively, in particular through a small brochure entitled *A short story about civilized aviation*, from which the following information is taken:

Our mission:
- to create the most respected airline in the world thanks to an uncompromising commitment to quality, innovation, attention to the consumer, and design;
- to become one of most admired companies in the world through our improvement of the lifestyles of men and women;
- to be Swiss.

Swiss values:
- quality
- prestige
- attention to the customer

- service
- efficiency
- reliability
- security
- cleanliness
- attention to detail
- elegance
- modernity
- luxury
- design
- coherence
- solidly Swiss.

This effort resulted in the definition of a new logo and an entire graphic identity, centered around a square with a red background, with the word "Swiss" in white letters and emblazoned with a white cross.

Two Swiss brands in a phase of repositioning, both with the desire to express Swiss values in their respective sectors, both coming up with the idea of two squares with red backgrounds and white letters. Coincidence, perhaps.

These considerations prompt us to submit for the reader's consideration a short classification of "national spirits" Jean-Marie Floch prepared using his "sign/meaning" square (see Figure 6.15).

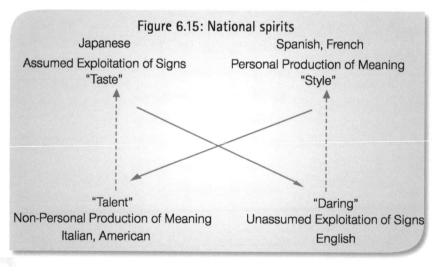

Figure 6.15: National spirits

Japanese
Assumed Exploitation of Signs
"Taste"

Spanish, French
Personal Production of Meaning
"Style"

"Talent"
Non-Personal Production of Meaning
Italian, American

"Daring"
Unassumed Exploitation of Signs
English

luxury **brand** management

The diagram might seem amusing, yet it corresponds to statistical typologies of consumers in the countries mentioned and confirms the assertions we made in the preceding chapter on the different national luxury customers.

In conclusion, the semiotic square has made it possible to formalize guidance concerning general positioning during the concrete projects we have had experience with. It complemented and put into perspective the concrete guidance stemming from the "hinge" studies. The semiotic square, by its nature, cannot offer exhaustive analyses. It nevertheless contributes to giving in-depth perceptions of domains that are too often neglected by the traditional instruments of marketing and strategy.

Semiotic mapping

Andrea Semprini takes the original semiotic square of consumption values introduced by Floch and turns it into a more malleable and more legible tool for marketers.[13] The principal semantic axis is transformed into the ordinate axis of a two-dimensional graph (Figure 6.16). All the nuances of value, from the most practical to the most utopian, can be located on this scale. The coordinate axis ("critical/diversionary") intersects the preceding one to form a semiotic "mapping."

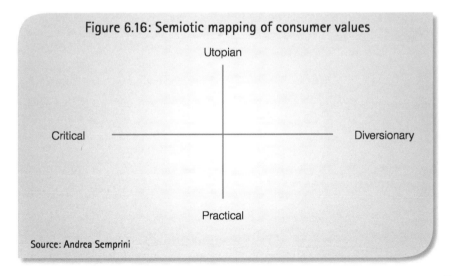

Figure 6.16: Semiotic mapping of consumer values

Utopian

Critical — Diversionary

Practical

Source: Andrea Semprini

The advantage that mapping has over the square is that a spatial continuity is created on which each positioning is relative to all the others. Its author rightly insists on the fact that the mapping, like the "practical/utopian" square, presents consumption values, not attitudes and behaviors. These individual behaviors (passion, enthusiasm, indifference, rejection and so on) will correspond to the strategies each consumer puts into practice to pursue the consumption values.

Semprini analyzes in detail the four quadrants delimited by the two axes (see Figure 6.17). The northwest quadrant is called "mission": the convergence of critical and utopian values leads directly to the will to surpass the present, project toward the future and seek innovation. It is the combination of duty and a constant striving toward different worlds. Benetton in the late 1980s (at the time of the launch of the "United Colors" campaign), with its billboards showing young people of all races, characterized this

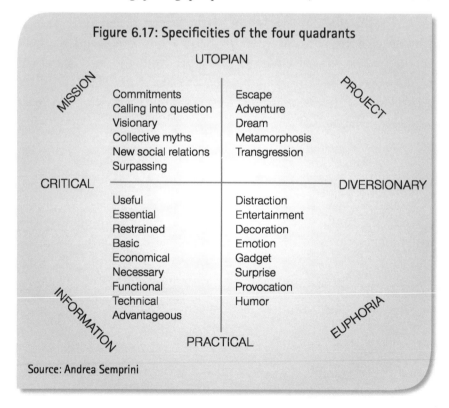

Figure 6.17: Specificities of the four quadrants

UTOPIAN

MISSION

Commitments	Escape
Calling into question	Adventure
Visionary	Dream
Collective myths	Metamorphosis
New social relations	Transgression
Surpassing	

PROJECT

CRITICAL — DIVERSIONARY

Useful	Distraction
Essential	Entertainment
Restrained	Decoration
Basic	Emotion
Economical	Gadget
Necessary	Surprise
Functional	Provocation
Technical	Humor
Advantageous	

INFORMATION

EUPHORIA

PRACTICAL

Source: Andrea Semprini

luxury **brand** management

positioning. The brand was offering an ideal world based on new types of social relations. The Body Shop, with its commitment to natural products, is another example of a brand located in this quadrant.

The northeast quadrant, called "project," conserves the willful dimension of the first quadrant, but the collective commitment is replaced by an individual quest for emotion. There is a strong propensity to embark on personal projects in the desire to find solutions to existential problems. Brands such as Swatch and Ungaro are positioned there.

In the southeast quadrant, "euphoria," the convergence of diversionary and practical values is propitious for brands such as Oasis or Gillette, whose discourse is positive, reassuring and relatively pragmatic. These are the brands that focus on the intrinsic attributes of their products: serenity, good feelings, happiness for all. That, for example, is Calvin Klein's Eternity perfume. A variant of this quadrant is made up of brands like Moschino that entertain using surprise, humor and provocation.

The southwest quadrant is the most immediately understandable. At the crossroads of the practical and the critical, the values presented are resolutely linked to the quality aspects of the products offered. The essential, the advantageous, the strictly necessary, the rational and the useful are uppermost. This is the "information" quadrant, where mass-retail brands such as the Wal-mart and Kmart hypermarket chains are positioned.

Semprini also uses his mapping to analyze the brands' discourse concerning time, space, passions, relationships and so on. The instrument proves to be just as powerful as the square, versatile, and more flexible to use. It introduces an infinity of combinations, focuses, and differentiations of consumption values that make it possible to comprehend a significant part of the complexity of brand identity management. Figure 6.18 presents an attempt at positioning several brands.

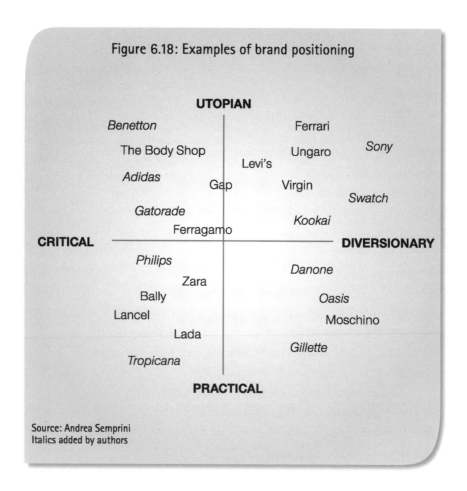

Figure 6.18: Examples of brand positioning

UTOPIAN

Benetton

The Body Shop   Ferrari

Adidas   Ungaro   *Sony*

          Levi's

          Gap   Virgin

Gatorade   *Swatch*

Ferragamo   Kookai

CRITICAL ———————————————————— **DIVERSIONARY**

Philips   Danone

          Zara

Bally   Oasis

Lancel   Moschino

          Lada

Tropicana   Gillette

PRACTICAL

Source: Andrea Semprini
Italics added by authors

The narrative schema

The last tool is also semiotic in nature, but has less analytical power than the signifier/signified hinge and the semiotic square. It nevertheless constitutes a useful method of structuring a brand's discourse. This is the narrative schema, originally developed in 1928 by Vladimir Propp for analyzing Russian fairy tales. Propp's conclusions greatly influenced the work of Greimas and structural semantics. Propp's initial schema was used by Jean-Marie Floch in his work on brands.

Floch did not use such a tool by chance, since one objective of semantics is to categorize the invariant elements of any form of discourse. If a brand can be understood as a complex ensemble of projects or actions that are undertaken within the framework of a system of values, then we are in fact dealing with discourse, with narrative, with stories, to which the semiotic methods used by the discipline of narratology can be applied.

In narratological terms, the four "episodes" that make the logical sequence of any story are contract, skills (or competence), performance or action, and sanction. In the first stage, the protagonist accepts a contract (challenge, promise, leaving to seek adventure); he or she then acquires competences (the classic initiatory stage); in the third, the protagonist successfully carries out the action or program with the aid of the competences acquired, and within the framework of the system of values (contract) that defines his or her action. Finally, the protagonist is rewarded (or punished): the sanction is the measurement of performance of the initial contract.

Applied to a brand, the schema becomes as shown in Table 6.1. In the case of Taurus (Table 6.2), the schema was used to synthesize numerous elements that had been developed using the hinge and semiotic square techniques. We see that the narrative schema is more a synthetic instrument than an analytic one.

Table 6.1: The narrative schema applied to brands

Contract	Competence	Performance	Sanction
The brand ethic	The company's business area	The company's activities	The brand's perception: Its image
The company's philosophy. Its world view	Human resources Distribution network Financial resources	Products offered to target customers	Level of renown, desirability and purchase of the
"What it stands for"	Quality of management (vision, coherence, clarity, determination, etc)		brand's products as opposed to its competitors'

Table 6.2: The narrative schema applied to Taurus

Contract	Competence	Performance	Sanction
Promote a new conception of luxury	A modern European spirit, capable of combining vitality and refinement, energy and subtlety	Taurus creates products that engender emotions based on aestheticism and sensuality	Perception of the brand and economic results
By proposing a lifestyle based on generosity, freedom, and the ability to appreci-ate what is refined and original	Being capable of offering a modern and dynamic lifestyle Being in control of all the technical, logical, and aesthetic aspects of the luxury world	The products are precious yet not outrageously expensive	A true luxury house, dynamic, innovative, original and international
By cultivating your own originality rather then following fashion trends			
By staying away from ostentatious products			

OTHERS ANALYTICAL MODELS

The analytical models presented so far have been far from exhaustive and represent those that we have had the opportunity to use with professional satisfaction.

We will nonetheless present another model that we find very much in tune with our postmodern times: the Rosewindow from Marie-Claude Sicard[14] (see Figure 6.19).

The brand is considered as a trace (like a scar, a footprint, etc.). It is drawn from the field of cognitive sciences, where each situation of communication is the result of the overlapping of seven contexts, namely:

- physical and sensory
- spatial

luxury **brand** management

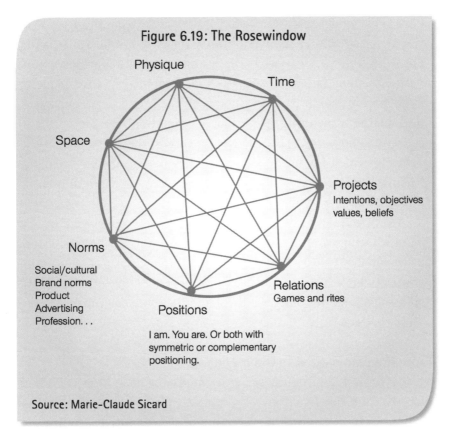

Figure 6.19: The Rosewindow

Physique

Time

Space

Projects
Intentions, objectives
values, beliefs

Norms

Social/cultural
Brand norms
Product
Advertising
Profession. . .

Positions

Relations
Games and rites

I am. You are. Or both with
symmetric or complementary
positioning.

Source: Marie-Claude Sicard

- timing/historical
- positional (of the two actors: the customer and the brand)
- relational (social context determining the quality of the rapport between the two)
- normative (the cultural context of socially shared norms and rules)
- actors' respective and perceived intentions (called "projects").

These seven contexts are then represented as seven poles of equal importance, constituting a network where any impulse on one transmits to the whole system. Brands need to play on at least three poles, with at least one in each group (tangible and not).

The more poles activated, the richer is the brand identity. Strong brands use seven out of the 21 possible itineraries (at least four poles). This model represents a major departure from the previously presented approaches as it maintains that the brand itself has no "soul," no nucleus. It is what the brand managers (various actors) and the customers make of it. The brand identity is then made up of the most frequent itinerary taken by the brand between several poles during a meaningful period. We mention this model for its originality; however, the absence of a core to the brand identity, as we have defined the brand ethics and aesthetics, makes it difficult to manage. Moreover, it does not define what good brand identity management should be.

We will leave aside all the other models developed by the American school around the notion of brand equity, made of economic and symbolic values, which is based largely on the perception consumers have of brands in terms of awareness, recall, recognition and associations. We don't use them and therefore don't feel qualified to discuss them fully.

From the semiologist to the manager

Of the first five instruments presented, the last four are taken directly from the discipline of semiotics. We have pointed out that such tools, to be applied to managing brand identities, require that we accept the following—quite reasonable—hypothesis: brands are systems of meaning. Some people might object that many brands seem to do exactly the opposite—essentially producing nonsense instead of sense, and insignificance instead of significance. But we're only playing on words a little. A semiologist would object that all meaning, even the most aberrant, is still an analyzable process.

Nevertheless, from a manager's perspective, the tools we have described have a decisive advantage in that they elucidate and control the brand's discourse. And paying careful attention to this discourse and to the meanings it intends to produce, for us, is an elementary part of a responsible manager's professionalism—and also of a responsible consumer's vigilance, since consumers are the primary recipients of the brand's messages. We will return to these questions later.

luxury **brand** management

The minimum of respect due to each of the participants—brand, managers, consumers—dictates that the brand "make sense." This seems to go without saying. But it's also a much simpler means of being competitive. Amid the media bombardment we are subjected to today, having something interesting to say is a first condition for effective communication. In fact, semiotics and advertising have had a privileged relationship from the start. After all, what is advertising's task if not the intentional production of meaning using signs?

All of the semiotic tools discussed must be used with an awareness of their limitations. Clearly, we can't ask semiotics to do the following, which it is incapable of doing:

- It is never able to create.
- It cannot invent a style or a best-seller.
- It does not attempt to substitute itself for the creativity of designers and publicists.
- It is never exhaustive in its approach.
- It cannot deal with problems of management.

On the other hand, it does deal with the mechanisms of the creation of meaning, and therefore can:

- point up the brand's fundamental invariants, if they exist
- provide a framework within which everything that "speaks" about the brand, and therefore all its manifestations, must be situated: it determines the domain of the possible and that of the plausible
- manage the coherence of the different signals sent out by the brand
- manage the brand's consistency with its past and present
- facilitate the strategic choices directors of brands must make.

We might even go as far as to insert the position of semiotician into the standard organizational chart of a brand. That is what we suggest in Figure 6.20.

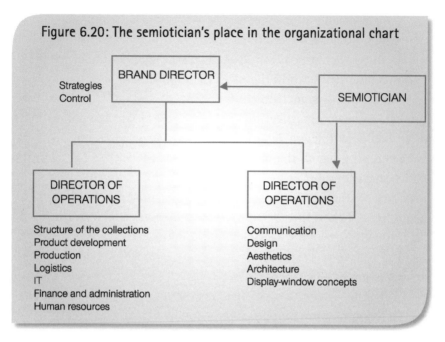

Figure 6.20: The semiotician's place in the organizational chart

BRAND DIRECTOR

Strategies
Control

SEMIOTICIAN

DIRECTOR OF
OPERATIONS

Structure of the collections
Product development
Production
Logistics
IT
Finance and administration
Human resources

DIRECTOR OF
OPERATIONS

Communication
Design
Aesthetics
Architecture
Display-window concepts

Semiotics is at its most effective when it is coupled with a good, in-depth trend survey on the society or the chosen consumer segments, and with good basic sales sense. In cases where semiotic analysis doesn't initially show solid results in identifying the brand's ethical invariants, other elements taken from market studies must be brought in. Semiology is then used to rework these elements and draw practical recommendations.

Later we will discuss the notions of a brand's coherence and relevance. We can say here that semiotics aids in the management of coherence, but is only marginally helpful in managing relevance. Even so, it is one of the rare tools that can get away from the subjective considerations of the different players and pose the question of the brand's identity objectively. This is in no way a guarantee of creativity, but in the context of the collectivity any company represents, that objectivity already represents considerable progress.

Brand identity and consumer identity

What is involved in the passage from identity to image? As we

luxury **brand** management

have stressed, identity is emissive in nature, while perception—the culmination of communication with the consumer—is receptive in nature. The two notions are independent. Between what I want to say about myself and what I get across to my recipient, a lot of shifting, pollution, interference, omission and unconscious revelation goes on. These unavoidable alterations represent the dynamic aspect of any process of communication.

The message of the brand's identity, consequently, undergoes changing interpretations as a function of who is on the receiving end. And a brand's discourse is aimed at winning consumers' approval. Its relevance depends strongly on the lifestyle, customs, values and tastes of those consumers. Like any speaker, any issuer of discourse, the brand must take into account the identity of its recipients. And since a brand hopes not only to be heard but also to be adopted by the consumer, to become one of the signs of his or her identity, the issue takes on crucial importance. Between the brand and individuals' identities, there is necessarily a cultural identity, structured by the cultural codes of a given social group. The brands, in communicating their identities through their various manifestations, will generate what could be called social and individual representations.

This has two important consequences for brand management. First, it must be accepted that perceptions of the brand will always be multiple, and that their diversity can only increase as brand awareness increases. Second, human society changes, and so does the identity of the individuals and the cultures that make it up. To continue to "speak" to them, the brand must also renew itself, change its own identity, without losing its fundamental substance. It must be able to change without getting lost in the process: that is the challenge we all face each day as social beings, and it's one that brands also face.

Single identity/multiple perceptions

Codol and Tap give the following definition of an individual's identity: "Identity is a structured, differentiated system, anchored both in a past temporality (roots, permanence), in a coordination of current behavior, and in a legitimated perspective (projects, ideals, values, and style)."[15] This definition applies closely to a brand's identity; the vocabulary is largely the same.

Psychoanalysis, anthropology and psycho-sociology have all studied the notion of the individual's identity, bringing out the intrinsic duality on which it is founded: on the one hand, personal judgment; on the other, comparison with others—in other terms, the purely individual dimension versus social existence. Psychoanalysts such as Erik H. Erikson hold that identity is constructed both by internalization of cultural and social models and by the imagination of the body and its impulses. Cultural anthropology places the accent on the collective dimension of identity. It sees each culture as tending to produce personality models.

In more semiological terms, these approaches have in common the fact that they temper the idea of universal communication: I can't really say the same thing to everyone, at least not if I hope to be understood by everyone in the same way. The perception of a brand's identity (values, signs) is conditioned by the values, judgments and models developed personally and in a specific environment by each individual.

Of course, we can't take the position that each individual's subjectivity is irreducible either. Human society appears to be "layered" by many determinisms—depending on culture, region, age, income level and so on—that can in part be elucidated. But no matter how refined the analysis, the perception of a given message by the individual members of a given group cannot be unique. Therefore, this duality inherent in identity must be dealt with.

The generation of multiple perceptions from a single brand identity is an absolutely normal phenomenon. All brands face this reality, particularly when it comes to geographical extension. In terms of communication and creation, there are two extremes in dealing with it.

First there is monolithic management, which deals with a standardized consumer. This is the case of the luxury brands,

luxury **brand** management

which produce a single communication campaign and collection for the entire world. Even in this case, there is still an implicit segmentation. The brand aims at an urban public who have a high income level and are fond of traveling. It relies on these strong determinisms to eclipse geographical specificities.

Then there is a more flexible form of management that adapts products or advertising campaigns to local cultures. L'Oréal is probably the best example of how cosmetic products and their relative communication can be adapted to different cultural markets. Another example that could be cited is certain liqueurs (such as cognac) for which modes of consumption vary greatly from one country to another. The automotive industry is another.

Such a range of individual and cultural identities makes all segmentations possible. Certain groups have realized this and take multiple actions in this direction (segmentation by brand, or intra-brand). The criteria are geographical, demographic, economic and sometimes psychosocial. "Mood segmentation"—which breaks potential markets down according to consumers' moods—has recently appeared.

Ms Consumer is walking down Fifth Avenue. She feels successful and seductive, or wants to; she buys an ensemble at Christian Dior. Or she's a little depressed, feels like a victim, not at ease with herself; Prada offers her the refuge she needs. She's at the top of her form physically and mentally, exuberant, in love with life; Loewe can provide her with the products that reflect Spanish energy and *joie de vivre*. A few days later, feeling a little guilty about all the money she spent, she feels she needs to find a bargain, a product she'll use every day, in good taste and at a reasonable price; she goes to Max Mara on West Broadway and, to soothe her shopping-tortured feet, buys a good pair of Ferragamo shoes.

Consumers have become multifaceted, very difficult to catch in the net. What's interesting in this example is that all these "images" are aimed at the same consumer, who will choose one or the other according to her mood. The choice of Christian Dior, for example, will appear daring to some and frankly unreasonable to others. We are looking at the difference between brand identity and what is called "brand image." The same identity crystallizes into a multitude of perceptions depending on place, social milieu, personality or mood.

There's nothing to be gained by fighting this diversity. On the contrary, it represents a form of wealth. It constitutes a portfolio of images, each of which enables different reactions to innovations and the risks they entail for a company. So perceptions are multiple. But they are not unstructured and accidental. Semiology, by analyzing the mechanisms by which meaning is produced, is fully aware of the polysemy of its subjects. But this multiplicity of perceptions does not contradict the need to guarantee, upstream, the coherence of the message.

The more coherent the identity, the more it lends itself to a wealth of interpretations. Messages that are vague, on the other hand, either through structural weakness or because of a desire to "cover all the bases," to be an aggregate of all trends, melt away under the light of interpretation. An identity that borrows from too many categories runs the risk of collapsing under the weight of its referents.

The need to evolve

Coherence of identity does not mean rigidity. A brand's identity must evolve. How many brands have disappeared because they haven't responded to that need? The evolution of mores and sexual liberation were responsible for the initial success of Paco Rabanne, with his metal dresses; that same liberalization of lifestyles took the polish off his image, and very quickly made him more marginal than original.

A brand's decline is an inevitable phenomenon if nothing is done to counteract it. The reasons, both internal and external, are numerous. First of all come errors in the brand's management–loss of relevance in a market, inefficient operations, incoherent strategies, inappropriate investments and so on. Then there is the competition, ever stronger and more battle-hardened. There is also what we call the "entropy" of brands. Any brand, through the wide use of its products and the repeated broadcasting of its advertising, engenders a certain demystification. It loses some of its mystery, and thereby part of its attraction. In the contemporary context of the race toward novelty, this wearing effect of success is more rapid than ever.

Finally, there is the evolution of the fundamental trends of our civilization: needs, fashions, technology, tastes, etc. We often cite the example of the history of the color blue, brilliantly told by Michel Pastoureau.[16] In Greco-Roman times, blue did not play a role in social, religious or artistic life. It was hardly used by the Barbarians. It was not until the thirteenth century and the windows of the cathedral of Chartres that blue took on more importance in liturgical life.

This is because a new theology of light had developed. Light was seen as an emanation of God, the ineffable made visible. The thesis that light and color were identical in nature won out over the idea that colors are only a material artifice. Blue and gold were used to represent that light. Within a few decades, blue became an aristocratic color; it was seen in clothing, artistic creations, religious life. It became the color of the sky, then of the Virgin Mary, and finally that of kings. Blue was never to lose that importance. From the uniforms of soldiers, policemen, and postmen in the nineteenth century to the blue jeans of today, blue became the most-worn color in the Western world. It is also, before green, the favorite color of Westerners. The Japanese, on the other hand, prefer first white, then black. Tastes change with time and from country to country.

For all these reasons, a brand identity that is too rigid, defined with too many constraints or in too much detail, hampers the ability to move rapidly with the market. But this does not necessarily imply renewing the brand's ethical and aesthetic invariants. In fact, the need for evolution expresses itself differently in these two domains.

The need for change is greater on the aesthetic level. More than changing invariants, the need is for keeping an aesthetic in step with the tastes of the time. For example, while Loewe's aesthetic was defined as "minimalist baroque" in 1996, today it can become "pared-down baroque," since minimalism is disappearing from circulation. While respecting the brand's identity, piloting creative approaches in this way allows the same diversity of offerings to customers.

As for the brand ethic, there is no question of changing the basic values of the brand, but rather of putting a stronger light on those values that seem best in phase with the mood of the markets, and therefore capable of generating the best sales. Evolution does not mean ill-advised transformation of the invariants, but rather making marginal corrections, variations in focus that will stay on good terms with the markets without altering the brand's substance. Rather than of permanent invariants, we can speak in terms of a stable continuity of the brand aesthetic and ethic.

Finally, we would point out that the need for change is greater for brands whose ethic is based on fashionable values, which by definition are not permanent. In this area, there is "old money" and there are the *nouveaux riches*: Bentley or Hermès will be able to rely on a brand ethic that focuses on elitist and aristocratic values for some time to come. On the other hand, evolution will very probably be more difficult for Prada or Roberto Cavalli.

THE LIMITS OF THE CONCEPT OF IDENTITY: STRATEGIC AND OPERATIONAL IMPLICATIONS

Throughout this chapter, we've made a point of defending the notion of brand identity and providing tools for getting a grasp of it. This is because we are convinced of its usefulness. Though still not a widespread concept, it is of primary importance for intelligent brand management. While necessary, this concept is not sufficient. Using a concrete example, we will now try to illustrate the areas where it can come into play directly in order to determine its advantages and its limits.

Operational implications

Once formalized, the brand identity represents a framework that will serve to manage all, or nearly all, of the manifestations of the brand's existence. Figure 6.21 is taken from a real case—that of a brand of moderately priced jewelry that launched a review of its brand identity in 1998. It shows all the operational projects that came out of that study.

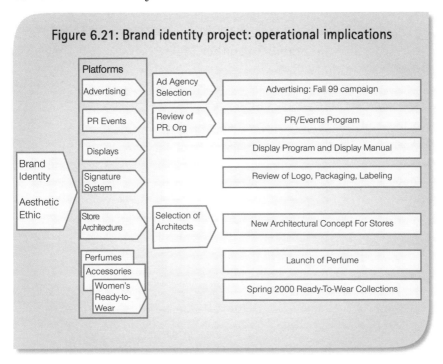

Figure 6.21: Brand identity project: operational implications

A brand identity study serves first to verify the brand's strategic positioning in relation to its competitors and its target markets, and then to provide a common language and guidelines for verification of all the brand's manifestations:

- products, choices made by creative departments
- advertising campaigns, the choice of media and models
- events, relations with the press
- the architectural concept of the stores and offices
- display-window concepts
- signage, labels, stationery—the signature system in general
- salespersons' uniforms, and so on.

In short, it is a federating framework to aid in eliminating, at the outset, all elements that are incompatible with the identity.

The place of the brand identity in company strategies

Figure 6.22 is taken from the Taurus project. It shows the relative place of the brand's identity within a more complete project of strategic redefinition. It clearly shows the need to launch the brand-identity study—on which the other considerations will depend—before any other project.

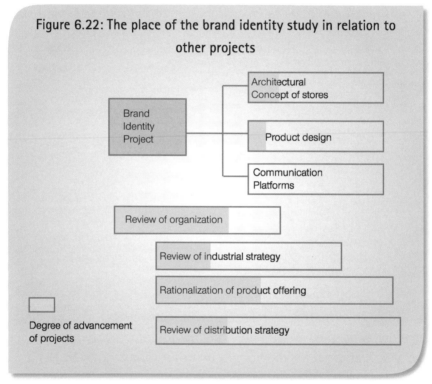

Figure 6.22: The place of the brand identity study in relation to other projects

As can be seen, other projects (organization, products to be offered, and so on) begin in parallel with the identity project, but with a slight time delay. This diagram was used, among other purposes, as a set of indicators (the darker parts showing the portion of the specific project already completed) of the progress of these projects.

Still, the brand identity as such cannot be used to act directly on the choices the business makes in terms of structure of the

luxury **brand** management

product offering, determination of prices and margins, choice of target customers, or organizational, industrial and retailing choices. These choices, which also have an impact on the brand's perception, must of course be taken into consideration, but the identity study alone is not sufficient to guarantee that the best decisions will be made.

The company's strategic approach defines the scope and the limits of the brand's identity. The overall strategy of a company can be broken down into "specialized" strategies (products, customers, retailing, communication, production, logistics and organization). We can see that while the brand's identity plays a central role in any strategy of communication, it is also affected in turn by decisions made by other functions. There is no activity in a company that does not affect or reflect, in one way or another, the brand's identity.

Figure 6.23 shows the degree of influence the logic of the brand identity should exert in the overall strategy of the company. For companies that share our approach to management of identity, the organizational implications are numerous. We will return to these later.

Figure 6.23: Place of brand identity in company strategies

		Influence of brand identity
Products	- categories	
	- structure of offering	
	- prices	
	- aesthetic	
	- functionality	
	- quality	
Customers	- targets	
Distribution	- networks	
	- aesthetic	
	- service	
Communication	- advertising	
	- PR and events	
Production		
Logistics		
Organization	- structure	
	- personnel	
	- culture	
Finance & admin		

Determining influence   Partial influence   Minimal influence

Limitations of the concept of identity

Another limitation of the concept of identity has to do with the paradox inherent in the definition of "identity" itself. Merriam-Webster's *Collegiate Dictionary*, which we cited at the start of this chapter, mentions identity as being not only the distinguishing character or personality of an individual, but also "sameness of essential or generic character."

Sameness and generic. Identical and unique. The individual and the multitude.

Is identity, then, the state of being both unique and like another? It swings back and forth between the tendencies of the mass market toward uniformity and radical uniqueness, and probably exists only in terms of this dialectical tension.

These considerations take us back, indirectly, to the difficulty of defining and formalizing an identity that is completely independent of the way in which it is perceived—or, more precisely, of the brand director's perception of the way in which the brand is seen by the target market segments. To try to define a brand's identity in a closed circle, independently of considerations related to trends and to the dominant perceptions of the brand in the most significant markets, is a dangerous oversimplification.

Figure 6.24, taken from a study we did as consultants for a brand of jewelry, illustrates this need for taking the competitive context—in the broad sense—of the markets into account beyond the pure semiotic approach.

We have seen that one of the conditions of a brand's existence is the differentiation of its identity. This implies that a brand exists in relation to other brands from which it is different. Pepsi would not exist without Coca-Cola; Coca-Cola would probably not be as important without Pepsi. The right balance must be found between the general conditions of the market and the degrees of flexibility of the ethical and aesthetic constants.

Providing the return on investment that shareholders demand, satisfying the expectations of existing customers, but also the expectations expressed by customers of the competitors of reference

luxury **brand** management

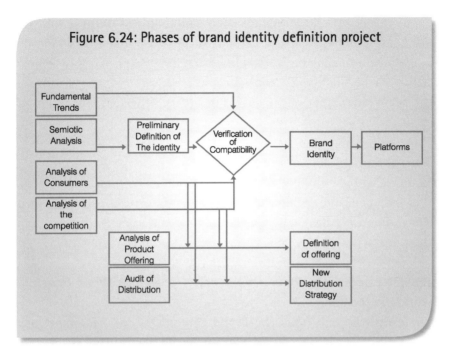

Figure 6.24: Phases of brand identity definition project

(that is, the more meaningful competitors), all without losing the brand's soul: such are the dilemmas brand directors face every day. Ours is an anthropomorphic approach, applying the principles of identity to systems like brands, whose objectives are essentially economic. It opens up an area for more detailed research into the nature of the interfaces between brand identity and cultures and consumers' identities, and into the mechanisms that trigger the act of purchase.

The goal of brand management being to lead consumers to buy the brand's products, consumers must position themselves in a positive way in relation to values and an aesthetic they can perceive. Are these values that are aspired to, or ones already acquired? Is a purchase an act of affirmation, of compensation, of protest? The projection of an image of the self that is desired, or actual? We leave this field of research to other disciplines and other books.

Meanwhile, the notion of brand identity is gaining ground, and is being used more and more in the industry. Suzy Menkes (Fashion Editor of the *International Herald Tribune*) had this to say about the debut of the Winter 2002 collections: "Brand identities are being eroded. Just as a calmer Gucci and a sexed-up Prada no longer seem to spar on well-defined territory, even Armani is now trying to be all things to all people."[17] Or, as another edition of the same newspaper put it in this headline: "Houses: a question of identity."[18]

The responsibilities of the company

If, as we are convinced, we look at brands as factors for progress, it is indispensable to remind directors of their responsibilities at a time when they deal with the concept of the brand's identity, and therefore with crucial choices for the future of the company.

What to present? What dream can I present? What possible world can I offer?

These are the questions the brand director or the CEO must ask when reflecting on the identity of the brand, examining the degree of liberty left by the semiotician.

How to present it? How can I make people dream about the possible world I present?

These are the questions the CEO considers with the director of communication. The problems have to do with execution. Needless to say, economic considerations are uppermost. All the resources of experience and intuition will be mobilized to present the facets of the brand's identity that are most differentiating, most in phase with the mood of the moment; the ones that will make the brand the most competitive.

But that is not enough. In order for brands to become a factor of progress, beyond simply contributing to the perfecting of commercial transactions, they must be able to activate in people (consumers and employees) the qualities that are necessary for progress: innovation, curiosity, a sense of action and of risk, a desire for conquest, the will to surpass oneself, solidarity, a love of hard work, confidence in one's own abilities, and so on. Contrary to

luxury **brand** management

what one might think, many brands contribute to putting people in a position where progress can be generated. All brands that procure, in one way or another, material or psychological comfort for their clients fall into this category. The same reasoning could be applied to brands that use seduction (the spirit of conquest), even though the field seems more crowded and it is therefore more difficult for a brand to differentiate itself in it.

When a brand has the power to influence a great number of people, it must be careful what it presents for people to dream about—and how it presents it. The CEO of BMW knows something about this. In February 2002 he withdrew an ad showing a nude couple on a bed, with one of the partners' heads covered by a magazine showing the latest BMW. Unfortunately, this need for responsibility is not felt strongly enough today by directors of brands, creative directors and directors of communication. The same happened to Marithé and François Girbaud in 2005 when they published an advertisement showing the Last Supper composed of languishing ladies and men in unequivocal attitudes, and were forced to withdraw the ad.

Provocation has been utilized extensively in luxury brand communication, but we feel that it is a dead end. If provocation is based on infringing existing social taboos, it has its own in-built limitations. When all taboos have been infringed, what is left to express? We are convinced, however, that it is very possible, with talent and taste, to promote values like seduction, sensuality, eroticism, and sensual pleasure without crossing the line into the vulgar or the shocking. That was not the choice made by the Sisley brand—whose advertisement in February 2002 showed a young girl stretched out on a bed, looking at us as she touches herself. For a brand director to engage in this kind of advertising is to show a lack of respect for potential customers and the rest of the population. Not everyone shares or even knows about Sisley's approach to managing brand identity as interpreted by photographer Terry Richardson, who decided to position the brand in the domain of "pulp provocation."

We do not feel that the systematic use of gratuitous provocation and vulgarity is a factor for progress. We therefore suggest that two questions should govern the activities of brand directors, beyond the usual economic considerations:

- Does my brand encourage in consumers qualities or sentiments that can, directly or indirectly, lead them to be factors for progress themselves?
- In all the brand's manifestations (products, advertising, and so on), is there a fundamental respect for the dignity of the audience?

To us, these two questions are fundamental. They will reappear several times in our arguments. If brand managers can answer these questions in the affirmative, then they will have found, at the same time, what to present to consumers and how to present it—the two decisional areas that, for us, characterize their responsibilities. If not, then consumers will step in and save us. The consumers' power is such that it is already contributing to restoring order in the world of brands, and accelerating a movement toward responsibility whose beginnings are already being felt.

These basic and simple principles are going to be particularly useful in the creative activities that we will explore in the next chapter.

Endnotes

[1]Banco Sabadell newsletter, first quarter 1998, No.11. Translation by the authors.

[2]Jean-Marie Floch, *Sémiotique, marketing et communication: sous les signes, les stratégies*, Paris: PUF, 1990.

[3]On this subject, see *Graphisme en France*, review published by the Delegation on the Plastic Arts of the French Ministry of Culture, 2001, on "La commande."

[4]In *No Logo*, Naomi Klein, Alfred A. Knoff, Canada, 2000.

[5]Cf. W. P. Margulies, *Harvard Business Review*, 1977.

[6]"Chrysler sharpens its brand identity," *International Business Week*, November 1983.

[7]D. Bernstein, *Company Image and Reality: A critique of corporate communications*, New York: Holt, Rinehart and Winston, 1984.

[8]David A. Aaker, *Managing Brand Equity: Capitalizing on the value of a brand name*, New York: Free Press, 1991.

[9]Jean-Noël Kapferer, *Strategic Brand Management*, New York: Free Press, 1994.

[10]Our examples are simplified. We are leaving out, for example, the acoustic image (the sounds I hear in my head as I read, before forming an image), which is itself a valid level of interpretation. The signifier/signified differentiation has been the subject of complex debates, but they take nothing away from the fruitfulness of the distinction made by Saussure.

[11]Jean-Marie Floch had also used the same technique in defining the layout of a hypermarket in the Lyon area in 1986.

[12]Jean-Marie Floch, *International Journal of Marketing* 4 (1998) (North–Holland).

[13]Andrea Semprini, *Le marketing de la marque*, Paris: Éditions Liaisons, 1992.

[14]Marie-Claude Sicard. *Ce que marque veut dire*, Editions d'Organisation, 2002.

[15]*Revue internationale de psychologie sociale*, No.2, 1988, p.169.

[16]Michel Pastoureau, *Bleu: histoire d'une couleur*, Paris: Seuil, 2000.

[17]Suzy Menkes, *International Herald Tribune*, 5 March 2002.

[18]*International Herald Tribune*, "Special report on fashion," 12 March 2002.

chapter 7

MANAGING
Creation

In this chapter, we will focus on the creativity that a luxury brand needs to apply to its products or services. Needless to say, creativity and innovation in all business functions are the main sources of competitive advantage in all industries, and even more so in the luxury sectors, where the customer is naturally expecting a great deal of originality within what he perceives to be the aesthetic characteristics of the brand. He also expects the product to be recognizable and carry a part of the dream inherent in the brand.

At Louis Vuitton, for example, the seasonal variations made on the LV monogram (graffiti, cherries, new colors, new materials, embossed LV, etc) have recently served these purposes and confirm Marc Jacobs' creative talents and the opening of the brand to outside artists.

Managing creative people has never been an easy task, even for themselves. In this chapter, after presenting a description of the nature of creative activities for a luxury brand, we will delve into the organizational matters related to it, with real-life examples of design structures and their underlying logic. This will show how product management interfaces with the creative work. We will also propose some insights into how the notion of brand aesthetics can help in solving some of the creative management issues, and finish the chapter by talking about the bridges that exist between a brand's creative activities and arts.

THE NATURE OF CREATIVE ACTIVITIES

Most frequently, the creative process in the luxury business starts with a specific market segment being identified by those within the business or commercial part of the company. We refer to the people identifying the market opportunities as "the prescribers" because their function is similar to that of an architect prescribing the use of certain materials or a doctor recommending a certain cure. The prescribers in turn commission the product, giving the creative department a list of specifications regarding function and price. In U.S. and Anglo-Saxon companies, the marketing prescribers are known as "merchandisers."

Figure 7.1 shows the typical sequence that a luxury product follows, from its concept to its presence in the distribution networks.

For the design of technical products, the prescriber can be the marketing or commercial department or the CEO, depending on the type of organization. There, the creation function would be split between product concept, design and engineering. For reasons of simplification, we will follow the model shown in Figure 7.1, which is prevalent in luxury ready-to-wear or accessories, where the prescription emanates from the merchandising manager. (For the mass-market brands, it would come from the product manager.)

What is common to any typology of product or service is that the design/creation activities, always and systematically, follow a business idea.

luxury **brand** management

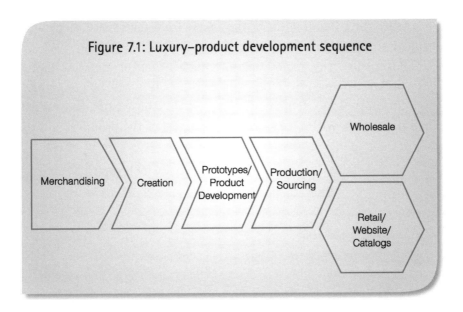

Figure 7.1: Luxury-product development sequence

Merchandising → Creation → Prototypes/Product Development → Production/Sourcing → Wholesale / Retail/Website/Catalogs

It may sound banal, but the luxury industry is famous for believing too often that the designer's genius transcends any market considerations. It may take all the long years of experience of Christian Lacroix in the LVMH group—from the creation of his *maison de couture* in 1987 until its sale to the Falic Group in 2005 without ever reaching a balanced income statement—to prove that sheer and recognized creative talent needs to be framed by a competent business prescriber.

The merchandiser gathers all the market information from the company's own retail and wholesale networks and from the competition, synthesizing this into a Collection Plan, which describes the number of groups, models, occasions of use, expected sales volumes, places and prices at which the products can be sold. The price indications determine the maximum cost at which the product can be manufactured because the retail and wholesale direct gross margin cannot fall below certain limits. This may not be a problem for high-margin brands such as Louis Vuitton, which look for a 55% gross margin at retail and an absolute minimum of 30% at wholesale. Table 7.1 illustrates a simple price structure scheme. This would have a direct impact on the choice of the quality of leather for a handbag or of the fabric for a man's suit, decisions typically made by the designing team.

After receiving a specific assignment from the merchandising department, the design team, working closely with the company's own prototyping department or with those of contracted manufacturers, will need to realize samples of the products.

Table 7.1: Theoretical price structure for luxury ready-to-wear and leather accessories		
Theoretical retail price	320	**100**
Minimum theoretical retail margin	165 (55%)	55
Wholesale price	155	45
Minimum wholesale margin	55 (35%)	15.75
Direct cost	**100**	29.25

The efficiency of the link between design and prototyping is a main source of competitive advantage for the luxury industry. Since most of today's designers do not have the technical knowledge to transform their own concepts into real objects, the need for efficient "*modelisti*" is very acute. *Modelisti* are handicraft professionals who are able to interpret the designs and ideas of the creative team, and are increasingly difficult to find. (Numerous great Italian shoe *modelisti* are spending their retirement as consultants for Chinese manufacturers.)

Gone are the Salvatore Ferragamos or the Cristobal Balenciagas who could construct their creations with their own hands. Today's designers are "visual," draw in 2D and therefore need talented product developers.

When the prototyping activity is integrated into the company, we often see the design and development departments merged, as the competences are complementary. The product development phase is not made of pure prototyping capabilities. In the case of shoes, for instance, the fit is a whole science, jealously protected

luxury **brand** management

and rarely formalized, mastered by only a few individuals who come into play at the time of prototyping and pre-production of small series. The prototyping department is also responsible for integrating the production constraints, as illustrated in Figure 7.2.

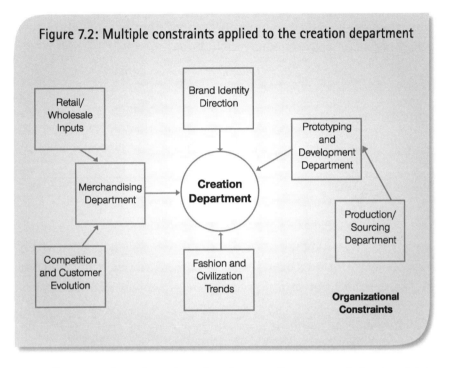

Figure 7.2: Multiple constraints applied to the creation department

The creative function is the confluence point at which commercial, financial, image-related, technical and logistical considerations come into play.

This leaves the most natural constraint within which the designers have to work: the respect for and constant upgrade of the brand identity. The invariant aesthetic components of the brand identity are still rarely formalized and it is left to the designers' talent and sensibility to interpret the aesthetics of the brand, to keep it relevant with respect to the fashion and the longer-term social trends, and to ensure that it continues to reflect the brand values. A clearly formalized brand identity, expressing the invariable elements of what we have called the ethics and aesthetics of the brand, acts like a Brand Bible and should be on every designer's

managing creation

desk, from the office junior to the creative director.

Adding to the complexity of luxury creation is the sheer volume of creativity required of the design departments of multi-product brands such as Gucci, Vuitton, Loewe, Celine, Coach, Ralph Lauren or Ferragamo. For a brand aiming at a lifestyle status, the minimum number of products to be presented in each collection every season is approximately as follows:

Ladies' ready-to-wear	150 pieces
Men's ready-to-wear	100 pieces
Handbags	50 pieces
Other leather goods	100 pieces
Silk	100 pieces
Total	500 pieces

For any model chosen for the season's collection, we estimate there will be an average of three prototypes. This happens twice a year. **That is, for any brand with ambitions to reach the lifestyle status, at least 3,000 products have to be conceived and prototyped every year.**

To create this volume of products within the demanding time, functional and cultural constraints requires rigorous coordination of resources.

Creation in the realm of service brands (restaurants, hotels, resorts, cruise, air travel and so on) focuses more on the physical comfort given to the customers and the communication.

Organization of the creative function

There are as many organizational models as there are luxury brands. A great deal depends on the number of product categories, the cultural approach to design, the simplicity of the brand aesthetics, the existence of strongly recognizable graphic codes, the designer's reputation, the size of the company and so on.

To get an idea of the diversity and the organizational importance of the design function, we'll look at how this works at some leather-

luxury **brand** management

goods brands, at different stages of their brand lifecycle.

Leather-goods brands

Michel Vivien, "*chausseur à Paris*," designs women's shoes under his own name. He has them prototyped and manufactured by an Italian factory and he sells them to the market himself through professional fairs. He has one design assistant, to whom he gives creative direction, and he does much of the creation himself. Not only does he directly control all creative activities, he manages all other functions as well. He probably sells fewer than 50,000 pairs a year, and his turnover is probably around €1 million.

At Robert Clergerie, where, in 2004, the volume of shoes produced was several hundred thousand pairs and the turnover around €30 million, the prototype design group consisted of four people; and, as the company also had ambitions to develop into the handbags and small leather-goods sectors, an external handbag designer was contracted. The company also used an external consultant as a creative director.

Christian Louboutin operates somewhere in between Michel Vivien and Robert Clergerie.

Loewe's turnover at the end of the 1990s was in the region of a few hundred million euros from activities spanning leather goods, ready-to-wear, silk accessories, gift items and fragrances for men and women. All products were designed in-house. The design function was spread within each of the four business units (leather goods, ladies' ready-to-wear, men's ready-to-wear and fragrances) and comprised 20 people. In 1997, Narciso Rodriguez was hired to design the ladies' ready-to-wear and the CEO functioned as Brand Identity manager, coordinating all these creative talents as well as the communication and retail departments.

At Bally in the late 1990s, the company was losing money, with a declining turnover of around €500 million. The sale of the company to the Texas Pacific Group, a U.S. private-equity fund, provided a good opportunity to restructure the brand to enable it to realize its ambition to become a lifestyle luxury brand reflecting perennial Swiss values.

The management started by clearly identifying the main culture and the competences needed to reach its objectives. Figure 7.3 explains the rationale underlying the revised organizational chart.

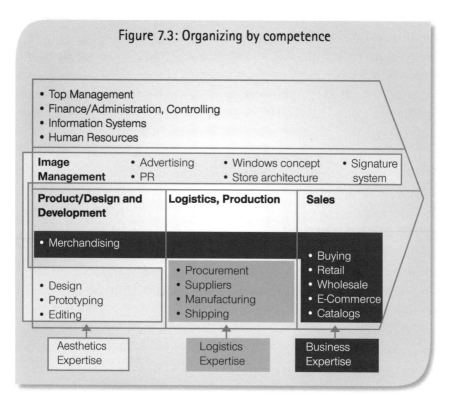

Figure 7.3: Organizing by competence

The business expertise is made up of "merchants," who not only sell the goods through Bally's own shops and wholesale customers, but are also responsible for prescribing the kind of collections they want (number of groups, models, prices, function, etc). Under such a scheme, the sales and gross margins are clearly the merchandiser's responsibility. He launches the development process and coordinates the various departments involved through establishing multifunctional teams. It is important to establish the rule that merchandisers never get involved in aesthetic matters, leaving 20% of the collection to be defined freely by the designers with no constraints whatsoever.

The logisticians produce and move goods. Decisions regarding suppliers, whose selection may be of strategic importance, are made in conjunction with designers and merchandisers. Then, all activities requiring a strong aesthetic sensibility, such as creation and communication, are regrouped.

In Bally, the organization chart for everyone involved in the creative activities in 2000 was structured along the lines shown in Figure 7.4.

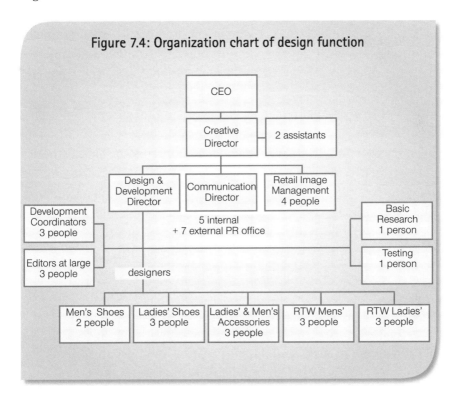

Figure 7.4: Organization chart of design function

The Design and Development functions were merged under a single responsibility to ensure a maximum fusion between 2D designs and prototyping. "Editors at large"—fashion reference personages, opinion leaders in the luxury world—were appointed in Paris, Hong Kong and New York to keep the company advised on recent fashion trends, on what the competition was doing and to give feedback on past and current collections. Not counting these or

managing creation

other outside staff such as the PR offices and the design departments dedicated to the watch and golf shoe licenses, a total of 31 internal creative staff were involved in the process. The financial effort needed to sustain such a multi-product brand strategy is enormous, but this is what the global lifestyle brands have to face.

Mass-market vs. luxury brands

The examples drawn from the leather-goods industry highlight the numerous models that can coexist within the same sector. Looking at the luxury industry as a whole, the number of organizational solutions is almost equal to the number of brands, and this, we believe, stems from the difficulty of rationalizing the aesthetic dimension of the brands.

Within this apparent abundance of organizational solutions, we can identify two extreme and opposite models that both avoid the issues surrounding the management of intrinsic brand aesthetics without really solving them.

The first model is found in major luxury brands such as Dior or Chanel, where the aesthetic keys are handed to a talented and proven designer (John Galliano and Karl Lagerfeld, respectively) and the CEO has little power whatsoever in the creative function. Designer and CEO seldom meet except at cocktail parties, perhaps.

The second model belongs to mass-market brands like Gap, Zara, H&M, Celio, Springfield, and so on, where the design team (an army of anonymous individuals) works under the close supervision of the product manager, who imposes price and fashion constraints, and where creativity is reduced to following rigid commercial plans and what is currently hot in the market. This solution does not exclude specific initiatives with celebrities, such as that recently orchestrated by H&M with Madonna for a special Fall 2006 collection. The product manager is frequently referred to as the "collection manager" or, as at Cortefiel, the "buyer," which clearly reveals the main focus of their task. In this sector, the overall organization is quite simple. Besides the usual financial and HR functions, there will normally be three departments: the product

luxury **brand** management

department (merchandising, creation, sourcing), the communication department (advertising, PR, showroom management) and the retail/franchise department. The brand-identity tasks are spread across the organization chart.

The basic difference between the two solutions is in the importance given to the creativity function and thus to the decision-making power granted to the designer, which in turn reflects the brand's basic culture and way of competing.

Each of these systems has created legends. The luxury model thrives on the geniality and talent of designers like Tom Ford at Gucci. It becomes much more difficult when the serving designer does not have these exceptional talents. The second model has given birth to extraordinary success stories such as Zara or H&M in the past 10 years—successes based essentially on good merchandising and on an extraordinary logistical capability that can reduce time-to-market to 10 days.

Nonetheless, the optimal solution is more balanced; where the brand aesthetics are more coordinated and better oriented toward the constant reinforcing of the brand identity. But how can these goals be achieved given the complex set of brand manifestations, all promoting the brand identity, performed by so many typologies of competences, as illustrated in Figures 7.5 and 7.6.

Finally, who is in charge of a brand's aesthetics? Who has the broad view necessary to span the range of brand manifestations and the power to act upon them?

The ultimate brand aesthetics manager can only be the CEO. He is in a position to really balance the sometimes competing logics of business and aesthetics and make the necessary trade-offs between them. Not that we are asking him to be Giorgio Armani; such talents are given to very few. Neither are we suggesting that he be involved in actual design. Nevertheless, the CEO should be capable of working with both sides of the brain, and have proper aesthetic preparation and sensibility. In addition, a transparent and constructive attitude from all members of the top management team would help in producing an almost-optimal aesthetic decision-making system.

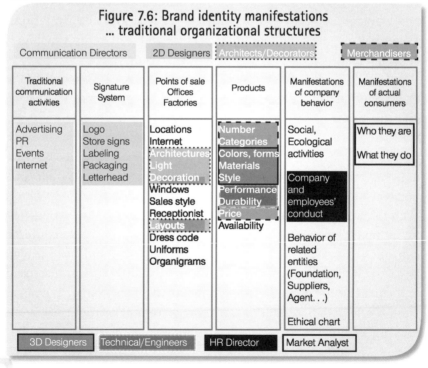

Figure 7.5: Brand identity manifestations... different competences

Style / aesthetics competences		Merchandising competences		Logistics/organizational skills	
Traditional communication activities	Signature System	Points of sale Offices Factories	Products	Manifestations of company behavior	Manifestations of actual consumers
Advertising PR Events Internet	Logo Store signs Labeling Packaging Letterhead	Locations Internet Architectures Light Decoration Windows Sales style Receptionist Layouts Dress code Uniforms Organigrams	Number Categories Colors, forms Materials Style Performance Durability Price Availability	Social, Ecological activities Company and employees conduct Behavior of related entities (Foundation, Suppliers, Agents. . .) Ethical chart	Who they are What they do

Corporate ethics competences   Indirectly controlled manifestations

Figure 7.6: Brand identity manifestations ... traditional organizational structures

Communication Directors		2D Designers / Architects/Decorators		Merchandisers	
Traditional communication activities	Signature System	Points of sale Offices Factories	Products	Manifestations of company behavior	Manifestations of actual consumers
Advertising PR Events Internet	Logo Store signs Labeling Packaging Letterhead	Locations Internet Architectures Light Decoration Windows Sales style Receptionist Layouts Dress code Uniforms Organigrams	Number Categories Colors, forms Materials Style Performance Durability Price Availability	Social, Ecological activities Company and employees' conduct Behavior of related entities (Foundation, Suppliers, Agent. . .) Ethical chart	Who they are What they do

3D Designers   Technical/Engineers   HR Director   Market Analyst

luxury **brand** management

Between the two extremes—creativity given free rein in the luxury industry, and a denial of creativity within the mass-market brands—there is room for more balanced organizational solutions whereby the respective logics informing the merchandising and creative processes can coexist and reinforce each other. The Bally solution presented earlier is, we believe, close to achieving that difficult balancing act.

MANAGING THE PRODUCT

Having covered product design and development processes, organizational set-up and the interfaces between merchandising and design, it is perhaps appropriate to say something about product management at this stage.

Product management is knowing what to sell, where to sell it, at what price and in which quantities, as well as monitoring the process from the concept stage through to distribution. The merchandiser has this responsibility.

In the case of the development of a series of goods, there are two key documents that govern the whole process: the Collection Plan and the Collection Calendar.

The collection plan

For each product category, the collection plan will ideally specify the following elements:

- The number of product groups, comprising those kept from the previous season and new products (a product group of a homogeneous set of products with similarities of material, form, occasion of use and so on).
- The number of products for each group and of models for each product.
- The occasions of use of the various group products.
- The expected volume of each model per specific point of sale.
- The expected retail price and therefore the maximum direct cost

of production. This will very often include technical specifications for construction or the type of materials required because this will have a direct impact on the manufacturing costs and design choices.

The collection plan frequently provides supporting analysis based on previous sales statistics, competitors' successes and the respective positioning of the various groups.

Let's take a real example from the men's ready-to-wear world. For reasons of confidentiality, we will call this Spanish brand "Don Juan." While the name has been changed, the data set out below are drawn from the real world. The brand promotes an identity centered around its Hispanic origins and tries to be trendy and up-to-date without being perceived as being excessively fashion-forward.

A collection plan is necessary for each product category. We will concentrate on the one prepared for suits. Below, we present a series of documents prepared by the merchandiser for the spring season 2007.

Figure 7.7 shows Don Juan's position compared to the competition with respect to the basic dimensions of price and fashion content.

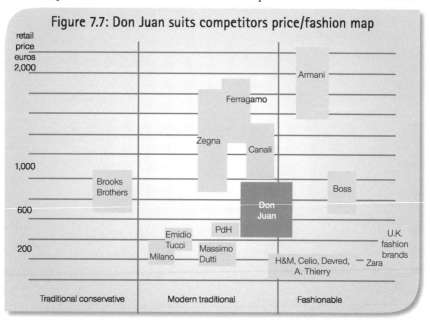

Figure 7.7: Don Juan suits competitors price/fashion map

luxury **brand** management

It is important to monitor the market on a constant basis and know where the brand wants to compete. The figure shows clearly that Don Juan is positioned between the mass brands competing on price and the global luxury leaders. Reinforcing this unique positioning in a field held traditionally by Italian, U.S. and British brands is the fact that it is the only brand daring to promote its Hispanic roots as a main differentiating element of its brand identity.

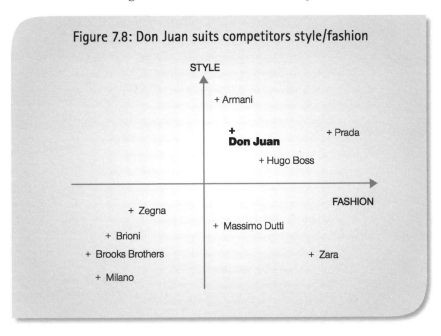

Figure 7.8: Don Juan suits competitors style/fashion

The second document, shown in Figure 7.8, positions the brand with respect to its main competitors in terms of style and fashion. We said earlier that merchandisers were not supposed to be involved with a brand's aesthetic considerations. Here, where the merchandiser defines the competitive frame into which the products have to be positioned (that is, that the brand needs to have more stylistic content), this is not the same as defining and designing that style.

The third document, shown in Figure 7.9, maps the five groups of suits according to retail price and fashion.

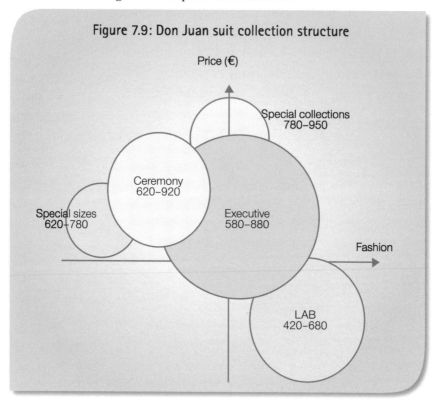

Figure 7.9: Don Juan suit collection structure

Price (€)

Special collections
780–950

Ceremony
620–920

Special sizes
620–780

Executive
580–880

Fashion

LAB
420–680

A general brief accompanies this, as shown in Table 7.2. As can be gathered from the real-life examples considered earlier, the merchandiser is the one really driving the whole development process of the collection and needs to have the tools to ensure that all the departments involved are informed and coordinate with each other. There are other documents covering, for example, the expected volume of sales for each product and each individual model, by point of sale. This information, which can only ever be estimated, is probably the most difficult to quantify and the one with most financial consequences. Commitments on fabric orders are taken very early in the process and drive the business gross margins. This is the exercise in which the real professional merchandisers stand out.

Table 7.2: Suit Collection Development Directions for Spring–Summer 07

- Strong drive toward improved quality and more style
- Continue the search for quality Spanish fabrics, in addition to Italian and British. Negotiate more exclusive fabrics
- Continue developing a strongly Spanish modern style, with more recognizable details on the products (lining, stitching, labeling)

EXECUTIVE collection:

- Only semi-traditional construction
- 30 different new fabrics. Continuation of the five permanent fabrics
- Keep the two- and three-button models. Start working on a double-breasted model for Fall–Winter 2007

LAB collection:

- Only fused construction
- 25 different new fabrics. Five to eight can be common with EXECUTIVE
- Extend the concept of the younger LAB line concept to all the other products for Fall–Winter 2007
- Special sizes: only plain basic suits. Both industrial and semi-traditional construction. Limited to 15 fabrics
- This season's Special Collection will be designed by the famous Spanish architect,"X"

A special design team with members of both parties is being set up
Respect scrupulously the three sub-collection shipments to the stores

The collection plan can vary in its format and in the information given depending on the type of merchandise. It is the contractual document binding all the departments involved in the development process.

Note that the essentially strategic decision to add a new category of products—say, shoes—to the brand offer would be analyzed within the Merchandising Department.

The collection plan can take very different forms according to the product category. For a ladies' shoe collection, there are likely to be lines instead of groups, classified by construction, occasion of use, specific soles or materials. Each line will specify the desired retail price in the reference market, the heel height, and all the different materials that can be applied to it.

For a handbag collection, there are likely to be diagrams of groups positioned with respect to price and occasion of use, from the more formal to the more casual.

For a tie collection, things will be simpler. There will generally be two big categories separating printed silk from jacquard (woven), with a number of repeated and new patterns.

The collection calendar

The collection calendar formalizes the important moments in the collection development process agreed to by all the departments involved: ordering materials for samples and for production; intermediary meetings to review the design progress; final editing of the collection; ordering from the stores, and so on. It is the most shared common tool of all the departments involved in collection development.

Figure 7.10 illustrates a real example of a ladies' shoes collection calendar, showing all the different steps involved. It is clear, for example, that prototype validation is a three-step process, with the line and model requiring approval before its final realization as a prototype.

The number of professional fairs attended by the designers and merchandisers is also indicated as well as the regular involvement of the commercial department right up until the presentation of the sample collection to wholesale clients and store buyers.

The product empowerment teams

Despite all the examples of monitoring tools and reports, more often than not the different cultures and specific operating objectives of different departments give rise to a lot of friction in the development process and, ultimately, to poor quality, late deliveries, higher costs and higher prices.

To reduce the possibility of such problems arising, in 2000 Bally decided to launch what was called the "PET" (Product Empowerment Teams) project. The intention of the project was to focus people's attention on the virtues of teamwork and to streamline the product development process.

Figure 7.10: Ladies' shoes collection calendar

	Fall–Winter 2006	September	October	November
1.	Think-tank creative brainstorming			
2.	ANTEPRIMA fair in Italy			
3.	Finalizing of Collection Plan			
4.	PREMIERE VISION fair in Paris			
5.	Work on volumes by design team			
6.	Materials first proposals and choice of colors			
7.	Proposal of first volumes and validation			
8.	Proposal and validation of three or four lines for U.S. early show			
9.	Validation of re-proposed lines			
10.	Validation of colors and materials			
11.	**Order of materials for prototyping**			
12.	Validation of U.S. models and final prices			
13.	Validation and finalization of new lines			
14.	Validation of models of re-proposed lines. Price decision			
15.	LINEAPELLE fair in Bologna			
16.	Validation of models on new lines			
17.	Meeting with sales executives			

		November	December	January
18.	Validation of prototypes for U.S. and price decision			
19.	New York fair			
20.	Validation of other prototypes and price decision			
21.	**End of creative work**			
22.	Buying of 30% of material			
23.	Meeting with sales executives			
24.	Launching of the production of the seven sample collections			
25.	Final pricing			
26.	Selection of advertising and catalog models			
27.	End of production of sample collections			
28.	Buying session from own stores			
29.	Participation in PREMIERE CLASSE fair			

Legend: fairs | process steps | meetings

A multi-functional team was created for each product division (men's shoes, ladies' shoes, men's accessories, ladies' accessories, men's ready-to-wear and ladies' ready-to-wear). Each team, coordinated by the divisional merchandise manager, comprised the category head designers, the category developer, and a member of the supply management team, and each team worked in conjunction with retail operations and the wholesale, communication, information system and finance departments. The focus of these teams was to make things happen, quickly.

In order to give substance to this set-up and make the team responsible for the performance of the division, we introduced financial incentives based on the objectives of the overall project, with the CEO directly monitoring the team performances.

Table 7.3 shows the key performance indicators introduced.

Table 7.3: Performance indicators for Product Empowerment Teams

a) PERFORMANCES	b) INDICATORS
Volume	Sales
Profitability	Sell-through
	Net gross margin
Immobilized capital	Inventory turns (FG, WIP, RM)
Speed	On-time delivery
	Time to market
	Time for re-assortment [replenishing retail stock during season]
Quality	Returns
Costs	Team operating costs
Team effectiveness	Initiatives and problem solving. Number of inter-department conflicts
	Interfaces with retail, wholesale, communication ...
	Team cohesion, communication, atmosphere ... fun

luxury **brand** management

The efforts were worthwhile, as we rapidly reduced the shipping delays, improved product quality and remained within the planned prices.

It should be clear from this section that putting the right product in the right place, at the right time, at the right price and in the right quantities is not a simple task.

BRAND AESTHETICS

In Chapter 6 we introduced a definition of brand aesthetics that differs from the usually accepted philosophical meaning of a discipline dealing with beauty. We took a semiotic approach, using the term to encompass all of the brand elements belonging to the sensory world: the brand manifestations, which not only include the visual elements (forms, colors, light treatments, etc), but also sound, taste, touch and odor. We classified the manifestations into four aesthetic fields: products, communication, space and behavior. The creative activities of a luxury brand operate at the center of the brand's aesthetics. But is this relatively new notion really relevant for brand management?

Relevance of brand aesthetics

There are three main factors that establish the relevance of brand aesthetics:

- First of all, there is a strong trend within society toward aestheticism, which is easily noticeable in the consumption of products and services. From the birth of Design in the early 1950s, initially applied to small series or industrial machines, to the arrival of the likes of Ikea, Conran, Alessi and Habitat in the market, this phenomenon is clearly manifest. Today, Design is everywhere. There are no successfully competitive products that have not been submitted to an aesthetic optimization. This is most evident in the extensive use of color is such objects as refrigerators, cellular phones—which have risen in a few years to the status of fashion accessories—or personal computers.

- The simple fact that certain forms, colors, contrasts or harmonies are more noticeable and easier to memorize than others, or trigger emotions in those exposed to them, proves the importance of aesthetics. Isn't the objective of any creator and communicator to generate emotion and remembering in the target customers? An advertisement showing a young lady with a nail in the forehead (Nell & Me) or monsters and mutants (Brema, Lee Cooper, Thierry Mugler's fragrance Alien and so on) generates uneasiness, rejection, fear; all effects desired by their creators. There are proven statistical preferences for rectangles obeying the golden mean ratio. It has been medically proven that colors and light have a physiological and psychological impact on human beings. There is an infinite number of examples that show that mastering brand aesthetics can assist in managing a brand's effects on its public.

- The third aspect of the relevance of the notion of brand aesthetics is its ability to untie some tight corporate knots.

Issues better treated with the notion of brand aesthetics
We are convinced that the notion of brand aesthetics can go a long way in helping to resolve issues related to creativity in brand organizations. In fact, the aesthetic notion allows us to tackle, with an innovative approach, communication, organizational and cultural issues.

Communication issues
The willingness to manage brand aesthetics in a systematic and rational way leads to some simple and immediate questions:

- Is the brand's aesthetic (or a specific brand manifestation) contributing to communicate the brand ethics efficiently and therefore consolidating the brand identity?
- Is the aesthetic treatment of a specific brand manifestation serving the brand's communication purpose (visibility, ease of memorization,

luxury **brand** management

special message to convey, specific emotion to generate, etc.) while remaining compatible with the brand aesthetics?

- Are the brand manifestations coherent among themselves?

Organization issues

We saw earlier how difficulties in rationalizing the management of brand aesthetics can lead to two opposite and equally unsatisfactory organizational models: one giving full and unchallenged decision-making power to the designer; the other submitting the designer to the constraints of strict commercial rules. Rationalizing brand aesthetics would provide the necessary tools to allow a more fluid, balanced and open rapport between all the direct and indirect participants in the process of creation.

Cultural issues: the missing dictionary

Design personnel tend to hold the "merchants" in perfect contempt. For their part, the merchants do not hesitate to criticize the bad collection design when sales do not meet expectations. Meanwhile, the production and development people look on everyone as extremely frivolous and uneducated about what a good product should be. These legitimate tensions often end up at a higher hierarchical level and condition the relationship between the head designer or creative director and the CEO or COO. In the confrontation between the manager—who lives among figures, statistics, budgets, consumer-behavior theories, board meetings and financial analysts—and the creative designer—who is aware of the glamour of the position, sensitive to fashion and taste, mixing with the fashion jet-set and the press, and perhaps dreaming of imposing a specific aesthetic viewpoint on the world—the relationship is not always naturally easy and rarely allows for a rational and **constructive dialogue**.

"Why do you do that?" asks the CEO. "Because I feel it!" replies the designer.

The main reason for such irrational talk is that neither has really been educated in how to discuss brand aesthetics rationally and that very few tools exist that would allow them to establish a common vocabulary for doing so.

Given this, it is no surprise that most of the great designers have always had at their side a trusted person with whom they have had an exceptional symbiosis that has rendered unnecessary the need to explain. Yves Saint Laurent and Pierre Bergé are perhaps the best example of such a duo.

Possible tools for managing brand aesthetics

The analytical instruments introduced in Chapter 6–the brand hinge, the semiotic square, the communication chain and the brand manifestations–are efficient at framing all the complex processes by which a brand produces meaning, but they are not adequate to tackle the plastic dimension (light, color, composition, lines and so on) of brand aesthetics.

There are a number of tools that exist for managing the plastic dimension of the brand manifestations. We saw in Chapter 6 how entering into classical and baroque considerations helps in treating light, forms and volumes and above all these aesthetics elements relate to specific brand ethics. We believe that these can contribute in bringing the merchant and the creative cultures closer together.

Conclusion on brand aesthetics

Introducing the notion of brand aesthetics as a possible management tool presents a double challenge. The first of these challenges is to prove that the notion is powerful enough to introduce a new approach to solve real issues. The second revolves around the audacity of thinking that brand aesthetics can be managed. This is itself dependent on a basic axiom, a certain vision of the brand business world, a notion of corporate ethics that asserts that there is no such thing as a "no man's land" within a company. Entrenched within such a notion is the idea that everybody must be able to explain the decisions they make and demonstrate how their choices are coherent with the company strategy and culture and how they make the brand more competitive.

Our considerations on brand aesthetics lead us naturally to the rich and complex relationships existing between brands and arts.

BRANDS AND THE ARTS

Given that both brands and artistic activities share a central core of creativity as their *raison d'être*, we may expect to find a lot of bridges between them.

We may think that the main difference between the activities of the "commercial" designer and the artist is that the latter generally does not have a business prescriber. While this may be so in most cases, we should not forget the role of the promoting gallery: the commercial dimension is never absent from artistic activities. There is a big overlap between the two worlds.

When we consider that paintings by Klimt, Picasso and Van Gogh have reached prices well over €100 million at recent auctions, is there a real difference between the painter who has an exhibition every two years and sells his work through galleries and the ready-to-wear designer who stages a fashion show twice a year and sells his goods through mono-brand and department stores? Is there a big difference between contemporary art fairs and fashion fairs?

Was there ever a time when the artist created independently of any money or power considerations? Artists, designers; where is the border now that brands fully compete with movies, TV and literature in proposing new ways of dreaming? To analyze the convergence of the two worlds of art and brands, we first examine how each borrows from the other.

From brands to arts

Brands came to a rapid understanding of the benefits of being associated with artistic activities. Having a strong cultural dimension can never have an adverse effect on a brand's identity. On the contrary, this is very much in the spirit of our times. When the affluence of cultural institutions such as galleries and museums has never been so great and the level of education is steadily increasing, for a brand not to develop a strong cultural dimension to its identity puts it at risk of losing competitive ground.

The designer's work has a lot in common with the creative artistic process. Both the artist and the designer need to make decisions regarding shape, form and color. The genuine ones have their own style and both have concerns, ideals of beauty, ethics and values that they try to express through their work.

The associations between brands and art can take several forms that can be classified according to the depth to which the brand's involvement with art penetrates its brand identity. It may start from the merely episodic association of circumstance with a known artist or art piece, and progress to having an art dimension fully embedded in its brand identity.

From episodic associations to an art-based brand identity

Designers and communicators in the luxury field have long had recourse to art works, either to compensate for their own wavering inspiration or simply in paying homage to the artist. Here are just a few examples of products or advertising that have taken their inspiration from works of art:

- Loewe scarf illustrated with a drawing and verses of Garcia Lorca; Etro scarves representing the Scala theater.
- Elena Miro's advertisement reproducing Paul Gauguin's Tahiti paintings using live models.
- A full-page Telefonica advertisement in the *International Herald Tribune* showing an Eduardo Chillida drawing.
- Vanessa Franklin's work for Converse sport shoes in *Wad* magazine in 2005, in which paintings by Watteau, Boucher and Ingres were scanned and superimposed with contemporary figures wearing Converse products.
- The Lanvin brand has always been closely associated with art since the Art Deco period, which was cherished by the brand founder Jeanne Lanvin. The first page of its website is the interior of an opera theater and, like many other brands, it cultivates links with the cinema. Its men's ready-to-wear

Summer 2006 collection was directly inspired by a Jean-Luc Godard film. Another advertising campaign made use of paintings by Ricardo Mosner, and drawings reminiscent of Matisse were used in advertising the Eclat d'Arpege fragrance.

- A new trend has recently seen special collections supposedly designed by an artist. In April 2006, Tiffany announced a new partnership with internationally renowned architect Frank Gehry, who designed the extraordinary Bilbao Guggenheim museum, to create six exclusive jewelry collections. Similar initiatives are also in evidence outside of the luxury world; when H&M offered a limited collection "designed" by Madonna in 2006, the products sold out on the first day they reached the stores.

- Cinema—the seventh art—has been the main source of cultural legitimacy for a lot of new brands. It conveys modernity, movement and the public can identify easily with the famous actors, who have themselves become a resource much used by television and the Internet. Events such as the Cannes Film Festival are very coveted fashion shows for the luxury ready-to-wear brands, with actresses commanding astronomical prices to wear a specific brand. Canali's links to the Hollywood movie industry are promoted on its website, which lists the many recent movies in which its clothes have been used. But the use of the cinema is by no means a recent phenomenon: Tod's famous campaign showing Cary Grant, Steve McQueen and Audrey Hepburn wearing its loafers went a long way toward establishing the brand as an iconic product.

- In the 1980s, Louis Vuitton launched a series of scarves designed by artists and designers such as Philippe Starck, Sol Le Witt and James Rosenquist. However, since Marc Jacobs' arrival in 1997, a stronger drive toward art in general has been evident. The first daring and very visible project was Stephen Sprouse's graffiti on the traditional monogram canvas. The most prolific collaboration has been with Takashi Murakami, who worked for several seasons on new versions of the monogram and who himself is producing animations such as that presented at the Venice Biennale in 2003 and which are inspired by the brand. The creation of the exhibition room "Espace" in the Champs Elysées flagship store has been another major step in that direction. It currently shows the photographs of Vanessa Beechcroft, and Alphabet Concept, letters made of nude models.

- One of the earliest and most common manifestations of the links between brands and the art world has been the cultural foundation: for example, *"La Fondation Cartier pour l'art contemporain"* was created in 1984 and is dedicated to promoting the development and awareness of all contemporary art forms, such as painting, video, design, photography and fashion. Another example, though on a smaller scale, is the "fundacion Loewe." Created in 1988 with the objectives of developing music, drawing and poetry among young people, it has instituted a coveted prize for poetry in the Castilian language. In fact, most of the major brands are involved informally in sponsoring artistic activities, such as Ferragamo sponsoring the restoration of an old painting.

- Some hotels have been pushing their association with the cultural world to a higher scale. The Guggenheim Hermitage Museum, designed by Pritzker Prize-winning architect Rem Koolhaas, is located at The Venetian Resort-Hotel-Casino. The Museum opened in 2001 with an exhibition on *Masterpieces and Master Collectors: Impressionist and Early Modern Paintings.* This a very shrewd move for a service brand to link its identity with such mythical names and the highest standards in the cultural world. Past exhibitions have included *Art Through the Ages: Masterpieces of Painting from Titian to Picasso; American Pop Icons; A Century of Painting: From Renoir to Rothko*—all art topics of relatively easy access for a non-specialist public.

- Yves Saint Laurent's own genius with colors and lines found a perfect challenge in matching the ephemeral nature of fashion to historical masters, paying homage to Mondrian (1965), Picasso (1979), Matisse (1981), Van Gogh (1988) and Warhol in his couture collections.

luxury **brand** management

The utilization of art and artists by luxury brands has, in general, been quite successful and it is hard to see how such an association can harm a brand in any way. It **helps attract the press and public attention, it reinvigorates brand creativity, it brings a new relevance to the brand when it is associated with current celebrities from the world of art, and it provides proof of the brand's sensibility to aesthetics.** Therefore, we are sure that the interest demonstrated by the brands toward the arts is bound to increase in the years to come.

In fact, we are now at the stage where certain brand creations are reaching art status. The New York Guggenheim museum was the first one to break a taboo when it organized an Armani exhibition in 2000. The 2003 exhibition of Guy Bourdin's photographs from the 1970s advertising for Charles Jourdan are a good example of this change of status. Keep in mind that, 15 years ago, the word "fashion" was almost obscene in art circles. The rise of photography as an artistic activity has contributed to this change of perception, as well as the spread of fashion and design-related museums and exhibitions.

The similarities between brands and arts and their current convergence is very much a two-way street.

From arts to brands
Campbell art vs. Warhol brand

Contemporary art has tried relentlessly to demystify the classical notion of artistic creation based on academicism, ideals of transcendental beauty, harmony and so on. In the process, it has been instrumental in introducing into it elements that had never been incorporated before. Marcel Duchamp was a precursor to this when, in 1913, he presented a bicycle wheel on a stool as an artistic creation. He began incorporating into his artwork technical elements such as door knobs, plastic bottles and day-to-day objects. This was not completely new, however, as Picasso had already utilized the handlebar and saddle from a bicycle in representing a bull.

Duchamp refined his logic to incorporate the "ready-made" art pieces and the famous 1917 urinal. Here, the artistic position evolves into a purely editorial role, selecting objects from daily life and choosing the moment and place of the exhibition.

Is this so different from the way some of our current designers work, selecting from the myriad of prototypes made by their juniors the pieces that will appear on the catwalk? This extreme approach indeed leaves little room for real creativity.

Artistic activity reduced to the discovery of an original concept and leaning heavily on the techniques of provocation (all familiar words in the communication world) is something of which Andy Warhol was a master. He piled up Coke bottles, produced color pictures of celebrities, and painted the famous Campbell soup can. The art work reproduced the branded object without adding anything to it. Warhol himself recognized that there were no messages in his work, that he was "a commercial artist" and that, in fact, business was the most artistic activity of all. The difference between Warhol's signed poster of the Campbell soup can and the actual product lies only in the discourse to be had about it. **It is the art theory that makes the art piece.**

Without knowing the theory, you cannot possibly know it is art. You need to be part of the "avant-garde," this restricted group who know; hence the importance of communication in contemporary art.

If you do not know that a particular brand is hot, you are out of fashion. The artist is exploiting a relevant concept exactly as most brands are trying to do.

Postmodernism is crossed by a strong relativism. Everything is art, just like everything is communication.

Museum business

Another taboo is disappearing. In the great rush to cash in on any little piece of reputation or notoriety that companies, institutions or individuals may have gathered over time, the past 10 years have witnessed an incredible fever of brand-extension activities that have led many brands to propose the most bizarre and illegitimate product offerings.

The great museums were among the first to open little souvenir shops within their own facilities, selling posters, art books, slides and postcards to the cultural tourist. For institutions with names such as Le Louvre, the Museum of Modern Art (MOMA) of New York and El Prado, the temptation to extend these activities is enormous, when all the competition is doing it and when it has no harmful effects on the customers' brand perception.

Now, in downtown or airport boutiques we find an eclectic range of articles: impressionist ties, Van Gogh mouse pads, La Joconde T-shirts, Picasso refrigerator magnets, cubist Venetian glass pendants and Velazquez aprons. It did not take long for business to realize the potential of these activities, and brand logic invaded arts when specialized brands—"museum musei," for example, with its baseline "the art from all over the world"—were specifically created to promote art-related articles. This is certainly a form of democratization of the arts, though it is not universally appreciated. After all, isn't the single most obvious and most necessary determining characteristic of a museum the presence of objects within it?

The tangible museum boutique has also been made virtual through the Internet. Museumshop.com is a leader in offering thousands of products from hundreds of museums as well as its own inventions.

The artists themselves were among the instigators of such moves. Salvador Dali—whose strong commercial sensibility was such that his surrealist colleagues called him "Avida Dollars," an anagram of his name—churned out prints and lithographs during his lifetime. His heirs allowed for the successful development of a sizable perfume and cosmetics business under his name. Paloma Picasso developed an accessory collection and, for the past few years, anybody can drive a Citroën model bearing the name of the artist.

At the end of these converging processes of contemporary art proposing branded products as masterpieces, masterpieces glued all over with day-to-day consumer goods and brands borrowing creative legitimacy from the artistic world, the frontier between art and brands has become blurred.

Indeed, the two worlds converge at a number of points:

- The nature of their creative activities
- Their commercial aims
- Their customers
- The fact that contemporary art is becoming another element of lifestyle
- The brand logic applied to their business in terms of differentiation, ethics, aesthetics and the use of communication and distribution to serve their commercial objectives.

Today, brands and arts are indeed competing on the common ground of communication, trying to generate cash out of entertaining activities, offering both real and virtual experiences, trying to make people dream and helping them escape reality.

It's the same business, to the point where bridges between the two worlds may no longer be necessary: Their territories may now be completely contiguous, if not partly overlapping.

chapter 8

Communication

In today's world, everything is communication.

Brands and their underlying logic are omnipresent in our public and private lives. The advent of the seemingly overpowering postmodern brand is rendering obsolete many previously efficient management tools.

OBSOLESCENCE OF THE "4Ps"

In the second half of the 20th century, most business students were raised with Philip Kotler's "4Ps," which were presented as the most powerful marketing analytical scheme. In 1967, Kotler defined marketing management as "the analysis, planning, implementing and control of programs designed to bring about desired exchanges with target audiences for the purpose of mutual gain. It relies on **the adaptation and coordination of Products, Price, Promotion and Place** for achieving effective response"[emphasis added][1]. This is what is commonly called the marketing mix.

- The products category was made of product lines, quality, brand, package and services. Note that brands, at the time, did not have the overwhelming importance that they went on to acquire in the 1990s. They were merely one of the inherent attributes of products.
- The price category included basic price, allowances, deals, credit terms and transport terms.
- Promotion was made of advertising, personal selling, sales promotion and publicity.
- Places incorporated channel types and locations, market logistics and sales territories.

The model was born in the low-tension competitive context of the 1940s, and built entirely on the product and some commercial considerations. In the 1970s, the brand appeared as a sub-element of communication and rapidly developed into a new communication alternative to the traditional product-focused advertising. Viewing product and brand communications as alternatives in this way probably contributed to delaying a proper understanding of their respective natures.

In the 1990s, there was a very clear shift toward intangible values expressed by the communication and associated with the products. Symbolic and semiotic values became crucial. **The brand seized power.** Table 8.1 summarizes the evolution of the brand.

We have moved on from the modern brand that held sway from the 1950s to the 1990s—which was a mere communication instrument to promote the product—to the postmodern brand, which proposes meanings and "possible worlds," establishing complicity with the customer beyond the product and often anchored in services. **The brand has become a project of meaning, where the product is only one of its manifestations.**

The postmodern brand proposes fantasy worlds, dreams and values that give a specific meaning to the brand product or service consumption. It enriches the purchase experience.

Communication, which used to be one of the links in a chain,

Table 8.1: The evolution of the brand

Period	Number of brands	Selling values	Nature
1900–1950	Birth of the modern brand phenomenon	Products	Identification Differentiation
1950–1990	Explosive growth	Products/ Brand values	
1990	Brand portfolios consolidation Branding logics spread The postmodern brand	Brand values more intangible	Meaning process

has become the chain itself. Kotler's legendary 4Ps have given way to the communication chain, to brand manifestations and to the communication program.

The communication chain

Figure 8.1 illustrates the sequence leading from the brand project to the act of product purchase. It starts from a clear willingness to propose a brand project to the market. This is followed by all the perceivable elements of the brand identity, which we call the "brand manifestations." This is the sensory world of the brand, where its aesthetics transmit the values inherent in the brand's ethics.

The passage from the first to the second link in the chain (known as the "consistency and coherence transition") lies in the scripting and staging of the brand ethics into discourse and image (the "*mise en intrigue*" and "*mise en scene*"). The third step in the sequence comprises the multiple perceptions that the manifestations generate within the market, which lead in turn to the last link in the chain, the actual purchase. The passage between the second and third links is called the "effectiveness transition," which is then followed by the "relevance transition" to the final link.

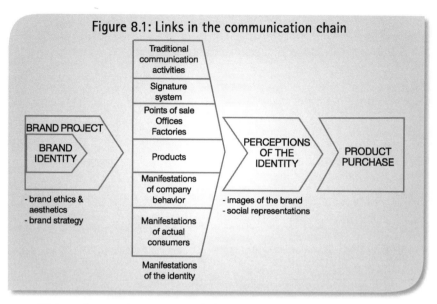

Figure 8.1: Links in the communication chain

This scheme is a powerful analytical tool that can serve multiple management purposes. The use of the communication chain as the basis for a methodological framework for a brand audit will be illustrated in Chapter 12.

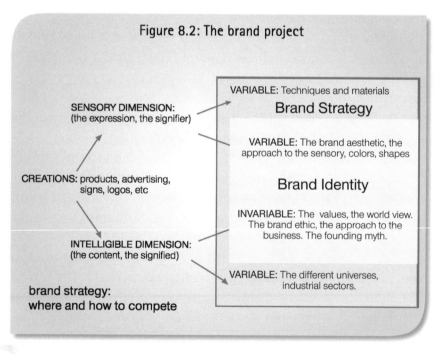

Figure 8.2: The brand project

luxury **brand** management

What we have called the "brand project" is shown in Figure 8.2, where the brand hinge (introduced in Chapter 6) can clearly be seen at the respective places and interfaces between the brand identity and the company strategies. This brand project notion has the advantage of showing that brand identity is born from a company's willingness, rather than from market reaction–in the form of feedback to the brand director–which only exerts influence on the identity at a later stage.

Brand manifestations

Brand manifestations go way beyond traditional communication activities such as advertising and PR. Most of them can be controlled internally and directly with the proper structure and processes. On the other hand, the look of the brand's actual customers and the behavior of its internal human resources and of their customers can be influenced but not fully controlled. However, they are an integral part of the brand manifestations in that they represent all the possible interfaces between brand and customer. They are complex combinations of traditional communication material, objects, spaces and people.

Figures 7.5 and 7.6 give a more detailed breakdown of the six broad categories of manifestations, which take us into the realm of brand aesthetics where we will talk about products, communication, and spatial and behavioral aesthetics.

With such a representation, the brand director (CEO, marketing director, creative director) is like a musician sitting at a keyboard, able to control (or at least influence) all of the brand manifestations that make up the sensory approach to the brand's identity, able to compose and play the brand "music"–the coordinated use of all the brand manifestations.

There are several possible strategies available here:

- The repetitive strategy, whereby, for reasons of efficiency, similar messages are expected from each manifestation. Even though fragmentary in essence, each of them should contain most of the identity values.

- The complementary strategy, by which different messages begin to make sense when merged; as, for instance, when a very classic store architecture highlights the baroque aesthetic of the products.
- The cacophony strategy (or better, the absence of strategy), which unfortunately covers the majority of cases, where each manifestation tells its own story.
- The symphonic strategy, where each type of manifestation is used to its maximum efficiency in order to contribute to the easiest possible perception of the brand identity. We know, for instance, that the Internet can communicate more comprehensively and exhaustively on conceptual matters than the product, and that advertising can communicate more easily than architecture on brand ethics.

The communication program

Having introduced the exhaustive classification of manifestations, we concentrate now on how to use them and consider the objectives of brand communication.

What is a brand trying to achieve through communication: to inform, to draw attention, to generate positive attitudes and desires, to be preferred, to be remembered? All of these, certainly; but there is still something missing.

The missing element, which triggers the whole chain of consumer reaction, is simply that the brand has to make sense. Brands are complex processes that need to generate meaning to be competitive. As Marie-Claude Sicard has pointed out, communication is what provides meaning to information.[2] The semiotic approach to brands (outlined in Chapter 6) clearly establishes that without meaning it is impossible to build an identity. What does not make sense to people is unlikely to attract their attention and is even less likely to generate in them a desire to acquire the product.

In Figure 8.3, we complete the consumer's behavior model by adding the brand meaning—the necessary trigger for the chain reaction leading to the act of purchase. We have also added the memorization step: without brand recall, no attitude can be developed.

luxury **brand** management

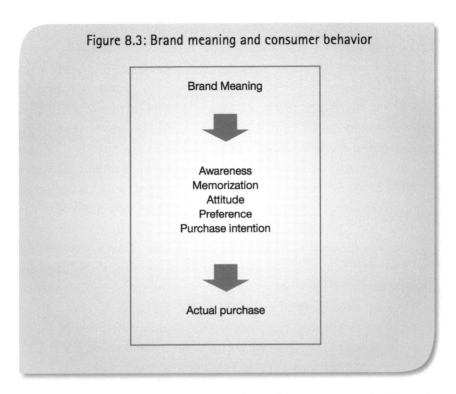

Figure 8.3: Brand meaning and consumer behavior

Brand Meaning

Awareness
Memorization
Attitude
Preference
Purchase intention

Actual purchase

Brand meaning is the brand's ethics expressed through its aesthetics; that is, the combination of all of the brand's manifestations. A brand's success in selling its products or services is dependent on the relevance of its ethics to the customer vis-à-vis those of its competitors. It asks the customer to consider the question: "How is this brand related to my needs, concerns, ambitions, dreams, desires and ethical values?" The manifestations express and make concrete the brand's abstract ethics. Communication becomes the system through which the brand project is presented to the market.

The Massimo Dutti eau de toilette launched in 2006 provides a concrete example of what we mean when we talk about a brand generating meaning. Massimo Dutti is a Spanish brand belonging to the Inditex group and offers men's and women's ready-to-wear. It has 400 stores in 29 countries and is positioned for a middle/upper-middle-class market. (You can see its relative positioning in Figures 7.7 and 7.8 of the preceding chapter.) The full-page magazine advertisement shows a traditional eau de toilette bottle in the bottom-left quadrant, with a soft, blurred, double shadow occupying 80% of the surface. The rest is a white background. The contents of the bottle are beige and white and the shadows are almost the same color. "Massimo Dutti eau de toilette for men" is written at the bottom right of the page. It is difficult to imagine anything more "plain vanilla." There is almost no meaning attached to this brand manifestation: no dream, very little information, no originality. Still, it offers a few pieces of information: Massimo Dutti is offering an eau de toilette for men; and, with its choice of colors, traditional layout and lack of a product name, the brand is probably very discreet and conservative.

If you're curious, you can search the Internet for more information. There's nothing on the Massimo Dutti site, though. After a further search you may end up on the website of Myrurgia, a company belonging to Puig, the Spanish fragrance and fashion group. From this, you can deduce that this is a licensed product. There is a photograph of the bottle with the following text: "The fresh natural fragrance for the man who makes his own style." This provides a little more information about the product, but without differentiating it in any way from myriad competitors.

The brand makes little sense through this manifestation and is losing an opportunity to promote its identity. This is often the problem of licensing. In any case, given the competition in this field, one has to wonder how successful the project is going to be. Fortunately there are 400 stores.

In Chapter 6, you will recall, we looked at the "Don Juan" brand. Don Juan undertook a strategic review and decided to promote its Spanish identity in a more radical way in the field of men's ready-to-wear. Table 8.2 shows its communication program, a high-level summary of what needs to be achieved in its brand communication. This is a master document, reviewed every year, as part of the budget process or after a major analysis such as this. The communication director will need to match it to the targeted customers.

From this master document, more detailed documents and operating briefs are prepared for each of the major and secondary

luxury **brand** management

Table 8.2: 2006 Don Juan Communication Program

Brand ethics

Render perceivable and interpretable the following concepts:

- the modern Spanish way of life
- total look: Spanish elegance
- affordable luxury

Brand aesthetics

Present new graphic chart (name, logo, colors, packaging, etc) and light baroque brand aesthetics

Products/Services

Promote best choice of European fabrics

Promote great tailoring. Excellent fit. Made-to-measure

Promote Superior Service in stores and after sales

Explain collections structures (lab, Executive, Ceremony, special collections)

Teach technical aspects of tailoring

Distribution

Inform on new store locations

Present new architectural concept

Cultural dimensions

Architecture, cinema and design

Solidarity dimension

To select projects related to the rest of the communication

manifestations. (Examples of such briefs are included in Chapter 11.)

This example of a communication program will help us identify the different categories of communication objectives a brand may have. These include:

- **Reflecting the brand ethics.** While it is almost banal to say so, it should be remembered that not all manifestations are equally efficient at doing this.
- **Giving factual information.** All brands have to inform on matters such as retail networks, solidarity projects, returned-goods policy, product maintenance, change of logo, brand history and so on.

- Generating emotions, states of mind, attitudes. In the Don Juan example, this is a reference to a Spanish way of life and elegance, which have been chosen as the basis of the brand imagery. It is the brand manager's responsibility to make people dream and relate to these aspects of the brand ethics through the various manifestations.

To this list we can add the two following objectives inherent in any type of brand communication:

- having a visual impact
- being remembered

In this short list, we have identified what we call the "communication efficiency criteria."

The communication chain gives an overall view of the meaning and the sales-generating process of a brand, highlighting the respective roles of the brand identity, ethics, aesthetics and their manifestations. We now look at how each manifestation identified in Figure 8.1 contributes to meeting the brand's communication and economic objectives. In reviewing these, we look at the extent to which they meet the communication efficiency criteria and the specific ways in which they can be used by luxury brands.

ADVERTISING

This is a powerful tool for expressing the brand ethics and is the most commonly used manifestation of the luxury brand. The competition for preferred placements and timing in the media puts upward pressure on prices, in much the same way as is happening in the real estate market. At this game, those with deeper pockets tend to win and the smaller brands need to be creative in their advertising activities.

The media

There is a wide range of media at the communication director's

luxury **brand** management

disposal: fashion and specialist magazines, newspapers, radio, television, street advertising, the Internet and so on.

The fashion magazines, which owe their existence to the luxury brands, have evolved into huge publications where 75% of the content is advertising. Mass and luxury fashion brands follow the seasonal cycle. The customer discovers the new campaigns (and products, when shown) in February, March, September and October. Fragrance, cosmetics, jewelry, watches and car brands are spread over the year and follow the calendar of their respective fairs. Hotel and in-flight magazines are often preferred by the luxury brands because of the natural segmentation they offer: airline magazines appeal to brands offering small products that can be sold on board (fragrances, ties, scarves, pens, watches, wallets, optical frames, etc.). Those not selected for in-flight sales will not find advertising space in the airline magazines. A similar reasoning applies to articles in the fashion magazines: those that don't advertise in them won't get any articles.

Vying for attention in a 250-page magazine full of generally similar types of pictures, products and models isn't easy and often leads to a bitter fight between brands to command the best possible pages.

In 1993, Ferragamo introduced one of the few innovations in magazine advertising: the gatefold, which is simply a doubling or tripling of the front-cover page opening from the external edge. That year, thanks to a gatefold in the *New York Times Magazine*, the Italian luxury brand succeeded in doubling its U.S. business in ties.

Other innovations seen in the fashion magazines in the past 10 years have been the special attached leaflet and the glued samples of fragrance and cosmetics. In addition to the institutional magazines with worldwide coverage such as *Vogue, Elle* and *GQ*, there are strong national magazines such as *Marie-Claire, W, Vanity Fair, Burda, Amica, Telva, Female* and so on.

Fashion magazines have long been the preferred advertising venue for luxury brands for a few simple reasons: they are big, they look luxurious and they project the right demographic image. However, the growing trend these days of adding all types of accessories—purses, bikinis, bracelets—as promotional tools is only serving to dilute the luxury appeal. As a result, the luxury brands have started to move to more selective, cultural, luxurious lifestyle magazines such as *Wallpaper, Quest, Monitor* and *Intramuros,* which feature a mix of architecture, design and fashion. The most fashion-forwards brands tend to go for the new avant-garde magazines like *Wired, Dazed, Blast, Exit, (T)HERE* and *AD!DICT.*

The daily newspapers have improved their position in the past few years with the introduction of color printing, despite their lower-quality reproduction. They tend to be used mainly for announcing forthcoming sales periods. Most daily newspapers have also introduced weekly magazines, which are often used by the luxury brands and in clear competition with the fashion magazines.

Television, because of its costs and wide coverage, is only useful for certain product categories that have the proper advertising budgets. In general, cars, fragrance and cosmetics make systematic use of television in their advertising.

Radio is rarely used because sound is greatly inferior to images and text for transmitting brand identities. Nevertheless, it is quite efficient for advertising factual information such as the dates of sales, the opening of a new store and so on.

Street advertising has been growing steadily as a very efficient medium. New types such as digital screens, and special films applied on buses, cars and buildings have added a new dimension to the more traditional billboards, posters, bus stops and scaffolding. Its big advantage is in its surgical precision, which enables the brands to pick up only those cities in which they have points of sale. A store window, which is also street advertising, or a bus covered with your latest campaign picture is bound to command more total attention time than a page in a magazine.

The Internet has transformed brand communication. It allows brands to use their own websites or those of relevant third parties. Though, in general, luxury brands do not advertise on other brands' sites, they may well be found on Style.com, the website created by *Vogue* and *W,* or on LVMH's eluxury.com or on intershop.com.

The advertising process

The communication program introduced earlier develops specific briefs for each brand manifestation. Table 8.3 shows the advertising brief of the Don Juan brand for the coming season.

Table 8.3: Don Juan advertising brief

A real story (authenticity, likelihood)

No pose, no artificial set up and attitude

Intensity of person's experience

No obvious Spanish cliches

Modern Spanish cultural elements

Spanish models

Luxury feeling

Include Spanish architectural and design elements

Situations: Exteriors and interiors

Business, travel, seduction, urban adventures,

No sport, no 100% nature.

The communication director's task is to match what the brand wishes to communicate (the communication program and advertising brief) to the target audience, with geographical and product priorities determined by the constraints of the communication budget. There are a few indicative guidelines for the breakdown of the communication budget: ready-to-wear and accessories brands allocate approximately 4–6% of their sales to traditional communication, but brands like Gucci may do more. Since sales are a mix of retail and wholesale, these ratios are not very reliable. Brands in the fragrance and cosmetics sector may even allocate as much as 50% of their sales in the year following a product launch, but this would then drop to 10–15% the year after.

The basis on which the communication director selects media and allocates funds is determined by a number of factors:

- The directions and constraints set by the communication program, the advertising brief and the budget.

- The specifics of the chosen medium. The visual image is supreme in conveying arousal, but weaker on informative statements. Table 8.4 attempts to evaluate the respective efficiencies of text, image combined with text, and speech. The communication director selects a particular medium or media based on their efficiency and effectiveness in conveying the required message.

Table 8.4: Communication efficiency of image, text and sound

Communication Efficiency Criteria ↓	Image advertising	Image + text advertising	Radio advertising
Reflecting the brand's ethics	efficient	very efficient	efficient
Giving factual information	weak	efficient	efficient
Generating emotions	very efficient	very efficient	efficient
Having a visual impact			none
Being remembered		dependent on realization	

This diagram is a statistical tool and is not intended for use across the board. In fact, its usage is dependent on a number of communication factors that will vary from case to case:

- The audience, circulation, exposure or coverage—the number and characteristics of the target audience; the expected duration and frequency of exposure (that is, the number of people who see the advertisement multiplied by the number of seconds of attention they give to it).
- The costs with respect to exposure.
- The context—the immediate physical environment in which

luxury **brand** management

the advertising takes place; for example, a full-page advertisement appearing precisely before that of a competitor or being placed before (or in the middle) of an article on war or a natural disaster.

- The location of the targeted customers. The luxury customer is not difficult to track down. It belongs to a global species, has more or less the same habits and behavior worldwide, and can be tracked down through a multitude of marketing studies.
- The geographical priorities. These are generally established on the basis of the density and performance of the existing distribution network, as well as specific efforts in developing or threatened areas of special strategic interest.

The communication director synthesizes the choices made in a media plan that specifies the media selected, the specific pictures and format to be used, the timing and duration of the campaign, and so on.

The advertising agencies

Advertising agencies play a more important role than simply buying space in the media. (In general, the major luxury brands have internalized this function.) The agencies provide creative services to the luxury brands in presenting a more precise and better formulated brand identity than their counterparts who deal with mass-market brands. Often, the main choices regarding the photographs and models to be used and the creative direction are made by the brand itself.

There is a certain comfort in selecting the most famous photographers, top models or architects, as the major luxury brands have been doing for a while. They may not get a super-differentiated image, but it at least reduces the chances of blunders occurring. There are examples where the agency becomes a de facto creative director. The U.S. agency Doyle Dane Bernhach (DDB), for example, has been creating Volkswagen advertising since 1959 and has contributed to building the brand identity almost as much as the products. In fact, in some senses the ads are more in the luxury field than the products themselves. In any case, a good agency should never be a substitute for strong internal creative direction. After all, who should know better how to promote the brand identity than the brand's own resources?

The role of advertising is probably overestimated today. The main function of many magazines is to distract people in the dentist's waiting room. The explosion in the number of publications and the increase in the number of pages of advertising; the constant race toward more provocation, which alienates the majority of people; the emergence of new media like the Internet; and advertising on public and mobile media—all contribute to diminishing the influence of this type of brand manifestation.

Zara (though not in the luxury category) is a fine example of a successful brand. Positioned in the intensely competitive clothing sector, it is giving Gap, H&M, Mango and Kookai a run for their money. In 2005, Zara had annual sales of €6.7 billion from its 2,692 stores around the world: all of this after just 20 years of existence and virtually without advertising (its advertising is restricted to newspaper ads twice a year to advise bargain sales).

PR, EVENTS, WEBSITES AND PROMOTION

Because of overexposure, advertising is losing ground to PR in communication. Press relations (as it is known in the fashion industry) is, as its name indicates, mainly responsible for the establishing and maintaining the company's rapport with fashion journalists. This is its original activity. PR directors are supposed to develop personal relationships with the most influential journalists, even though, as we mentioned earlier, the number of articles that appear in any given magazine is proportional to the brand's advertising budget allocated to that magazine.

The global brands lean on a worldwide network of PR agencies, and it is not unusual for them to contract six or more worldwide. This requires strong logistical capability: if the various magazines and newspapers around the world are to take pictures of products,

luxury **brand** management

obviously they have to have those products available to them. To meet this need, the brands specifically manufacture numerous samples and send them to their selected PR agencies. The costs of this worldwide structure and of the sample collections make this prohibitive for the small brands, which need to rely on other brand manifestations.

For the past 10 years, we have witnessed a strange phenomenon: certain fashion editors being used by some brands to select (edit) from among their products the items that are going to be most fashionable. The fashion editors are in an ideal position to follow the latest fashion trends and the overall evolution of a specific sector, so they certainly are competent to fill this role; and, clearly, the brands and the magazines find this mutually beneficial. However, this raises obvious questions about potential conflicts of interest and whether the editors could be seen to be exerting undue influence on behalf of particular brands.

Creating the buzz

The other fast-growing function of the PR office is managing the social relationships with the taste leaders of this world: movie actors, artists, architects, designers, singers, bands, sport celebrities, journalists, politicians and so on. Much has been written about how to create the "buzz," the magical momentum that gets everybody talking about the hottest new product, brand, store, designer, event, etc. While it is still a mystery to most, it is essentially a social and communication phenomenon that depends on moving in the right circles and mixing with influential people. And this is where the brand designer, who is often part of such circles, can play such an important role in influencing the perception of his peers toward the brand.

Events

Events are generally managed by the PR office and fall into three categories:

- Those that are directly organized by the brand—fashion shows, store openings, brand foundation awards, exhibitions, etc.

Following the example of Dior with Galliano, the fashion shows have become real entertainment events much like movie premieres (the seating of the guests has become one of the most perilous of the PR director's duties). Their overall costs— of the dresses and accessories, the fees for the top models, the venue rental, the air tickets, hotels and fees offered to invited celebrities, gifts to journalists and so on—can vary from a few hundred thousand euros to a few million.

How, then, is the success of a fashion show to be measured? If it were purely on the value of the articles published the following day, it would not be worthwhile. Everything depends on the selective social dimension in which the brand participates and this is difficult to measure objectively. The show itself is ephemeral and has little durable communication effect beyond the video taped replays shown in the boutiques.

The opening of a store is generally a major event for luxury brands, matching in lavishness the investment made on the construction. Here again, how to measure the return on the construction costing tens of millions of euros? Certainly not on the magazine articles and photos that follow the grand opening, whose influence lasts mere days. A truer measure is the communication statement that the store, the products and the sales personnel offer as a shopping experience and how efficiently these promote the desired brand ethics.

- A second category comprises sponsored events such as the Louis Vuitton Cup or the Grand Prix de Diane by Hermès, where the brand appropriates part of the event's identity. Louis Vuitton was originally associated with stylish travel and can thus introduce a set of more modern values revolving around sports such as yachting, team spirit and images of the ocean. Hermès reinforces its link to horses, competition, tradition and aristocratic behavior. Sponsorship can bring surprises, however, when unexpected events or behavior occur. A newspaper headline in March 2006 announcing "Movilstar is sinking" caused momentary flutters among followers of the Spanish brand (a subsidiary of Telefonica) until it became clear that it was referring to the problems facing a sponsored yacht of that name at Cape Horn in the round-the-world race. Other brands have also had problems with artists or athletes used to promote their products being caught up in unsavory or illegal activities.

- The third category comprises events or ceremonies such as the Cannes Festival and the MTV and Grammy awards at which the brand has high visibility. When in the 1990s Madonna showed up wearing Prada clothes to receive one of her 21 MTV awards, this had an incredible impact for the emerging brand. Competition between the brands to have high-profile celebrities showcase their clothes is fierce, placing such activities well out of the reach of the smaller brands. The climbing of the red-carpeted stairs of the Festival de Cannes by movie actresses and directors has become the most famous fashion show in the world. The films themselves become of almost secondary importance as the journalists spend their time describing the jewelry, outfits and accessories on show.

Product placement—the introduction (for a considerable fee, of course) of specific brands and products into movies or television shows—also figures large in this category. Hamilton, a U.S. watch brand, benefited greatly from its association with the movie *Men In Black*. Ferragamo shoes are often mentioned in American movies. In the same way, Sarah Jessica Parker and *Sex and the City* made Manolo Blahnik into a household brand with deep resonance among a younger generation initially not familiar with these sexy shoes.

Websites

By its nature, the website can incorporate all the communication advantages of the press, television and movies, and, because of its interactive capabilities, can improve the efficiency of advertising and some PR functions. Though luxury brands have been reluctant to use it fully, things are changing, as we will see later when we discuss online sales.

Table 8.5 illustrates an example of a brief for the Don Juan website.

Table 8.5: Don Juan website brief

Communication functions
- Second main communication tool to promote the brand identity.
- Seasonal revamping according to the related advertising campaign
- Didactic role to explain the product offer and its specificities (fabric choices and fabrication)
- Giving news on company's life
- Special coverage on specific events in cinema, architecture and design (a few well chosen topics)
- Emphasize the brand solidarity initiatives (always related to cinema, architecture and/or design)

Selling functions
- To be treated as a separate project (the new store)
- Aesthetic compatibility.

• Promotion

The promotional activities employed by the luxury industry fall mainly under the label of direct marketing. **One of the specific characteristics of luxury brands is the way in which they manage the relationship with any single customer.** The technology available now allows them to follow individual customers separately and keep track of their overall purchasing record and of more personal data such as sizes, tastes and so on. There is no luxury brand today that is not equipped to capture and record at the cash register (with prior authorization, of course) a maximum of data on each of its customers. A little birthday gift or a simple call from the local store manager go a long way in gaining goodwill for the brand

and create a degree of intimacy with the client. Catalogs, leaflets, postcards and loyalty cards are all standard means by which the brand can build on this relationship.

While on the subject of cards and luxury, this seems an appropriate place to take a detour into the luxury world of the American Express Centurion Card, popularly known as the Black Card. Made of titanium and commanding an annual fee of about €1,770 in the United States in 2006, it is the world's most exclusive charge card, with fewer than 10,000 issued worldwide. The card is available only by invitation and requires minimum annual spending of about €177,000 on another American Express card. Certain requirements have been known to be waived for major celebrities and business figures.

The card offers numerous exclusive privileges, including complimentary companion airline tickets on trans-Atlantic flights; personal shoppers at retailers such as Escada, Gucci and Saks Fifth Avenue; access to airport clubs and first-class flight upgrades; membership in Sony's Cierge personal-shopping program; and dozens of other elite club memberships. Centurion membership also includes personal services, including a personal concierge and travel agent. The program offers many hotel benefits, including a free one-night stay in any Mandarin Oriental hotel worldwide once a year, as well as elite frequent-flier status on Delta, Continental and US Airways. American Express Centurion customers have been known to purchase Bentley automobiles with just a swipe of the card and make purchases exceeding €1 million without even a credit check. The card has no limit, the largest purchase ever made on it exceeding €25 million for a fighter plane. It has been mentioned in films (*Casino Royale*), songs and TV shows. The card has achieved mythical status in less than a year.

THE PLACE OF THE PRODUCT

The product has a special place among the most meaningful brand manifestations. First of all, it is the basis of economic results. At the fourth step of the communication chain process, it is the product that is bought and determines the success of the overall brand project. Beyond this essential role, the product carries much more communication content than any other manifestations, for a number of reasons.

Tangible attributes

The product is advertising in its most direct, evident, multi-sensory form, generating immediate impressions. The communication power of the product has several attributes:

- **Aesthetics**: colors, forms, materials, style. An Armani suit, with its cut, fabrics, labels...and price, tells you all about the Armani brand identity.
- **Functionality**: reliability, durability, reproducibility. Ferragamo's ability to consistently offer the same fit across different shoe models is part of its brand identity and allows for catalog and online sales.
- **Workmanship**: is especially important for the high-end luxury brands where it is still a cult and is a basic tenet of the brand identity. The product is the foundation of the brand's legitimacy in a specific sector. It is proof of expertise in a business area (the client is rarely aware of licensing or franchise agreements and is only marginally interested in them) and guarantees the "substance and authenticity" offered by the brand.
- **Availability**: has an impact on the way the brand is perceived, but can work both ways. Large distribution and sales can increase brand awareness, but can also make it standard and without interest. The creative work done by various designers on the Louis Vuitton monogram fabric could be interpreted as an attempt to fight this possible lack of originality. The product is therefore the foundation of brand awareness (except in specific cases such as Absolut vodka). The more it is sold, the better it is known, especially if the product is identifiable from across the street. This explains the use of logos, materials, colors, metal accessories and other style codes that are aimed at facilitating identification.

- **Merchandising**: collection structure, number of categories and models, and, obviously, price. Tiffany's collections are not structured or presented in the same way as Agatha's.

The key to the brand's relationship with the consumer

The product is the source of repeat purchases, of the confidence or the disappointment that is created between the consumer and the brand. The product spends a lot of time with its owner (certainly more than the distracted attention the consumer gives to a page of advertising in a magazine). An "affective" tie develops. Brands of cars, motorcycles, perfume, shoes and coffee know this well.

The principal dimension of creation and innovation

It is on the product that the bulk of research and creative efforts are concentrated. It is also where they are most visible. Stylistic and technological research go hand in hand. Audi is a brand that has concentrated its efforts in both areas, with visible success.

Always in context

At least in the store, the product is encompassed within the brand retail architectural concept—the window and internal displays, the music, promotional materials—and promoted by dedicated sales staff.

Zara, which communicates exclusively through its products, stores and website, is a good example of the communication strength the product can have. For luxury brands, it is the final test. A Daum vase carries all the brand mythology of l'Ecole de Nancy, but is also a specific crystal ("pate de verre"): no two pieces are exactly the same and they will not be found anywhere else under another brand name. The luxury product must be different from its mass-market counterparts.

The product must be managed with full awareness of its impact on communication. Never kill a best-seller: restyle it. Canceling a group of products that sell well, on the grounds that they no longer fit with a new style or a new brand identity, shows a lack of respect for the market. Certain brands have tried it and regretted it. It amounts to a massive "layoff" of customers—the same customers who could have become spokespeople for the brand's change, had the change been carried out progressively and intelligently. The automobile industry has been successful at this—the Volkswagen New Beetle and the new BMW Mini Cooper being good recent examples of how to do it right.

To summarize product communication power: bad advertising rarely deters a faithful customer, whereas poor product quality always will.

COMPANY BEHAVIOR

The Enron scandal in the United States, Nike's alleged use of sweatshops in developing countries, the disappearance of Arthur Andersen, and many other cases have shed light on certain malpractices. Company behavior can have a great impact on the way that brand identity is perceived and should certainly be included among the brand manifestations.

Uncontrolled behavior

In general, harmful impacts on the brand identity are caused by the uncontrolled conduct of individual employees. Newspaper headlines such as "Siemens is investigated for alleged bribery in the Iraq 'oil for food' program" (*Financial Times Deutschland*, January 2007), or "Beginning of court hearing of Ahold former executives for alleged accounting fraud" (*Le Figaro*, May 2005), can damage a brand greatly. Increasingly, consumers are interested in the conduct of the people managing their preferred brands, and there is strong evidence of the fact that the public is demanding more ethical business practice. A Millward Brown survey conducted in 2002 showed that 75% of a sample of U.K. consumers bought or boycotted a brand on the basis of the company's behavior.[3] This has led companies to tighten their controls, draw up ethical standards and adapt their structures and processes to minimize the potential for misconduct.

What is valid for the brand should also apply to all related entities such as foundations, suppliers, agents and so on. The

luxury **brand** management

resonance of the Nike story served as a clear warning to all brands in the world. Since the settlement of the Kasly lawsuit in 2003 for alleged misrepresentations of its labor standards, Nike has been receiving excellent ratings from organizations that monitor corporate behavior. In 2004, for the third consecutive year, Nike was given a 100% rating on the Human Rights Campaign's Corporate Equality Index Survey. Nike's Corporate Responsibility Report received 3.5 stars (out of 5) from the independent ethical rating agency Mapplecroft, which said: "Nike is to be recommended for its reporting transparency."

The brand has reacted very well to protect its identity and the whole brand sector has benefited from the lesson.

Controlled decisions

On the other hand, it may happen that some company behavior, although fully controlled, has a negative impact on the brand. For example, in September 2006 the management of Burberry decided to close one of its fabrication units in Wales, with a view to reopening it in China in March 2007. However, the Welsh workers succeeded in forcing the company to justify its strategic choice in the House of Commons. The media took the matter very seriously, highlighting the incoherence between a brand identity essentially based on a British sensibility and the intention of "abandoning the country and leaving 300 UK families without work."[4]

There is a price to be paid for abandoning brand values, as Arthur Andersen found out to its cost. If you do not respect your own brand identity, ethics and values, you weaken irremediably the credibility of the brand.

ACTUAL CONSUMERS

Brands do not always choose their customers and can never control the actions they take that may come to have an association with the brand products. In this respect, customers are also brand manifestations and may have an unplanned impact on how the brand is perceived.

There are unfortunate examples of brand products being associated with famous cases legal—the Bruno Magli shoes that were used as evidence in the O.J. Simpson murder trial, or the Berluti shoes offered to Roland Dumas, the former French minister implicated in a bribery scandal, are cases in point. While the media coverage in such cases may broaden brand awareness, it may not always be good for the perception of brand identity.

More difficult to manage are the cases when brand products are adopted by market segments that contradict the values the brand promotes. For example, Lacoste—famous for its crocodile logo and its links to tennis, and a symbol of the modern sporting lifestyle—has been adopted by young people of African and North African origin in the poorer outer suburbs of most French cities; a market segment not originally planned by the brand managers. When asked about the impact of this in an interview with *Presse Magazine* in 2005, the company's advertising manager Didier Calon replied:

> It obviously had negative effects on the brand image. Certain of our customers were upset that we could pursue this target, when in fact we have no control over it. Our sales decreased for three or four years. However, as well as the negative impact on the brand image, some customers have found that it positioned the brand in a more modern trend. It is difficult to fully assess the phenomenon.[5]

In this same vein, we find luxury tastes being demonstrated by rappers. Agenda Inc. prepared a list of the brands mentioned most frequently in their songs, as shown in Table 8.6.

(While it is somewhat comforting to see cars, drinks and accessories ranked ahead of weapons, the presence on the list of the AK-47 is very disturbing nonetheless.)

The Cristal case is particularly interesting, as it generated a public controversy that sheds light on the management problems it raises.

luxury **brand** management

Table 8.6: Brands in songs

	Brand	No. of mentions
1.	Mercedes-Benz	100
2.	Nike	63
3.	Cadillac	62
4.	Bentley	51
5.	Rolls-Royce	46
6.	Hennessy	44
7.	Chevrolet	40
8.	Louis Vuitton	35
9.	Cristal	35
10.	AK-47	3

Source: Agenda Inc.

Cristal is a Roederer champagne originally created exclusively for the Russian tsars. Jean-Claude Rouzaud, who managed the winery until his retirement in 2005, once said: "We make our champagne for that 3–5% of consumers who really know wine, and who take the time to taste it correctly." (This definition perhaps captures the essence of a luxury product.) Today, the most high-profile consumers of Cristal are rap artists like Puff Daddy, Snoop Dogg and Jay-Z.

The controversy stems from an interview given by Rouzaud's son Frederic, the current CEO. Asked if an association between Cristal and the "bling-bling" rappers' lifestyle could actually hurt the brand ("bling" is rap slang for chunky gold jewelry), he replied: "That's a good question, but what can we do? We can't forbid people from buying it. I'm sure Dom Pérignon or Krug would be delighted to have their business." In response to Rouzaud's comments, Jay-Z labeled these comments "racist" and declared that he would no longer support any of Roederer's products through any of its various brands—which include Rocawear, a €490 million clothing business, and the 40/40 nightclub chain. In an attempt to limit the damage, Rouzaud responded with a statement of love and affection for all forms of music, art and culture: "A house like Louis Roederer would not have existed since 1776 without being totally open and tolerant to all forms of culture and art, including the most recent musical and fashion styles which—like hip-hop—keep us in touch with modernity."[7]

WHAT IS GOOD COMMUNICATION?

Good communication is that which costs little and generates a maximum of sales over the longest period of time.

In this chapter, we have introduced the notion of communication efficiency criteria that we have applied to image, text and sound. Despite their subjective limits, we could also apply them to the whole range of manifestations as shown on Figure 8.4.

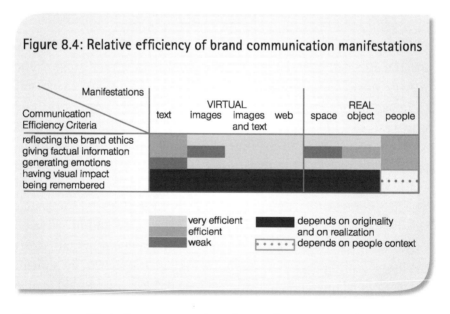

Figure 8.4: Relative efficiency of brand communication manifestations

Some manifestations are weaker than others on certain criteria.

- Text generates less emotion than image in the little time allowed by modern communication. That is not to say that a photograph in a newspaper is superior in generating deep emotions than, say, the poetry of Baudelaire. These are "statistical" considerations more than absolute judgments, not least because so much will depend on the author's creativity.

- Images are not as efficient as text in giving factual information. It is difficult, for example, to have phone numbers in a picture, unless text is added.
- Space alone will not give much factual information either. It can be very efficient at conveying moods and creating a favorable psychological context.
- The object does not always give precise information either, and often requires an explanatory leaflet on maintenance.
- People may be persuasive speakers, but it may take them much longer than images or objects to create the necessary fascination with the brand.
- A website can synthesize all the advantages of image, text and sound.
- Visual impact and the ability to be memorized depend essentially upon originality and actual realization of the communication element.

The diagram can be used more easily for an a *posteriori* assessment of communication documents.

Although we have dealt mainly with the aspects of good communication, we have not forgotten that that there are still too many examples of bad behavior from brand communicators in general. We have deliberately avoided mentioning here the communication excesses—the provocation, vulgarity, profanity, promotion of drugs, and so on—as we have dealt with this subject elsewhere.[8]

We believe that brands, if well managed, can be factors for progress. In Chapter 12, we will look at a method for auditing the whole communication of a brand, what good communication is and what it means to manage a brand identity well.

Endnotes

[1] Philip Kotler, *Marketing Management*, Prentice Hall, 1967.

[2] Marie-Claude Sicard, *Ce que marque veut dire*, Editions d'organisation, 2001.

[3] See www.millwardbrown.com.

[4] Quoted in *El Mundo*, 31 January 2007.

[5] www.pressemagazine.com (Authors' translation).

[6] See www.agendainc.com.

[7] www.usatoday.com.15 June 2006.

[8] See our book *Pro Logo*, New York: Palgrave Macmillan, 2004.

chapter 9

International
DISTRIBUTION

The word "distribution" can be misleading, as it deals with all methods of distributing goods, from the factory to the final consumer. This incorporates, of course, the stores where the products are sold, but also the systems used to take the products from Paris or Milan to everywhere in the world.

INTERNATIONAL "DISTRIBUTION SYSTEMS"

We said earlier that the luxury businesses are worldwide activities, which may give the impression that companies such as Givenchy or Max Mara have their own fully owned subsidiaries and their own stores in which to present their products to consumers. In fact, in much the same way that manufacturing is often subcontracted, so too is international distribution often handled by others.

In Figure 9.1, we start with the original company, which distributes its goods through distribution systems that include outside distributors, joint ventures or subsidiaries. It may also sign license contracts for products it cannot or does not want to manufacture and distribute directly. The licensees, in turn, select their own distributors around the world. (We will say more about the licensing issue in Chapter 11.) As a result, the original company has a presence in territories and in product categories that it does not directly control.

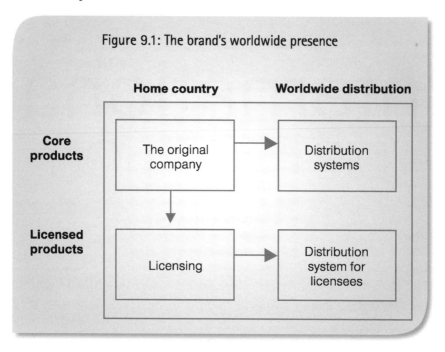

Figure 9.1: The brand's worldwide presence

THE DIFFERENT "DISTRIBUTION SYSTEMS"
We move now from the simplest to the most complicated systems.

Exclusive sales from Paris or Milan
This is how brands get started on exporting their products at the outset. They present their collections at the international fairs—in Paris, Milan or Frankfurt, for example—and sell them on the spot to individual stores or department stores in a given city or a given country.

luxury **brand** management

Most sectors have such fairs on a yearly or twice-yearly basis. In addition to the fabric fairs, there are also regular fairs for leather goods, jewelry, watches, optical frames, men's wear, ladies' ready-to-wear and so on. Here, distributors from around the world come looking for new ideas or new products. If they are attracted by a new brand, they may enter into an agreement, exclusive or otherwise, to sell the products in their stores in their home country.

In the luxury ready-to-wear sector, the different brands present their fashion shows in the same week or in the same fortnight, and all major purchasers come to town with their purchasing budgets (or "open to buys"). The fashion brands pay particular attention to purchasers from U.S. or Japanese department stores that can sometimes purchase large quantities of goods. At the end of the show, firm orders and cash down-payments are taken for the goods to be delivered later in the year: at the end of this process, fashion houses have a precise idea of their sales for the coming season.

Before they come to Paris and Milan, department-store purchasers will have prepared their "open to buy" budgets based on each individual brand's performance over the previous couple of years. Because budgets are predetermined, new brands experience difficulty unless they have discussed their ideas with the department stores beforehand. Without this, budget constraints would restrict the quantity that purchasers could buy, even if they were to love the new collection. Thus, the "selling" must be done well in advance and, if possible, at the headquarters of the main national department stores in major countries.

The exclusive sales system has many advantages. It is very low risk because generally there is a cash down-payment with the order, with the balance being paid by letter of credit on the date of shipment. With purchasers from department and multi-brand stores coming around every year looking for new brands and new ideas, it requires a minimum investment. In this way, brands can end up in some extremely high-end department stores, where their products can sell easily and at full price.

Of course, the disadvantage of this is that the brand has very little control over the choice of stores or distributors and is dependent on the goodwill of one or another of the major operators. When a brand wants to grow, it must combine such sales with additional, more targeted, points of sale if it wants to be represented in smaller countries.

Subsidiaries

It is a common misconception that "fully owned" subsidiaries are the most common system of distribution for luxury goods. However, this is seldom the case, and the majority of the business is not done through subsidiaries.

Subsidiaries are great because they can do a good marketing job. They also have the advantage that their sales are consolidated at full value (wholesale price), rather than at export price. A company with many subsidiaries appears bigger and more impressive at home and top management are very proud of managing or chairing, at a distance, a U.S., a Japanese or a Chinese corporation.

However, in many countries in the Middle East and Latin America, not to mention Indonesia, foreign companies cannot hold 100% of the shares of a subsidiary dealing solely with the distribution of products manufactured and imported from abroad. In some cases, such subsidiaries are forbidden. In other cases, the majority of the shares must be held by a local partner. In countries like Russia or China it is possible to have a fully owned subsidiary, but it is generally advisable to take a local partner that will, among other things, be responsible for dealing with local authorities.

Second, subsidiaries are expensive. Depending, of course, on the size of the country and the type of products involved, having a subsidiary does not make sense if expected sales are not reaching €4 million. Below that figure, the gross margin resulting from sales will not be sufficient to cover overheads and salaries. Also, budgets tend to be generally optimistic, but sometimes sales fall; a once-profitable subsidiary can then become a nightmare.

Third, subsidiaries require cash: the local inventory of products and the accounts receivables have to be financed by headquarters. When cash is tight, this is not necessarily the best way to operate:

luxury **brand** management

growing through a system of subsidiaries is slower than with a network of distributors.

There is also a misconception that subsidiaries are easily controlled and therefore unlikely to initiate parallel businesses or "grey market" operations. However, specialists in this area say that the easiest sources of products are general managers of subsidiaries that are behind their yearly budgets and who may be tempted to unload some products without controlling where they would end up.

For very large, established firms, subsidiaries may work well, but for small luxury-business firms this is certainly not the most common distribution system.

Local distributors

Local distributors purchase the products with their own money, build local inventories and sell in their own country. This is, of course, a low-investment approach for a luxury company looking to expand internationally.

A local distributor is generally granted an exclusive right to distribute a product or a brand in a given territory. Distributors generally represent several brands in order to spread the cost of their sales force between them. This also gives them better bargaining power with department stores or individual outlets, which can be an advantage for a smaller brand.

Local distributors assume all financial risks on the brand locally. But they generally know how to negotiate for the best location in a department store and how to arrange discounts on media advertising tariffs. All in all, they can generally handle a brand's day-to-day activities very effectively.

There are limitations, of course. They are not always easy to control and may, in some cases, do their own marketing locally, rather than necessarily following what the brand would like. They may also vary the way they operate for the individual brands they handle.

When a brand is very strong in a territory, paying a percentage of wholesale sales to a local distributor can be much more expensive for the brand than having a subsidiary. Distributors are ideal for starting and developing a brand; but when sales reach, say, €10–15 million, it may make sense to start a subsidiary. But moving between the two systems may not be easy, as we will see below.

The joint-venture system

Canceling a relationship with a distributor can sometimes lead to unpleasantness that may result in the distributor organizing a boycott of the brand among its closest customers. This has certainly happened in Japan when, for example, a particular department store has had its exclusive distribution rights and master license agreements for a given ready-to-wear or perfume brand removed when the brand decided to create its own subsidiaries.

The joint venture is a subsidiary that belongs in part to the brand headquarters and in part to a partner who could be, for example, the former local distributor. The system provides an elegant way of smoothing over some of the potential difficulties involved in starting up a subsidiary by leaving open the possibility for the former distributor to play a major role through offering office space, back-office activities and local market knowledge. Through such joint-venture agreements the way may be open for the principal to increase its shareholding over time and to end up with 100% of the business.

Having said all this about the distribution avenues available to luxury-goods companies, the "average" luxury firm will probably deal directly with some department stores, will have up to 10 fully owned subsidiaries, between five and 20 joint ventures with former distributors, and probably 40 to 60 independent distributors around the world.

PRICE STRUCTURES

Prices are not set at random. They must take several factors into account. First, it is more expensive to distribute a product in the United States than it is to distribute it in Panama or a small island in the Caribbean. Second, some countries have import duties of up to 100% as well as protective quota systems.

luxury **brand** management

But luxury-goods companies try to harmonize their worldwide prices. They work on three different price zones, as shown in Table 9.1.

Table 9.1: Pricing in different zones (perfumes and cosmetics)

	Paris/Milan	New York	Tokyo
Domestic market	100	85–110	135–150
Duty–free	80	68–88	108–120

(For fashion brands, New York domestic prices can be around 120 and Tokyo domestic prices can reach 200.)

The anchor is the Paris/Milan price, which we have put at an index of 100. Because there is no longer any duty in Europe, sales in other European countries are generally around 100 to 105 and duty-free prices are calculated at 20% below (that is, around 80).

For New York, the objective is to have retail prices at somewhere between 105 and 110. But in periods when the dollar is weak, such as we have known from 2001 to 2004, and in 2007, it is difficult to increase U.S.-dollar retail prices unreasonably and prices often end up as low as 85. Latin America and Caribbean duty-free prices follow New York prices, and for some brands in 2006, they were below European duty-free prices.

In Tokyo, where costs of operations are high, and where import duties still exist in different product categories, prices are generally in the 135–150 range. Duty-free prices are generally slightly more expensive than European domestic prices.

In countries such as Thailand or Brazil, where customs duties amount to 50% or more, retail prices would not necessarily be increased by that same percentage from the base of the price zone. The brand owner would look at the level of retail prices that would be acceptable to the local market and to tourists and would reduce its export prices accordingly.

The general rule is that there is not one given export price for everybody. In fact, the system generally works the other way round, with an agreement on the ideal retail price for a specific country, the calculation of a sensible margin on this price, and a specific export price based on these.

In fact, in the luxury business, there are often as many export prices as there are different clients. This approach is sometimes questionable, as in many countries price fixing is prohibited by law so that the price structure decided between the principal and the distributor is considered only "indicative," with only a "suggested" retail.

The price structure will be based, as in Table 9.1, on a Paris/Milan retail of 100 and will start from the most logical or effective retail price for the given country. Taking into account the standard retail margin (which varies from one country to another) and the impact of different levels of value-added or other local taxes, a wholesale price can be calculated. From this, the agreed distributor's margin and the agreed advertising budget are deducted to give a landed cost, which is the basic agreement between the distributor and the principal. From there, it is only necessary to know the specific import duties for a given country and the other costs (freight and insurance) to be able to define what should be the right export price.

Table 9.2 provides an example of how this might work for two European countries.

For the purposes of discussion, we have assumed that Country A would sell at retail at 105 and Country B at 110. Wholesale prices are the result of the retailers' margins, which are 50% and 47.7%, respectively. Subtracting the respective margins and the advertising budgets from the wholesale price gives the landed prices of 16.8 and 23. It is then necessary to take into account freight, insurance and duty, which produces an export price of 16.2 for Country A and 22.4 for Country B.

luxury **brand** management

Table 9.2: Cost structures for Europe (perfumes and cosmetics)

	France	Country A	Country B
Retail price	100	105	110
Wholesale price (irrespective of value–added tax)	50	52.5 (100%)	57.5 (100%)
Distributor's margin		25.2 (48%)	25.875 (45%)
Advertising and promotion budget		0.5 (20%)	8.625 (15%)
Landed price		16.8	23.0
Freight, insurance and duty		0.6	0.6
Export price		16.2	22.4
Product cost	12.5	12.5	12.5
Gross margin	75%	22.8%	44.2%

Although the cost structures in Countries A and B seem quite similar (agent's margin: 48%/45%; advertising budget: 20%/15%), the final gross margin figures are very different: 22.8% in Country A and 44.2% in Country B.

In the French case, the gross margin is very high (75%), but this is not really a fair point of comparison because the firm sells its own products directly and does not use a different structure to cover distribution and advertising activities. It is clear, though, that activities in Country A are not very profitable: a gross margin of 22.8%. There is a need for a very high margin in the French case to be able to feed the long distribution circuit as in Country A or B.

The advertising budget is generally integrated in the cost structure and this money is at the disposal of the distributor to be used in that country.

In the case of Europe, the difference between landed and export prices is limited. As we will see later, this is not always the case.

In Table 9.3, we have taken the example of two countries with higher duties and different costs of operations.

	France	Japan	Mexico
Table 9.3: Cost structures for Japan and Mexico (perfumes and cosmetics)			
Retail price	100	150	250
Wholesale price	50	90	78 (100%)
Wholesale price (second distributor)		67.5 (100%)	
Agent's margin		37.125 (55%)	35.1 (45%)
Advertising and promotion budget		10.125 (15%)	11.7 (15%)
Landed price		20.25	31.2
Freight, insurance and duty		2.94	8.89
Export price		17.31	23.11
Product cost	12.5	12.5	12.5
Gross margin	75%	27.8%	45.9%

In the case of Mexico, there is no major change from European cost structures except that, because of high import duties, the retail prices are much higher than in the United States.

For Japan, we have taken the case of an importer distributor who has no direct access to department stores or other outlets: very often in Japan the perfume counter, unlike the cosmetics floor, is not run directly by the department store but is farmed out to someone acting more or less as a rack jobber and working on a 25% margin. This piling up of intermediaries—from retailer to wholesaler to distributor—is specific to Japan and explains in part the high cost of operating there.

Within these cost structures, it should be noted that percentages run in different ways. They are calculated from the retail or the wholesale price on one side. They are also based on the export price to assess the freight, insurance and duty on the other side.

To simplify, people speak of the "coefficient" of a cost structure: the coefficient is equal to the retail price divided by the export price. Thus, in the Japanese cost structure the coefficient is 8.66 and for Mexico it is 5.62.

In discussions with different potential distributors in any given country it is necessary to compare the different price structures with which each of them wishes to work. Differences in the global coefficients are an indication of the economic advantage of working with one distributor or another. But it is also necessary to look at the advertising support included in the structure.

THE ADVERTISING BUDGET AND ADVERTISING POLICIES

In Japan's cost structure as outlined in Table 9.3, the export price is 17.31, while the advertising budget is 10.125–almost 60% of the export price. Why has the cost structure included a local advertising budget when this could have been added to the export price, and then spent directly by the brand principal? The only problem here is that, if the manufacturer were to invoice at 34.81 (rather than at 23.11) to include the advertising budget from Paris (as was done in the case of Mexico), import duties would have to be paid on the advertising money spent locally, which does not make sense.

This is why advertising budgets for perfumes and cosmetics are generally included in the cost structure. (For ready-to-wear, a percentage of local spending is written into the contract even if it does not appear directly in the cost structure.) The direct consequences of this are:

- The brand owner (generally called "the principal") feels it has reduced the export price of the products by this amount and therefore considers this advertising budget its own.
- The distributor considers that it is paying the right price for the products and therefore feels that it is paying the advertising budget out of its own money.

But the differences do not stop here:

- The principal is very interested in building brand awareness and its standing in a given market, so it tries to push for the largest part of this advertising budget to be spent in media investments.
- The distributor is more interested in the short term, so prefers immediate promotional activities. It may also try to include in this advertising budget costs that are necessary to distribute the product but that it would have to spend anyway on things such as sales staff, promoters or push money in the stores, which may have immediate sales impact.

What happens when everybody believes that to distribute, say, a perfume brand in the territory, the budget of 15% of the cost structure is not enough and an additional couple of million euros must be spent? Here again the points of view may differ:

- The distributor considers that as it has no long-term rights in the brand it is the principal's responsibility to meet these extra costs if it wants the brand to be better known in the territory.
- The principal considers that whatever happens in the local market is to the advantage of the distributor because it should have immediate impact on his sales; therefore, any additional investment in advertising should be made by the distributor alone.

Such discussions have the potential to be discordant and disruptive to both parties and, fortunately, the standard rule is to split the costs of "overspending" equally.

It is clear, then, that the management of the "distribution system" requires a lot of time and attention. Most companies have to deal with a mix of structures involving a few subsidiaries and a large number of distributors. Subsidiary managers are simply company staff—albeit far from home—and should be motivated as such. Distributors should be considered as individual partners,

luxury **brand** management

investing their own money for the success of the brand. Exclusive distribution contracts generally run from three to seven years and it is sometimes advisable to renew some contacts in advance so that a "partner" feels secure and motivated to continue developing the brand. There are also cases when joint-venture agreements must be discussed and signed.

Developing the distribution system is obviously the number-one activity for those who want to build a worldwide business and cannot afford to invest directly everywhere in the world. It is the responsibility of top management to know directly their distribution "partners," in the same way that they should know personally the merchandising vice-presidents of the major department stores in the world. This responsibility is particularly critical for perfumes and cosmetics and for wines and spirits activities.

THE SPECIAL CASE OF DUTY-FREE OPERATIONS

A large percentage of luxury goods are purchased by people traveling: for perfumes, for example, it is estimated that more than 30% of worldwide volume is purchased in duty-free outlets. For cognac and ties, too, duty-free purchases account for up to 20% of worldwide sales.

An estimate by the specialist research firm Generation put the total duty-free market in 2006 at almost to €20 billion (38% from Europe, 35% from Asia and 25% for the Americas). Of this total, wines and spirits represent €7.6 billion; fashion luxury goods and accessories €6.99 billion; and perfumes and cosmetics €4.87 billion.

Most duty-free stores are located in airports, where people generally have time on their hands and cash in their pockets. These stores are a good opportunity to provide discount prices and real customer savings in a sophisticated environment. When very few people traveled, it was a discount market reserved for the "privileged few." Now that everybody travels, it has kept part of the luxury characteristics because traveling by plane—or on cruise ships—remains a relatively upscale activity.

Though duty-free stores are located in major airports, there is not always a direct link between the number of passengers and the size of the business, as shown in Table 9.4.

Table 9.4: Estimates of duty-free activities at major international air/ferry ports

	Sales 2005[1] (€ million)*	No. of passengers 2006[2]
London Heathrow	560+	67,530,197
Seoul Incheon	490+	NA
Dubai International	350+	27,925,522
Singapore Changi	350+	35,033,083
Amsterdam Schiphol	280+	46,065,719
Paris Charles de Gaulle	280+	56,849,567
London Gatwick	210+	29,695,609
Frankfurt Airport	210+	52,810,683
Manchester International	210+	NA
Hong Kong International	210+	43,857,908
Bangkok Don Huang	210+	42,799,532
Silja Line, Finland	140+	NA
Honolulu Airport and Downtown	140+	NA
Tel Aviv Ben Gurion	140+	NA
Scandines, Denmark	140+	NA
Tokyo Narita	140+	NA
Viking Line Finland	140+	NA
Brussels Zaventem	140+	NA
P&O Ferries, U.K.	70+	NA
Taipei Chang Kai Shek	70+	NA

(1) Estimates of Generation database and Duty Free News International (DFNI) database
(2) Airports Council International
*These figures were expressed in U.S. dollars, but for consistency we have converted them to euros using an exchange rate of US $1= €0.7058.

The duty-free system

Duty-frees operate on two basic conditions. As the products they sell have not really "entered" the country, they are not liable for import duties. As they are not sold "within the country," they are not subject to a local distributor's margin. But while local duty-free operators do not pay import duties or local taxes, they do pay airport commissions, which can be two to three times higher.

Table 9.5 illustrates the workings of the duty-free system.

Table 9.5: Duty-free pricing system			
	French retail —domestic (€)	European duty-free retail (€)	German retail price—through a local distributor(€)
Full retail price	100		105
Retail without value-added tax (19.6%)	83.61		
Duty-free retail price		80	
Wholesale price	50		52.5
Export price		32	16.2

Note: For the German prices, we have used the Country A figures from Table 9.2.

As Table 9.5 shows, if, for example, a perfume company sells its product in a store in Germany at a retail price of €105, its export price may actually be €16.20, the difference being accounted for by a large distributor's margin and an advertising and promotional budget. When the product is sold directly to the duty-free operator at, say, Frankfurt Airport, the perfume company can invoice it at a price of €32; that is, at almost double the price it would sell for if it had to go through the German distributor's cost structure. Thus, everybody is gaining: the customer gets a better deal, and the manufacturer sells at a higher export price, even if there is no advertising budget built into the structure.

Table 9.6 explains how the system works from the duty-free operator's perspective.

Table 9.6: Price structure for the duty-free operator

	Total Amount	Percentages
Airport retail	80	100%
Airport commission	32	40%
Operator's margin	16	20%
Export price	32	40%

When the duty-free operator purchases at 32, it receives only a 20% margin; most of the difference between the export price and the duty-free retail price goes on commission paid to the airport operators. In fact, airports have two major sources of income: landing and parking costs for planes, and duty-free commissions; in many cases, the latter provide more than half of the total airport revenues.

Duty-free operators work with an airport concession generally awarded to the highest bidder. Such concessions can last from three to seven years, but the majority are for seven. In preparing their bid, the major operators study their forecast volume of business based on the number of planes, the destinations and the nationalities, and the types of the travelers (tourists versus business travelers, for example), and commit themselves to give a commission (which can range from 35% to 55% of their sales) and sometimes also a flat minimum for each year of the concession.

In general, for a large-volume airport this activity is very competitive, with most of the worldwide operators bidding.

Operators factor into their bids considerations such as new slots that may be given for new destinations or new airlines, and they use their own estimates of nationality and travel-type mix for each of the luxury-product categories: Japanese customers smoke more than American customers, but they smoke mainly Mild Seven, the

luxury **brand** management

highest-selling cigarette brand in Japan. Americans buy whiskies and cognac and, for cognac, their preferred brands are Hennessy and then Rémy Martin; and so on. Operators can then prepare a business plan with their best estimates of sales and the maximum concession fee they can offer the airport authorities.

Given the very high airport commissions (which can be more than half of the duty-free retail price), and in countries like Hong Kong, Guam, Singapore and Panama where there are no import duties, it makes a lot of sense to build downtown duty-free stores or large downtown galleries because then the business model will work without the payment of large airport concession fees.

But in this case, duty-free operators are back to square one: they are in the official territory of the domestic distributors, unless they can pressure the brands and find middle ground. Of course, even these downtown stores are the result of the specific duty-free system that pertains in each country.

With this system, products sometimes end up with very different prices, as can be seen in Table 9.7.

Table 9.7: Price differences for duty-free products in 2006 (€)*

Marlboro 200 cigarettes		Chivas 12-yr-old whisky (1 liter)	
China Airlines	€7	Beijing Airport	€15
Istanbul Airport	€13	Bangkok Airport	€20
Berlin Airport	€22	Sput Airport	€24
British Airways	€25	Salzburg Airport	€28
Vienna Airport	€32	Keflavic Airport	€32

Source: Duty Free Price Guide, 2006 (incorporating airports and airlines)
*These figures were expressed in U.S. dollars, but for consistency we have converted them to euros using an exchange rate of US $1= €0.7058.

There are huge price variations from one place to another, but this is generally the result of differences in local prices (cigarettes are very cheap in the Chinese domestic market) and different retail price strategies of airport operators. For example, the operators of the Amsterdam Schiphol Airport prefer to work on a lower percentage concession fee, provided the duty-free prices in many product categories are the lowest in Europe. This way, they believe they can attract more stopover passengers—going, for example, from Boston to Helsinki or from Houston to Hamburg—than London, Paris or Frankfurt.

The major duty-free operators

Eight or ten major duty-free operators manage more than half of all airport volume in the world. There is obviously a strong advantage to size: the bigger the purchase potential, the better the duty-free operators can put pressure on their suppliers for better export prices. And the lower the purchasing prices they can get, the better they can win new airport concessions by offering a higher commission to the airport authorities. The major operators, ranked by size, are described below.

The DFS Group (Duty Free Shoppers)

A division of LVMH, this activity was started in Asia by three individuals and now has estimated sales of around €1.5 billion. Most of its activities are in the Pacific region. The group headquarters are in San Francisco and it operates 150 stores located mainly in 15 Pacific cities including Hong Kong, Singapore, Hawaii, San Francisco, Los Angeles, Guam and Saipan.

Specialists in Japanese and other Asian customers, the group has very strong negotiating power in dealing with suppliers. It is also very strong in its downtown activities, operating under the "Galleria" name.

The Nuance Group

The Nuance Group had sales of around €1.4 billion in 2006. It operates at Geneva and Zurich airports; at most airports in Turkey; at Manchester, Bristol, Cardiff and London Heathrow airports, amongst others, in the United Kingdom; at Denver, Fort Lauderdale, Houston and Las Vegas in the United States; at Sydney and Melbourne in Australia; and at Vancouver. It also operates

luxury **brand** management

in-flight sales for airlines such as Edelweiss Air, SATA, TAP Air Portugal, Yesair and 20 U.K.-based airlines.

Its sales are well balanced, with 45% coming from Asia and the Pacific, 44% from Europe and 11% from North America. Sales comprise wines and spirits (37%), accessories (23%), perfumes and cosmetics (17%) and tobacco goods (14%), the additional 9% being accounted for by miscellaneous products.

Heinemann

Heinemann is a family operator based in Hamburg, with sales in the region of €900 million. It operates all German and most Austrian airports, has major airport operations in Spain and Portugal, and has a presence in Miami and New York.

It is strong in food and tobacco products and has domestic distribution activities in Germany.

Lotte Duty Free

This is a different operator in that it includes airport sales made mainly through downtown department stores, where purchasers can give their flight number and departure date and have their purchases waiting for them on board. Thus they can enjoy duty-free prices in the environment of a department store. Sales are estimated at around €700 million.

Dufry

The Dufry Group, with sales of approximately €500 million, operates airport duty-free outlets in Basle, Milan, Panama, Mexico City, New York, Singapore, Moscow, Nice and many other places. It also as a ship chandler (duty-free operators in major harbors for cruise ships and others leaving domestic waters) in Barcelona, Colón in Panama and in Croatia.

World Duty Free

This subsidiary of the British Airport Authority offers duty-free activities at Heathrow, Gatwick, Stansted, Southampton, Aberdeen,

Edinburgh, Glasgow, Naples and Budapest airports. In 2006, it dealt with 150 million passengers, offering 13,000 products at its 60 stores, and recorded consolidated duty-free sales estimated at €500 million.

DUBAI AIRPORT

This is the largest single airport duty-free in the world, with sales estimated at €450 million. Like Schiphol, its objective is to attract passengers in transit from Europe to Asia and vice versa. It offers very good prices and is famous for a lottery in which the first prize is a Ferrari. It also organizes special deals for Indian and Filipino citizens who have worked in the Middle East who want to take a television or a washing machine back home with them.

AER Rianta International, the Irish group that manages Dublin airport, Moscow's Sheremetyevo and many others, had sales of around €450 million in 2006.

Aelia with sales estimated at over €450 million, it has more than 100 points of sale, mainly in France (Roissy) but also in the United Kingdom.

In many places, including Greece, Venezuela and Argentina, small operators generally manage one or two airports and are often run with the blessing of the state.

The negotiation

Negotiating with any one of these major operators is always difficult for brands. While the brand executives want to achieve both visibility and maximum volume in the airports, there is a high price to be paid for the privilege. First they have to pay for each item to be listed and then for promotional support, which can include:

- Pricelist book advertising
- Shelf location
- Transparencies in the shop with the name of the brand, or an advertisement
- A special promotional program for the brand

luxury **brand** management

- Push money for the sales staff.

In most cases, sales staff are employed by the brands themselves and have to be paid. Together, all of these factors mean that it is very difficult for small brands to break into the potentially lucrative duty-free market.

THE PARALLEL MARKET: REASONS AND CONSEQUENCES

The parallel or "grey" market consists of quantities of products that are sold in stores that are not supposed to handle such products. Parallel operators purchase large quantities of products, if possible in places where they are at the lowest possible price, and bring them to stores that would not otherwise be able to get them. The parallel market is all the more developed for brands that have selective distribution practices that make their products hard to find and where prices vary greatly from one place to another.

The reason for parallel markets

We must distinguish here between different product categories.

For **perfumes**, products are very easily transferred from one place in the world to another. Grey-market operators reason that if they can buy perfumes at wholesale prices in Panama at a very low price, it may be profitable to sell them in Japan, where retail prices are generally higher. These "arbitrage" activities are much the same as take place for currencies or for grain futures. Their only work is to take the perfumes from where they are available at good prices and sell them where they are in demand and at a higher price.

Perfume brands have built their image on the concept of selective distribution. Most brands make sure that their products are not available in supermarkets or hypermarkets in Europe or in U.S. drugstores. Because they organize scarcity as part of their reason for being, they do not want to be found in huge display piles in a Carrefour hypermarket in the suburbs of Brussels the week before Mother's Day. This would damage their image of desirability and their exclusivity.

It is not easy for brands to keep their products out of the drugstores and hypermarkets because in most countries there are laws to prohibit manufacturers from selecting their retail outlets. They are supposed to offer their products to every store without discriminating between retail outlets. So perfume brands have defined policies stating that they will only sell their products to stores where the environment is exclusive and luxurious and where beauty consultants are available and knowledgeable about the products. They thus limit their sales to traditional perfume stores and beauty chains.

If they allow Carrefour to sell their products in the build-up to Mother's Day or Christmas, this is quite unfair on the traditional perfume stores that carry the brand all year round and that would be unable to cover their distribution costs, losing out to supermarket sales.

In the United States, sales of perfumes and cosmetics are concentrated in department stores, where brands fight to get good locations and large counters. If these products were also available in drugstores, it would dilute their overall image and reduce their negotiating power with department stores.

On the other hand, drugstores are interested in carrying top brands because this improves their image and broadens their product line into more glamorous categories.

So grey-market operators act as wholesalers and are ready to offer almost any perfume brand to the U.S. drugstores. All products are available, but not at the same price. Brands such as Estée Lauder and Chanel that are difficult to get will be sold at retail or with a 10% discount on retail (which means that when drugstores decide to carry them, they are ready to sell without making money), while brands that are easy to get on the grey market—Pierre Cardin, for example—can be found with a 60%–75% discount at certain periods.

Given that it is almost impossible for them to stay out of grey-market channels, the objective for perfumes is to be difficult to get; to be there at such a wholesale price that the retailer who handles the brand does so without making money.

luxury **brand** management

For **accessories**, the history is a little different. First, because fashion dresses are unique they are difficult to find in the grey market. Because they have a short shelf or store life, they are rapidly out of fashion. The main target for the grey market is accessories that are sold only in free-standing boutiques such as those of Prada, Louis Vuitton and Chanel.

Chanel or Louis Vuitton handbags often end up in the window displays of small leather-goods stores in Japan, for example. Clients are attracted to the stores because of these famous and exclusive brands, but once inside, sales staff do everything they can ("They are too expensive for the quality ... I can show you a much more fashionable product ...") to move the sale toward other brands on which they make higher margins. So the Chanel or Louis Vuitton products are there not to be sold, but merely as an attraction.

For **wines and spirits**, the issue is complicated by the fact that, in most countries, heavy taxes are levied on such products and this is reflected in the prices in the stores. The issue here is not only the selective distribution aspect but also the way to avoid the alcohol taxes. In some cases, products are smuggled into the country. To prevent this, some countries have tax stamps that are stuck on the collar of the bottles as proof that the tax has been paid. Of course, smuggled products are still available, but only from parallel, unofficial outlets, where customers buy at their own risk.

Collecting products for the parallel markets

Grey-market operators use all types of systems to gather merchandise. Some travel all over France or Italy in small trucks, visiting perfume stores and offering to purchase everything the store operators are ready to sell, at, say, retail minus 30%. If a store operator is behind his budget or if his inventory is too heavy, he might be tempted to unload. Needless to say, distribution contracts between each perfume brand and the retailer prohibit any such activities, but it is not always easy to trace back sales like this. There is a good lesson here for perfume brands and perfume salesmen:

it is very dangerous to push store operators into purchasing too much merchandise. It may be a very common and effective practice in food supermarkets for mass-market products, but it is very dangerous for selective luxury products.

For Louis Vuitton, Prada or Chanel handbags, the system is even easier. It is common practice for grey-market employees to pay passers-by to enter legitimate stores and buy different products for them. We estimate that for a brand like Louis Vuitton, more than €15 million-worth of merchandise will be bought from the different Paris stores each year and will end up in small, second-rate leather-goods stores, mainly in Japan. Some say that this system also involves getting official checks from small Japanese retailers to launder €15 million that will be put very officially in a genuine Japanese bank account.

But there are other sources of grey-market products. Distributors from countries buying at reasonable costs—Panama, Hong Kong, Paraguay and Singapore, for example—all know some of the parallel buyers and might be tempted to unload some of their inventories. They are prepared to run the risk of not having their distribution contract renewed if they are caught. The brands themselves may sometimes sell their old inventories to "jobbers."

What is sure is that luxury products can travel the world at a relatively low cost, compared to their value. Therefore a perfume bought in Singapore or a handbag purchased in Paris may well end up in a U.S. drugstore or a Japanese leather-goods store. In neither case will the products be sold in their normal environment.

How to fight parallel distribution
When a grey-market product finds its way into a particular territory, a distributor or the manager of a local subsidiary will complain to the brand's head office, and with some justification. They say: "Those products come from your factory, so you should know where they went and what happened to them." They have a point.

Brands that are serious about reducing parallel activities must ensure that they keep proper track of their products. About 15 years ago, manufacturers began putting laser identification numbers on each individual sleeve carton to enable them to keep track of if and how things came to be in the grey market. But the grey-market operators responded to this by discreetly removing all laser numbers from the cartons they acquired.

The next step, then, about 10 years ago, was for the brands to put a specifically located laser number on each perfume box so that each client would have a laser number. Then, even if the outer number were scratched, the client could still be identified. So the grey-market operators would also scratch other places on the sleeve, hoping perhaps to eradicate the identification of the distributor. While this was not always successful, it would often be sufficient to create uncertainty and make tracking difficult.

Today the perfume manufacturers that really care use boxes that have two bar codes: one for the product name and reference; the other with a number from one to several millions, which enables all products taken from the warehouse for shipping to a client to be recorded and tracked by computer and for each individual product to be identified by its destination.

Today, when a perfume appears in a store where it should not be, it is generally possible to identify the source. Although the distributor may not have acted illegally in allowing branded products to pass into the parallel market, what it has done is not good for the brand's standing. And in any event, in the absence of an invoice between a distributor and a wholesaler who has official links with a grey-market operator, it is still difficult to prove that a specific perfume comes from the distributor's stock. Needless to say, such invoices are quite difficult to get.

The U.S. customs appeared at one point to have invented a very effective system to counter grey-market activities: only the distributor who had a right to the brand registration in the United States could import the product and pay duty. But this still failed to take account of smuggling. What is sure is that the parallel operators will continue to disrupt the selective distribution system for many more years. For brands, therefore, the objective must be to limit the damage as much as possible. But the parallel market will probably always exist.

.

luxury **brand** management

chapter 10

Retailing

For the fashion and accessories sectors, retailing (either directly or through franchised distributors) is the number-one priority. Ladies' ready-to-wear products are sold in a variety of stores, including:

- **Free-standing stores**, having direct access to a street or a shopping centre.
- **Flagship stores**, which are the biggest, most impressive stores, located generally in the brand's home city (Paris, Milan or London, for example) or in other major cities such as Tokyo, New York, Shanghai and Hong Kong.
- **Shops-in-shops**, which are, as the name indicates, fully individualized stores within a department store. Sometimes such stores simply rent a space, but in most of the cases, the products belong to the department store operator and sales are recorded and paid in the store's standard cash registers.

- **Corners** in department stores, where branded products are sold from several counters in a space that is more or less "open," but where the brand still gets some specific identification.
- **Department store counters** where there is no longer a clear identification of the brand and the sales staff are employed by the department store, which is generally not the case for shops-in-shops or corners.
- **Sale in multi-brand individual stores** or store chains.

For perfumes and cosmetics and watches, there is generally a system of "stands," which are decorated by the brands and operated by the brands' own employees.

A great deal of research has been conducted on every aspect of retailing and many books have been written on the subject. There is a management research review, the *Journal of Retailing*, published by New York University, but unfortunately no research has ever been conducted in luxury retailing. In New York, the **Fashion Institute of Technology** publishes a lot of research on store branding or store positioning, but with this exception all research on luxury retailing has been conducted by the brands themselves and is proprietary.

BACKGROUND ANALYSIS

In this first section, we will put luxury aside for a moment and look at different aspects of retailing in general, which will give us some insights into the issues and what is at stake.

Store location and site selections

For the mass market, the first issue is to decide on the best location for a new store, for which there are several options available.

The central business district is the traditional downtown business district. It is the ideal place for shoppers during business hours or at lunchtime. It draws most of its customers from people working in the area.

Main street locations are generally in smaller towns. They may also be close to a smaller business center, but they also get customers who travel there to do their shopping.

Strip centers are small shopping malls with direct access to the streets or to a parking lot and where customers can do their shopping almost every day and with easy immediate access to the store.

Shopping malls are large centers in which no store has direct access to a parking area: customers must park and walk to the mall, and then enter their stores of choice from the lobbies of the mall.

Free-standing stores are stores that are built directly on a street and are not part of a shopping mall or a shopping gallery.

In their book on retailing management, Levy and Weitz[1] draw a table of advantages and drawbacks of these different categories, as outlined in Table 10.1.

In selecting a mass-market retail location, specialists define the trade area. From existing stores, they can check, through credit card information, the precise location of their customers and determine the percentage of residents within a five-, 10- or 20-minute drive they can attract to their stores. They draw up "pulling power" maps with primary or secondary zones as a function of the average purchase in their stores by residents of each area.

They also look at accessibility, sometimes by looking at the traffic flow at different points and, of course, counting the number of customers passing a target location. They can also check the flow of cars into the parking systems using aerial surveillance.

They must also take into consideration man-made and natural barriers such as highways, subways, bridges and rivers that may act as physical or psychological impediments to consumer access to their planned stores.

Indices of market potential are often available and these are also consulted by the stores as part of their planning processes. Then, of course, there is the question of competition to consider. It is often thought that being positioned close to a competitor is something of a disadvantage, but this is not necessarily the case. Studies have shown that when two or three stores of the same trade and of the same standing are positioned together, they multiply the

Table 10.1: Relative advantages of major retail locations

	Central business district	Main street	Strip center	Shopping mall	Free-standing
Large size draws people to area	+	−	−	+	−
People working/ living in area	+	+	+	−	−
Source of entertainment/ recreation	?	−	−	+	−
Protection against weather	−	−	−	+	−
Security	−	−	−	+	−
Long hours of operation	−	−	+	+	+
Planned shopping area/ balanced tenant mix	−	−	−	+	−
Parking	−	−	+	?	+
Rental costs	+	+	+	−	+
Pedestrian traffic	+	+	−	+	−
Landlord control	+	+	+	−	+
Strong competition	+	+	+	−	+

Source: Levy and Weitz

luxury **brand** management

attraction power of the location as a whole and this serves to offset part of the competitive disadvantage.

In-store behavior[2]

Many department-store studies have investigated how consumers behave as they enter a store and have observed the following recurrent patterns of behavior:

- They look straight ahead as they enter and only look around once they are in the store.
- They walk to the right.
- They use their right hand to touch the products between two aisles and they stay on the right, even in countries where people drive on the left.
- They look straight ahead.
- If there is a sign that they cannot read from a distance, they will not get close to it to read it. They will just forget about it.

Another study measured how long people would stay in a furniture and homewares store and found the following:

- A woman with a man: 4 minutes 41 seconds.
- A woman alone: 5 minutes 20 seconds.
- A woman with a child: 7 minutes 19 seconds.
- A woman with another woman: 8 minutes 15 seconds.

The time spent waiting to be served in a mass-market retail store is also perceived differently from the actual time spent, as shown in Table 10.2.

Table 10.2: Perception of time waiting for service

Actual time	Perceived time
Up to 90 seconds	Accurate
2 minutes	3 or 4 minutes
3 minutes	5 minutes
4 minutes	Much too long

But as soon as consumers have personal contact with a salesperson, they feel the waiting time is much lower: this is all the more important since waiting time is the number-one criterion consumers use to assess the quality of service in a store.

Table 10.3 lists what customers want to do and don't want to do when they are in a store.

Table 10.3: What customers want/don't want

They want	They don't want
To touch the products	To queue up
To look at themselves in a mirror	To have too many mirrors
To find things on their own	To be obliged to ask silly questions
To speak	To find unreadable labels
To be considered	To have the product they want out of stock
To get a "good deal"	To face intimidating sales staff

Retailing indices

The performance of a point of sale is always closely monitored. Some of the indicators looked at are:

- The number of pedestrians passing the store.
- Index of attractiveness: the percentage of passers-by entering the store.
- Conversion rate: the percentage of people entering the store who buy something. Even in supermarkets, the conversion rate isn't always 100%, because when two people go shopping together, they are counted individually; if they buy something they often leave the store with only one receipt from the cash register. Conversion rates can also be broken down by gender or generalized age categories (below 25, 25–45 and over 45).

(Obviously, in ready-to-wear, where the conversion rate is around 10%, it may well be that the merchandise is not suitable for the people entering the store. A study conducted in the United States indicated that the conversion rate increased by 50% if the sales staff initiate contact. It increased by 100% if the sales staff initiated the contact and the consumer tried one piece. Another study showed that when men try on a piece of clothing, 65% will buy. For women, the equivalent figure is 25%. On the other hand, when women look at the price of a dress after they have tried it on, 86% will buy. The equivalent figure for men is 72%.)

- **Average ticket:** this is of course a very important part of the sales performance. It can be registered by sex, by age impression or by local clients and foreign customers.

- **Average number of items purchased:** this can be a measure of performance of the sales staff. This is the case, for example, in shoe stores.

Other indices measure the store activity:

- **Inventory turnaround:** this is the ratio of yearly sales at cost-of-goods value and in-store inventory at cost value. For example, a food supermarket can have an inventory turnaround of 20 (it sells 20 times more in a year than what it has in stock on any given day), while a high-end jewelry store may have a turnaround of 0.66 (that is, it needs an in-store inventory of 150 at any given time to make yearly sales of 100). Of course, in those two cases, the financial attractiveness and the growth potential of new stores are quite different.
- **Ratio of bargain sales to total annual sales:** this affects, of course, the average gross margin for the year and the profitability of the store.

- **Sales per square meter:** a measure of the efficiency of the brand and of the store, calculated in general on the selling area.
- **Sales per staff:** this allows the efficiency of the sales force and the profitability of the store to be measured.
- **Sell-through:** this is the ratio of goods sold since the beginning of the season with respect to the number of goods purchased. This is a key indicator of how the sales performance for the particular point of sale relates to the amount of goods purchased. It can be done in units or in currency based on the cost value. It is an essential element in deciding the following season's open-to-buy budget. In a normal luxury ready-to-wear season, sell-through at full price (before discounted sales) should be around 50%; 30% in the sales period, and 20% going to outlet discount channels. Sell-through at full price for accessories like shoes or handbags should reach at least 60%.
- **Standard income statement per store:** this is the basic tool that enables all operating expenses to be related to sales.

Rules of thumb for internal display in supermarkets

In a supermarket environment, almost everything has been tested; for example, the impact of an increase in "facings" for a given product on its sales and on the sales of the product category. (For supermarket merchandisers, a product has one facing when it is alone on the shelf. Having two or three boxes/tins/packets of the same product– that is, two or three facings–on the shelf brings greater visibility and strength to the brand.) It always depends on the product category and on the market share of a given brand, but it is fair to say that as the facing for a product doubles, its sales increase by approximately 50%. But while sales of the product are increased, sales per linear foot decrease, unless the doubling of such a facing has had another impact on some items of the same product category, which it always has. There is therefore a difficult balance between the objectives of a given brand and the objectives of the retailer. In luxury retail, double or triple exposure does not necessarily have an impact on the sale of an item. If the product is

luxury **brand** management

hot, it will fly off the shelf. If it is a dog, it will not sell no matter how much exposure it receives. This is evident at end-of-season liquidation sales: luxury products that are not desirable, do not even sell on discount.

Studies have shown that when products are placed on promotion with an end-of-aisle display, sales are multiplied four or fivefold.[3] What is strange is that this increase is the same whatever the competitive situation of the brand: a strong market leader and a smaller-volume brand will each increase their sales by this amount even though the latter may have an end-of-aisle display with 10 times less volume. This explains why store operators are interested in promotions for high-volume brands.

In these studies, it was also found that end-of-aisle displays are less effective for new products than for old ones, which comes as a surprise. Also, when the products on display have a deep price cut (at least 20%), they do not sell significantly more than when there is only a nominal cut or no price cut (0 to 10%). In fact, on seeing a product on end display, the consumer assumes that the price is really reduced, and does not check. In one-third of the cases, the price has not really been reduced significantly.

What is the impact of the levels at which products are displayed on the shelf? Faced with a wall of products, consumers first scan from the top left, then move down and across to the center. They then look to the right before their eyes move down. This probably explains why locations at eye level are more effective than locations at hand or floor level.

But how many of these supermarket rules can apply to a luxury retail environment? In fact, these rules can be usefully adapted to the context of a fashion store or a perfume counter. The idea here was to extract from mass-market studies the rules of thumb and the reflexes that could also be applied to luxury retailing.

A perfume on promotion will behave exactly the same way as a detergent. Doubling the facing of a brand of champagne on the shelf will increase its sales, but will not necessarily increase the volume in the product category. Customers entering an upscale department store or a specialty store will first go straight, looking straight ahead, and will not necessarily see the first line of perfume counters if these are too close to the entrance.

RETAILING IN THE LUXURY FIELD
Store location and leasing systems
Strangely enough, in luxury the location of a store is not determined by pulling power and trade area analysis. The brands look at the trade potential in any given city in which they are considering opening a store. Even at this level, they rely heavily on the competition: "Cartier has a store in such or such city. They have X clients entering the store every day. Does that provide enough potential for a Bulgari or a Boucheron store?" This is more or less how the issues are analyzed and discussed.

Store location
Once a city has been selected, store location is relatively simple. There is, in every city, a best location for a luxury-goods store. In Paris, it used to be Avenue Montaigne or Rue du Faubourg Saint Honoré, but the Champs Élysées and Saint Germain have challenged this assumption in more recent times. In Milan, it is around Via Monte Napoleone, Via San Andrea and Via Della Spiga. In Hong Kong, the choice is between Peninsula Plaza, the Landmark or Pacific Place. In Tokyo, it is between Ginza and Omotesando.

In this regard, then, for the location of a brand's first store in a major city, things are quite simple. There is only one place to be. Nevertheless, even in such a place, there can be huge differences in business potential from one side of the street to another. On Rue du Faubourg Saint Honoré, sales are great on the North side of the street. On the South side, the business is not there (though rental costs are almost identical) and there are few passers-by. Generally a very strong brand, through its very high pulling power, attracts a large number of customers who also end up entering other stores in the area. The Rue du Faubourg has the Hermès flagship store, but customers are focused solely on it and seem to have no time to visit neighboring stores.

The point is that, before selecting one side of the street rather than the other, or the second floor of a luxury shopping center rather than the ground floor, it is important to count the passers-by. Knowing the coefficient of attractiveness of a given brand, it is possible to get an idea of the volume that can be expected.

The worst decision is to make do with second-best, believing, say, that the adjacent street will be just as good. In reality, on most occasions a street that is only adjacent to the best street is dead. A nice address is not necessarily a pointer to a profitable business.

There are still difficult tradeoffs for a luxury brand to consider. For example:

- Is it better to have a small store in a top location or a large store in a second-choice location for the same rental cost?
- How should you move from one store in a given city to two stores, then three?

The answer to the first question is not too complicated. A small store in a top location is a very effective set-up. For many years, Lancel had a small store in the Peninsula Hotel in Hong Kong, across from a large Louis Vuitton store. It did extremely well despite having a very high rent. It also had a much larger store in Swire House, close to the Landmark, which presented a very large collection of products but sold very little because it was 20 meters away from the right traffic flow. While location is extremely important, for luxury it can be looked at more as a function of what the competition is doing than as a matter of working through pulling-power maps.

The second question is a difficult one. Louis Vuitton has two stores in Beijing and yet only one in Shanghai, where business potential is the highest in China. Is this a mistake or simply a question of concentrating all of its customer strengths in a single location in Shanghai? The situation of Hermès in Paris is quite similar. Apart from its flagship store, it has only one other small store in Avenue George V and a shop–in–shop in the Hilton Hotel of the Left Bank; Louis Vuitton has five locations in Paris, while Salvatore Ferragamo has nine free-standing or shop-in-shop stores, not to mention about 10 additional multi-brand retailers also selling its products. Hermès certainly has the customer base to open a second flagship store on the Left Bank, but it hasn't done so, probably because it wants to maintain its unique situation as the last genuine luxury brand cultivating the principle of managed scarcity. But how much does it lose in sales as a result? If its existing flagship store was as large as that of Armani in Milan, how much additional business would it do? And how much would this increase its competitive image in Paris?

Such discussions currently taking place in Paris and Shanghai are almost certainly echoed in New York, Tokyo and London for many brands grappling with similar big decisions. This is, of course, a question of corporate objectives and priorities. But it is also a question of investment capabilities.

The different leasing systems and their costs

Securing a top location in a major city is not an easy matter: they are seldom available and generally expensive. Very often, it is necessary to pay a large amount of "key money" upfront. There are several leasing systems that apply around the world, each with its own rules and peculiarities.

The American lease system generally does not include "key money." The lessor rents a place for nine or 10 years, after which the lessee has to negotiate a new lease, at market price, for a specified period. If the parties cannot agree on the new lease, or if the lessee wants to get out, no money is due either way.

The American system is balanced and very open, but there is a catch to it: where a store is losing money, or where sales drop dramatically overnight (as happened after 9/11), the lessee is bound by the contract to continue paying rent for the entire period of the lease.

Many foreign luxury brands have found themselves in such a position, and sometimes unable even to sub-let the premises. Even if the original contract does permit a sub-lease, contractual

luxury **brand** management

clauses governing product category and brand positioning can be very restrictive. In difficult times, lessees may be faced with the prospect of sub-letting at a lower rental and having to make up the difference for the duration of the lease.

If prospective lessees are careful, they organize an exit clause by creating a fully owned legal subsidiary for each store they open in the United States: if things go sour they can bring the subsidiary to Chapter 11 bankruptcy and rid themselves of the rental commitment. But then, prospective lessors also have a way around this. When they see that a subsidiary is signing the lease, they ask for a guarantee from the head office.

In many parts of South East Asia, the American system prevails, but with only three- or four-year leases. While this probably makes the relationship between lessor and lessee more balanced than in the United States, it also gives the lessor the opportunity to increase the rent every three years in line with current demand for that location.

The Japanese lease system is even more to the advantage of the lessor. In Japan, leases are long (10 years), but on signing the lease, the lessee is obliged to pay a deposit equivalent to 10 years' rent. Though this deposit is returned at the end of the lease if the lessee does not wish to continue the arrangement, the lessee is, in effect, giving the lessor an interest-free loan. If the lease is renewed with a higher rent, the lessee pays an additional deposit to cover the difference in rental amounts.

Because the system works very much to the advantage of the lessor, many foreign luxury brands found it very difficult to move into Japan and open stores: they just could not afford it. To get around this, the brands developed through shops-in-shops with department stores. Louis Vuitton, which had a policy of opening only free-standing stores around the world, was forced to make an exception in Japan and move into department stores. At the end of 2006, Louis Vuitton had 54 stores in Japan, only six of which were free-standing: the rest operated as shops-in-shops within almost every Japanese department store chain.

The slowdown in retail development from 2000 to 2005, led to a reduction in the payment of "key money" from 10 years to five. Also, luxury companies seem to have decided to purchase land and become owners of their own stores, but this too requires a lot of money upfront and easy access to bank loans.

Unlike these other systems, the **French system** works to the advantage of the lessee. The lessor rents a store for a period of nine years, but the lessee can exit unilaterally every three years. If after nine years, the lessee decides to stay, the lessor must renew the lease for a further nine years, with a rental increase that is determined in line with a national construction cost index. Lessees have no obligations other than to stay a minimum of three years, and have the right to stay in a place as long as they want. If the store is in an area much in demand, the rental will become much cheaper over time compared to that paid by more recent neighbors.

But the lessee also has another option: he may leave the place and ask for key money from a new tenant. Informing the landlords of the change is sufficient for all obligations to transfer to the second tenant.

This key money will appear as an investment in the balance sheet of the new tenant, who will hope to sell it at a much higher price later on. The lessee has the possibility of making money and the system was probably created to give small shopkeepers sufficient money to live on when they retire.

To sum up: selecting and renting a store in a major luxury city is always a long-term investment. It can cost huge amounts in "key money"—sometimes as much as the equivalent of one year's sales—and can prove very risky if, as in the United States, there is no way to cut costs when the location produces poor results.

For shops-in-shops or corners in department stores, the situation is quite different as the stores provide floor space in a given location in exchange for a given percentage of margin. In the worst cases, department stores also demand a minimum payment each month. The brand has to pay for the decoration of the space, for the salaries of the sales staff and for all promotional activities.

luxury **brand** management

Budget, planning and control

The planning system starts, obviously, with a budget. This budget starts with a sales target, then an inventory forecast so that the purchasing can be consistent with expected sales.

The sales target

The sales target depends on the pulling power of the brand, the size of the store and the width of the merchandise offering. The expected volume must be forecast for each month. (For fashion stores there will be a higher ticket average for the winter season than for summer.)

For a new store, sales grow for at least two years and then plateau when it has found its base of repeat customers who are used to the new location. When a store is doing well, moving it elsewhere, even 200 or 300 meters away, could be a mistake because, again, customers would have to familiarize themselves with the new location.

For a new store, the sales budget is often preset at the level committed in the pre-opening financial analysis. As a rule of thumb, in Europe, rental costs should be less than 10–20% of sales. In Asia, rental costs can reach 20% and in some cases 30% of the sales target, but the overall profit-and-loss picture is different, with a more limited staff cost in percentage terms.

When, after six months, the store fails to meet its sales objectives, management has the tendency to remain optimistic and to wait for an improvement. Unfortunately, this improvement seldom comes unless the merchandising mix or the sales staff is modified.

Inventory forecast

With the sales forecast and the gross margin target (which is different from the theoretical gross margin) in place, it is then possible to prepare an inventory forecast by month.

But this forecast must be divided into different product categories: ready-to-wear and accessories, and within accessories, leather goods and other accessories. Within the ready-to-wear category, the inventory should be split between the classics (which are there all the time and can be sold this year as well as next year) and the seasonal products (which have to be sold by the end of the season, either through bargain sales or in factory outlets).

Actual sales results and inventories should be followed up each month for each large product category and even down to the single-model level. Each store must have a scorecard each month against which remaining inventory is compared with budgeted monthly and cumulative sales. If, say, cumulative sales are 30% below forecasts and this trend continued until the end of the year, the scorecard would show the need for a dramatic reduction or a cancellation of orders for future deliveries, or for major changes in the selling approach. This monthly scorecard is absolutely necessary to enable the store to react very early to lower or higher sales than expected. It is even more necessary for fashion brands where seasonal purchases are the name of the game.

Purchasing plan

As mentioned earlier, department stores refer to the purchasing plan as their "open to buy." For perfumes or permanent accessories, these are forecast on a monthly basis, and are based on the sales forecast made on the previous year's sales. So the system is very tough for brands that have lost ground in the preceding 12 to 18 months. Their open-to-buy is arithmetically reduced and there would have to be a very good reason for this rule not to be respected.

The purchasing plan ensures that the store has enough merchandise to meet its sales target, but with a monthly readjustment between the planned sales target and the "most probable" sales level.

In luxury retail, an important driver of the nature of the seasonal merchandise "purchased" for each point of sale is the number of models or stock-keeping units (SKUs) that the internal display system allows. If, as should happen, all models purchased by the store are displayed, then the number of models purchased is directly dependent on the store's internal display set-up. An 80-

luxury **brand** management

square-meter store will not be able to show the full collection that a 400-square-meter store can. Therefore, the number of models purchased will depend on the overall shelf space available at each point of sale. The depth of the purchase will depend on the open-to-buy budget.

Margin control

As mentioned earlier, the theoretical and actual gross margins are not always the same. This is the result of bargain sales (if they have not been carefully forecast and accounted for), special discounts and pilferage.

Special discounts are given by the sales staff to their favorite loyal customers. Brands such as Louis Vuitton or Cartier do not offer discounts at all, but some give loyalty cards to regular customers that entitle them to, say, a 10% discount. In many places, journalists or VIPs get up to 40% discount if they are on the right customer list. Such actions can reduce actual margins significantly, but it is a systematic process that is relatively easy to control.

A number of brands allow sales staff a degree of discretion (within predetermined limits) in offering individual discounts in circumstances when such an offer can make a difference in the customer's thinking or when there is a chance, say, of the customer purchasing a second item. But this must be carefully planned and controlled, on a day-to-day basis if necessary.

Pilferage can happen in the warehouse or in the stores. In department stores, it is believed that the majority of products disappearing from the shelves, from the warehouse or from the counter are stolen by staff. In luxury stores, this is probably less so. But it is necessary to do frequent physical inventories (at least for each season and immediately after the bargain sales) to keep track of what is happening.

The store information system

In most luxury companies, the cash register of every fully owned store, wherever it is in the world, is linked to a global computer system. This gives the company an on-line inventory report that enables it to follow up on the inventory forecast and the products on order in real time. This is necessary to reduce working capital and ensure that all stores are working as efficiently as possible. With this system, for example, it is possible to organize product transfers from different stores in the same town, every day.

It is also possible to view the performance of each store online and to see how close they are to meeting their budget targets. The system enables accurate sales forecasts and streamlines the supply chain, as will be explained in the next chapter.

Staffing, training and evaluation
Staffing
The tendency is to hire people who have worked for the competition and who can bring with them a good reputation and a good customer address book. But it is sometimes better to bring in new talent and to give them company-specific training. This may be the more difficult path, but new staff have no preconceived ideas of how things should be done.

The same is true for store managers. It is good to promote managers from within the sales staff, but several major brands are moving top university graduates into managerial roles to see how they develop in the company.

Training
Obviously, a sales person who is efficient will increase the conversion rate and the average sales ticket. This is a question of attitude, empathy with the client and responsiveness.

In some of our retailing seminars in Paris, we sometimes send executives as mystery shoppers to visit luxury stores and assess the quality of the service. Often, the results are great, but what is very striking is that two different teams sent to the same store —one in the morning, the other in the afternoon—can sometimes come up with completely different impressions. It is likely that they

luxury **brand** management

have not spoken to the same people, but what is clear is that even for top luxury brands there is plenty of room for improvement in the area of customer service.

Sales training is one thing, but product training is something else again. Recently in New York we asked a sales girl in a Coach boutique if a particular handbag was made in China (actually it was indicated inside, on a large label). She answered: "I don't know, but it may be the case because we are looking for top-quality craftsmanship, and I think, today, some Chinese workshops provide the very top quality." This was obviously a rehearsed response, but it was impressive nonetheless.

Product training is generally well done for a brand's main products. Montblanc sales staff are very good on fountain pens, just as Longchamp sales staff are very good on leather goods. But what about a Montblanc watch? Or Longchamp ready-to-wear? The level of staff expertise is not necessarily as broad and complete as might be expected.

The solution is, of course, frequent internal training (on the products) and external training in general sales practice and techniques. But this is not simple when the annual turnover of sales staff is 50% in Europe and is even higher in South East Asia.

Evaluation and motivation

Every brand, particularly those that rely heavily on their own stores or their own department-store counters, looks for the best way to evaluate and to motivate staff. Formal evaluation should take place twice a year.

Incentive systems vary from one brand to another. Brands such as Louis Vuitton do not give commission on sales because they are very concerned about grey-market sales and want to ensure that staff never push for sales. But there are other approaches, including:

- Commission incentives for individual staff or for the staff as a whole, which can come into effect on every sale or start only after a monthly budget target has been met.

- A special bonus given when the monthly target (individual or at store level) is met.
- A mix of the above.

The system chosen will depend on the brand's objectives. An individual incentive requires a system of turn-taking so that each sales person in turn has the first contact with the customer. But this system can lead sales staff to be unpleasant to customers that they perceive as having little sales potential and thus to pick and choose the people they wish to serve. On the other hand, team incentives require a strong team spirit and a strong sales manager.

Retail consumer-response management

Modern information technology systems enable brands to know their consumers well: details such as their names and addresses can be obtained via check or credit card payments, for example. The customer-response management (CRM) system will then build a profile of individual consumers: how often they visit the store; how much they buy during a year; which products they buy; whether they buy mainly at full price or at bargain sales prices. All of this information can be put together to produce different promotional programs. For example, top clients could be invited to special fashion shows or in-store cocktails for the presentation of the new collection. Major clients could receive different catalogs and could be targeted for special events.

A CRM system could be limited to a given store, to a specific country or, more likely, could operate in all countries in which a brand is present. The international system makes all information available to the brand headquarters, which can then give restricted access to staff in specific countries or individual stores for promotional activities, as necessary.

To sum up: retailing has changed very rapidly in the last 10 years and has become more professional. In addition to the aspects covered above, there are other issues—such as visual merchandising

luxury **brand** management

and advertising—that need to be addressed and which can present further challenges.

THE STORE AS A COMMUNICATION TOOL

Because of its expected visibility, a luxury store is always a part of the overall image a brand can create for itself, and this is why store design is a very important part of the retailing process. Brands generally want their stores to use the same concepts and create the same atmosphere so that consumers, wherever they are in the world, feel as if they are in the main store in Paris or Milan.

There is an exception to this rule: Bulgari tried a completely different system and has achieved beautiful, bold, statements through its retail architecture. Each of its stores is different and striking. Its New York Fifth Avenue store has nothing in common with its Tokyo store or its London store.

Most of the other brands work on one concept that they adapt to the different shapes and sizes of their stores and to the respective customer flows. The same architect will be in charge of all the stores to ensure a continuity of look. Architects and designers such as Peter Marino or Anouschka Hempel specialize in this activity, working to give the brands a distinctive style and atmosphere. Even when a brand strives toward having identical stores, this can't always be achieved, as concepts change over time and there may be periods of overlapping styles as a new design comes into play. Brands are careful, though, to ensure that design changes are not so marked as to have an impact on the brand identity, which changes very little over time.

But store design can vary as a function of the brief. Some brands want their stores to be primarily for ladies' ready-to-wear. Other brands want their stores to be for both men and women, which is quite a challenge. Others want the emphasis to be on accessories. Whatever the chosen emphasis, this is usually obvious to consumers as soon as they walk in.

Again, there are exceptions to this general rule. Take the case of Diesel Jeans stores (although this is not really a luxury brand, it's worth mentioning anyway). The company's objective is to present the merchandise in such a confusing way that customers are forced to ask the sales person for assistance. It wants its customers to be disoriented and has created an unfriendly environment so that the customer has no choice but to interact with the sales staff. Only brands with strong customer awareness and a strong identity can force the customer to do it their way.

We said earlier that customers like to touch the products. Louis Vuitton or Hermès stores are almost like exclusive jewelry stores in that their products are presented inside glass counters and generally cannot be touched. To get a closer look at a product, it is necessary to ask the sales staff.

The concept and design of a store is very much a part of the brand identity discussed in Chapter 6, and can be a strong statement that the brand communicates to its environment in general, and to its clients in particular.

This is why the treatment of the space where employees and customers spend time has become the new competitive frontier. The ability to deal creatively with spaces, living 3D environments, requires a talent that does not often exist within a brand's general human resources. There are specific aesthetic and functional aspects to consider—often requiring enormous financial investments—in creating a context that expresses what the brand stands for, while generating the necessary revenues. Bernard Arnault has described architecture as a form of image-making.[4] It was no surprise, then, at the end of the 1990s to see the global luxury brands competing to attract the best architectural talent. This trend is now reaching much smaller brands too.

Landmark projects

Set out below is a summary of some of the most creative and spectacular retail projects realized in the past 10 years. This is a mere glimpse of what has been achieved and is by no means exhaustive.

luxury **brand** management

New York

- In 1999, Christian de Portzamparc, winner of the Pritzker Architecture Prize in 1994, was chosen to create an original symbol of the LVMH group presence in the United States. He created the 23-story LVMH tower on 57th Street, with a very innovative fractal façade and the "magic room": a four-story glass cube at the summit. He later went on to create LVMH's new corporate headquarters on Avenue Montaigne in Paris.
- Rem Koolhaas, the Dutch architect and the winner of the Pritzker in 2000, designed the Prada store on Broadway. Opened in December 2001, the store, costing €32 million, has 2,300 square meters of retail space. Koolhaas was given great freedom by the owners, Miuccia Prada and Patrizio Bertelli, and went on to design Prada stores in Los Angeles and San Francisco.
- John Pawson, the British high priest of minimalism, conceived Calvin Klein's "ice palace" on Madison Avenue.

Tokyo

- Opened in the Ginza shopping district in 2001, Maison Hermès is the brainchild of Renzo Piano. The architect's design is that of a traditional Japanese magic lantern. In daylight, the translucent facade gives a hint of what is beyond, the events and objects blurred by the thickness of the glass blocks. At night, the entire building glows from within. The tall, narrow, elegant building (45m long by 11m wide) is classical yet innovative and stands out like a piece of well-crafted jewelry. In terms of its location, respect for traditions, cosmopolitanism and innovation, it would be difficult to be truer to the Hermès brand identity.
- Following the success of the Koolhaas store in New York, Prada continued its radically innovative retail architecture drive in 2003 with a store in Tokyo's fashionable Aoyama district. The intent behind Swiss duo Jacques Herzog and Pierre de Meuron's design was "to reshape both the concept and function of shopping, pleasure and communication, to encourage the meshing of consumption and culture."

Milan

- Giorgio Armani commissioned Tadao Ando to design a spectacular fashion theater in the former Nestlé building in the canal district. Ando's 3,400-square-meter reinforced-concrete theatre (long pillared corridor and modular movable catwalk with seating for 680 people) leads into a dining area and water courtyard. The building incorporates Armani's showroom and commercial offices.

- For the design of the vast new Armani Casa homeware store on Via Manzoni, Armani chose Michael Gabellini, the minimalist American who rose to fashion fame as the creator of Jil Sander's limestone-floor temples in Milan and on Avenue Montaigne in Paris. Armani said that for his new stores he wants a neutral background, not an architectural statement. "The problem with famous architects is that they become so instantly identifiable," he said. "It is better to work with different architects."

- Peter Marino, the U.S. architect and decorator, rates a particular mention. His name is synonymous with excellence in design and quality in construction and he is internationally admired for his commitment to historical preservation and adaptive reuse of existing buildings in the pursuit of the integration of art, architecture and interior design. He has the most impressive track record of any of the famous architects who have worked for luxury brands. His recent projects include five stores for Chanel from 2001 to 2005; two stores for Fendi in 2005; four stores for Louis Vuitton in 2004 and 2005; three stores for Dior in 2002 and 2003; Armani's New York store in 1999; and Barney's department stores in New York and Beverly Hills.

- Smaller brands are starting to follow the trend, though with more limited investment capabilities. Nonetheless, there have been some recent success stories, including two spectacular projects completed by Future Systems: the bright, modular Marni store on Sloane Street in London, where the clothes become part of the overall composition and design; and Comme des Garçons in Tokyo.

luxury **brand** management

The big luxury brands have chosen to use outside architects and designers because of the reputation and kudos they bring and because they are unlikely to create anything uninteresting. Furthermore, there is a natural dissociation between products and store creativity. The case or jewel box is of a different nature from that of the content. It is not sold. It is shown and it helps show the product. The store is a symbol of power and a permanent link to culture. For fashion moguls, architecture is the new strategic subject. Governments have long been the main sponsors of modern buildings, but it looks as if luxury brand owners may become the new renaissance princes of patronage. They have understood that architects (from serving clients with avant-garde tastes) tend to be one step ahead in aesthetic trends, which then filter down into product design and fashion.

The same logic applies to office and factory design. The factory of Forge de Laguiole, the legendary French knife, was designed by Philippe Starck and its original architecture is attracting busloads of foreigners to the little town of Aubrac.

The communication power of the store

The store's role in communication is unmatched by any other single brand manifestation. This communication power is made possible by several factors.

First of all, the store presents **the product in context**, where different brand manifestations converge to give the most complete brand experience a customer can get. Customers are under the simultaneous influence of the architecture, the product and the sales staff aesthetics. It is also a **multi-sensory experience** where products, music, odors, decoration, light, logo and advertising materials are physically accessible. It is interactive by nature and should be the place where the customer can obtain the maximum of information about the brand and receive luxury service.

Nike Town, Disney stores, Hermès Tokyo and Louis Vuitton Champs Elysées are places of entertainment, able to propose the most complete "physical" experience of the brand, in an overwhelming and multi-sensory manner. The smallest Timberland boutique, with its well-planned and controlled environment (products, apple aroma, temperature, materials, colors, the feel of wood underfoot) can create and convey a feeling of being in a log cabin in the Himalaya.

The "Don Juan" brand example introduced in an earlier chapter showed how the table of brand manifestations can be utilized in communication management. In formalizing its identity and reformulating its competitive strategy, the brand established an overall communication program to frame all the messages it needed to convey and applied it to each brand manifestation to determine what part of the program each could most efficiently promote. In this systematic way, the company was able to orchestrate an overall communication drive where each manifestation had a specific role, while remaining coherent with the rest.

Figure 10.1 shows, in particular, the role of the points of sale in promoting the messages of the communication program. The same exercise could be conducted for each type of manifestation.

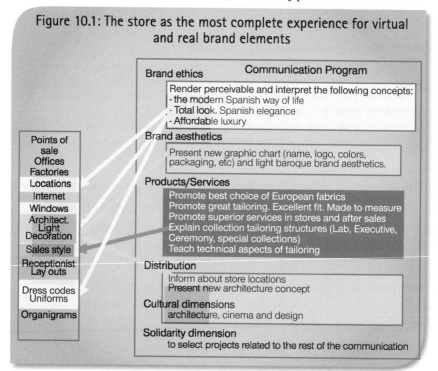

Figure 10.1: The store as the most complete experience for virtual and real brand elements

luxury **brand** management

Personnel communication

It all starts with the doorman at the entrance of the store, the receptionist or the customer-services telephone operator. These very often form the first points of contact a customer has with a brand and first impressions die hard.

One of the major features of the luxury industry that distinguish it from mass-market brands is salesmanship. The way luxury-store sales staff engage with, talk to and deal with potential customers is very particular. They have to adapt to the customer, lending assistance when asked and knowing when to leave the customer alone. The aim is to establish a relationship that goes beyond the pure commercial transaction. Many personal relationships between sales personnel and their clients are born in this way. The sales staff are a very valuable brand asset. In 1999, when Texas Pacific bought Bally and decided to develop a luxury-lifestyle brand strategy, the first thing the CEO did was to cancel the retail policy in which sales staff were measured on their ability to sell a leather jacket to any customer who entered the store.

The uniform and grooming of the sales staff is always important but more so in the luxury industry. The make-up of a L'Oréal sales girl should be as perfect as the shoeshine of a shoe brand salesman or the CEO.

Internal and external display

Traditionally, in each city or each country there is a retailer with a reputation for having the most beautiful window displays. The Christmas windows of Saks Fifth Avenue in New York have enchanted generations of children; Loewe windows in Spain were eagerly awaited in the 1950s and '60s; queues form in front of the Hermès store windows in Faubourg Saint Honoré whenever the display is changed. **This is a hallmark of the luxury industry**. Louis Vuitton has invested heavily in this field, hiring known artists to decorate and prepare complex and spectacular window displays that are genuine artworks. To replicate such displays in 400 stores worldwide requires a huge investment and complex logistical and advertising capabilities.

Windows are part of street advertising and have the same function as a billboard or a poster. In fact, advertising elements like campaign photographs and products are often on display. Internal display, which is usually the responsibility of the window-dressing team, involves rigorous training and strict adherence to the guidelines and rules set out in internal manuals.

Selling online

If the luxury brands have all now developed informative websites of their own, many have been slow to accept the Internet as a distribution channel. The eLuxury website (www.eluxury.com) lists almost 100 brands, including Louis Vuitton, Tiffany, Gucci, Celine, Blumarine, Marc Jacobs and Emanuel Ungaro. But many are not on the list, including the likes of Rolex (which warns readers that its products cannot be bought online) and Harley Davidson. This reluctance was based on a combination of several factors, the main one being that online customer service was perceived as being much inferior to that which generally characterizes the luxury industry. It is difficult to replicate virtually the multi-sensory experience that luxury brands strive to give their customers at the point of sale—touching the material and handling the products. Brands with wholesale distribution networks also felt it necessary to protect their third-party distributors.

Times have changed. More and more multi-brand boutiques offering luxury brands are opening online. It is now possible to buy Hermès online (www.hermes.com) from its own site and even Prada shoes are available on kelkoo.com.

THE RETAIL MODEL VS. THE WHOLESALE MODEL

There is considerable disagreement among luxury executives as to the ideal luxury distribution model. According to some, it should be like Louis Vuitton and Hermès, a network of directly controlled mono-brand stores. Others believe there should be exceptions to this rule.

luxury **brand** management

The "ideal" model

In this model, probably best exemplified by Louis Vuitton and Hermès, the brand sells only in its own stores. In the case of Louis Vuitton, it has no perfumes that require wholesale distribution. Hermès perfumes are sold at wholesale in Europe and some other parts of the world, but in the United States and parts of Asia, they are sold only through Hermès stores.

In every major city of the world, there is at least one Louis Vuitton or Hermès store, and these are the only places where their products are available. The brand positioning is very clear and simple. For the most part, all the stores are fully owned and controlled from headquarters, which enables promotional activities to be coordinated for maximum effectiveness.

Inventory systems are well organized. Classical items are shipped automatically to the stores and store managers can select seasonal or specific items. This system is quite effective. If independent stores want to carry the merchandise, they must buy it through grey-market operators, and in some countries, the brand protection is so strong that they may not be legally authorized to do so. The system works well for powerful brands: there are no license agreements for some products and, apart from shop-in-shops operations in some countries, no department stores to deal with. Within the retail price zones decided by brand management, there are no price differences from one location to another, except those arising from transport costs and customs duties.

The system is simple, very efficient and makes a lot of sense for very powerful brands.

Exceptions to the "ideal" model

The first exception to this model is that a brand that has difficulty breaking even in its flagship store cannot hope to develop through free-standing retail stores. If the flagship stores lose money, this is probably because brand awareness is limited and the brand attractiveness is further reduced. The first priority for a brand in such circumstances must be to deal with its problem of attractiveness and the necessary changes to its product merchandising. This is a time-consuming process and there is no guarantee that it will succeed in recovering lost ground.

Some products require an extended presence. This is certainly the case for perfumes, which must be available almost everywhere. This can also be the case for products that are a complement to ready-to-wear (underwear, for example). The answer is very simple. The brand's own stores should not carry such products, as they run the risk of upsetting their customers if they charge more for the products than their other local distribution channels, which can often sell at a discounted price.

This is also the case for technical products such as glasses. Louis Vuitton wants to sell its glasses solely in its own stores, so confines itself to selling sunglasses. Chanel, on the other hand, also wants to sell optical frames and has signed a licensing agreement with Luxottica, which distributes the Chanel optical frames in many upscale stores in the world. Is this hurting the Chanel brand?

And where do duty-free sales fit into the picture? Even Hermès does not comply entirely with the "ideal" model because its ties appear in some very exclusive duty-free stores. Louis Vuitton also has some shop-in-shops arrangements with DFS Galleria in Asia.

The point here is that the "ideal" model may be great for some, but it is not at all applicable for less-powerful or more middle-range brands. Brands that are contemplating opening a store in, say, Shanghai or Chicago and are not sure of breaking even in their first year of operations should look for another system if they want to grow quickly and develop.

The management of retail and wholesale

In our view, a mixed system—a few exclusive stores; shops-in-shops; and, in some cases, department store corners or counters—is probably best. For a middle-range brand, visibility and accessibility are essential. People will probably drive 20 kilometers to purchase a Hermès gift. They would probably not do the same for a Kenzo scarf or a Guy Laroche wallet, whereas if these products were available in their local department stores, they would buy them.

Of course, brands have to be careful in their selection of the wholesale stores that will sell their scarves or small leather goods and, where legal requirements in the country allow, prices must be carefully monitored.

Cartier provides a good example of a mixed system. It has its own exclusive stores, but also sells watches and a select number of fine jewelry pieces to individual jewelers. This requires a very well-organized product line, to ensure coherence between the two channels. Bulgari decided some 10 years ago to copy Cartier, and has moved from a "pure retail" system to a mixed retail and wholesale system. This accelerated the company's growth when it entered the stock market and, so far, has worked to its advantage.

Where there is coherence between systems, it works to everybody's advantage. The best system is one that takes into consideration the brand's specific strengths and weaknesses in determining what is best for the brand. Exclusive boutiques are great, but department stores or upscale specialty stores can also do a good job for some brands. We will return to the issues of exclusivity, accessibility and visibility in our discussion of licensing in the next chapter.

Endnotes

[1] Michael Levy and Barton A. Weitz, *Retailing Management*, Irwin, 5th edition, 2004, p.234.

[2] Unless stated otherwise, all research findings presented in this chapter are taken from: Paco Underhill, *Why we buy: The art and science of shopping*, New York: Simon and Schuster, 1999.

[3] Three studies on this subject—Dillon, Michel Chevalier and A and P—give figures of 4.20, 4.72 and 4.93, respectively. References for these studies can be found in: Michel Chevalier, "Increase in sales due to in-store display," *Journal of Marketing Research*, November 1975.

[4] Bernard Arnault and Yves Messarovitch, *La passion creative*, Paris: Plon, 2000.

chapter 11

LOGISTICS AND
Licensing

LOGISTICS

More often than not, luxury brands have had a reputation for neglecting the logistics function. Goods are often late at the beginning of the season, it is normally impossible to reorder fashion items, and anyone wanting a Kelly bag from Hermès has to join the waiting list. We will use the word "logistics" in a broad sense, grouping together the movement of the products from the components and materials purchase to the finished products in the stores.

Moving the product

One of the major differences between mass-market and luxury brands is that the former excel in developing and moving their products very rapidly. They are competing in an environment where they need to react quickly to market movements. They have, therefore, developed business models where the logistics function is very advanced. They make early commitments on materials, fabrics and components, well before they have actual orders in their hands; that is, they work on speculation, taking risks on the volume they will sell. Zara, the uncontested leader in this, keeps its fabrics un-dyed until it becomes clear which colors are in demand and then responds accordingly.

On the other hand, the luxury brands, which try to impose their taste on the markets, have concentrated more resources in communication and distribution and tend to make their final commitments on materials, manufacturing only when they receive actual orders from their wholesale clients and their own stores.

Under competitive pressure, things are starting to change. The old luxury system—one shipment at the beginning of the season and the withdrawal of the unsold merchandise after the sales—is obsolete and many companies have abandoned it. Now, the design of the order-processing system depends on retail, wholesale, warehousing and production factors. These include:

At the retail level:
- The store's size and display system; that is, the number of store-keeping units (SKUs) that can be shown at any time. This supposes that the rule in the store is to show all existing SKUs to the customer.
- The size of the store's storeroom.
- The frequency of shipments to the store.
- The frequency with which goods are withdrawn from the stores. (Advances in information systems technology help a lot in this crucial task.)

At the wholesale level:
- Delivery dates and the size of clients' orders.
- Order periodic requests for information (on the status of orders, for example).

At the central and regional warehousing level:

- The size and location of the warehouses.
- The logic of central stocking of permanent items (those that will remain unchanged across seasons).
- The frequency of shipments to retail and wholesale outlets.

At the production level:

- the size and location of warehouses for factory-finished products.
- the frequency of shipment to warehouses.

In 2000, Bally launched its DOT (Delivery On Time) Project to ensure that goods would never arrive late for their own network of stores or for their wholesale customers. Late delivery is a recurrent problem for many luxury brands whose focus is more on managing image and creativity than on logistics. Bally's six-month DOT study incorporated most departments—merchandising, design, manufacturing, shipping, warehousing, information systems, wholesale and retail. It took two-and-a-half years to implement all the changes and consolidate the new procedures, but in 2003, the leather-goods industry recognized Bally's logistics system as the best in the sector.

The introduction of multi-collections during that period have also had numerous positive effects. The stores receive new merchandise at least three times per season, which is a good reason for customers to make several visits. It has had the effect of spreading the production volume over a longer period, flattening the peaks and filling low-activity periods, and has reduced the average stock levels in the stores.

Performance measurement: Time-to-market

The development time necessary to transform a concept into a product available in the retail network is called time-to-market. It has become a key competitive element in all industries, at a time when the product lifecycle is shortening. It may range from a few years in the automotive industry, to a few months for luxury clothes, accessories and fragrances, to a few weeks for mass-market fashion.

It is a major performance indicator and can be broken down into all the intermediary constituent processes: design; preparing the prototype; testing; initial production series; actual production; and shipping to stores.

The usual time-to-market for luxury goods can be anything up to 10 months because of the brands' unwillingness to gamble on manufacturing products for which no definite orders have been received. This is bound to change in the future. Traditionally, luxury fashion brands have struggled to deliver fresh supplies of seasonal goods that have sold out. They can now restock some items within four weeks and some have even initiated "design-in-season" programs. After a new collection has been in the stores for four weeks and it is clear what the best-sellers are, the brands produce and deliver more of these models within a period of four to six weeks. This necessitates a very specific program on materials and factory production space. The logistics model of the mass-market brands will eventually make its way into the upper part of the market.

Outsourcing

There are two strategic considerations linked to the manufacturing function: whether to maintain direct control and whether to keep a "made in ..." label coherent with the brand identity.

Maintaining direct control

The merchandising/design/prototyping functions are generally the basis around which luxury brands build their competitive advantage. For a considerable number of brands, particularly at the higher end of the market, direct control over manufacturing is a key element of their brand identity and thus has to be kept within the company's operations.

The Hermès brand identity is strongly anchored to handicraft skills and it has always striven to preserve and develop exceptional craftsmanship. All of its production sites are in France and its legendary Kelly and Birkin handbags are still produced in its Pantin factory near Paris. The brands that Hermès has acquired over the past 20 years have all been characterized by specific luxury manufacturing know-how. These include the hat-maker Motsch; the shoemaker John Lobb; the goldsmith Puigforcat; the crystal manufacturer Saint Louis; and the glove-maker Saint Junien. These brands have not become global, but they hold their ground and maintain a professional know-how that may well have disappeared had they not become part of the Hermès Group. The company's commitment to genuine, high-quality craftsmanship has led it to incorporate pleating made in Morocco and jewels from North Africa into its products. Here the "made in wherever it is made best" mentality prevails over the "made in France."

Chanel, too, has focused on maintaining direct control of manufacturing. In the past 10 years, it has acquired several of its small, specialist providers—the lacemaker Lessage; the accessories-maker Lemarié; the hat-maker Michel; the shoemaker Massaro—to ensure perennity.

Louis Vuitton, which owns seven leather-goods factories in France, has always insisted on keeping full direct control of production. When it decided to develop a shoe business in the late 1990s, it acquired an Italian factory. The products it has manufactured in Spain and California are also made in group factories.

The same logic applies in the luxury motor industry. Ferrari may sub-contract its design work to brands such as Pininfarina from time to time, but the engineering (the really creative part) and final assembly are kept inside the company. The same approach has been adopted by Ducati.

In 2006, Ferruccio Ferragamo declared that all Ferragamo products would continue to be manufactured in Italy—a decision with far-reaching consequences! The Ferragamo industrial model is a smart variation on the above. In the 1970s, it was decided that all the manufacturing (apart from a reduced fabrication line for small series and prototyping) should be outsourced. The purpose of this was to reduce the investment in production facilities and machinery and to simplify management by eliminating the need to deal directly with the trade unions. The company set up a series of third-party owned factories to manufacture its shoes exclusively. Ferragamo specified the manufacturing process and supplied the leather and components.

This example shows that **the key to successful outsourcing is to retain manufacturing know-how within the company,** choosing and controlling the suppliers. This is what we could call the "luxury" solution.

This is an ideal situation, but it applies only to products for which there is existing expertise, or when a brand decides, like Chanel and Louis Vuitton, to acquire production facilities of strategic importance to their development.

In 1999, Bally restructured all its processes. On the industrial side, it had to choose between a Hermès-type solution, keeping all manufacturing inside the company; the Gucci model, subcontracting 100% of its needs; or an intermediary position between the two. The decision was to keep only one factory, located at the company's new worldwide headquarters, with a production capacity of 200,000 pairs of shoes per year (10% of the volume needed). There were several reasons for this:

- to keep the production of the models that required particular expertise
- to retain the flexibility required for producing small special series (special collections, models needing quicker time-to-market, test series, etc.)
- to maintain the close links between modeling and production
- to retain the industrial know-how (manufacturing and materials)
- to maintain control over suppliers and subcontractors
- to provide technical knowledge to other company functions (commercial, design, etc.)
- to ensure that the company did not lose money (200,000 pairs per year being the breakeven benchmark).

 luxury **brand** management

By 2007, the factory had more than doubled its internal production.

Deciding not to produce directly

Most of the brands whose identity is based on a style or brand ethics not related, directly or indirectly, to the mastery of particular manufacturing skills have never had their own production facilities. They have had no choice but to subcontract production. As we saw in Chapter 4, this also applies in the case of brand extension into new products that are not the natural domain of the traditional business. When Ferrari decided to develop into different market segments—selling T-shirts, miniature replica cars and videogames to motor racing fans—it had recourse to licensing.

The decision to outsource a production function previously held within the company is based on pure economic and flexibility considerations: to reduce fixed costs inherent in the production infrastructure; to benefit from lower unit costs; and to have the flexibility to choose from several suppliers.

The process of outsourcing is fairly standard. In the leather industry, for example, it may start with the decision to buy cutting tools from, say, China. In the shoe industry, the first part of the actual production process to be outsourced is the stitching of the upper shoe. From there, it is an easy step for some basic models to be outsourced entirely. The obvious risk in this, of course, is the possibility that basic industrial know-how will be lost, forcing the brand to rely on its suppliers for new product development, quality, feasibility, price and so on.

Then comes the "made in etc..." question.

Made in China

Philatelists will remember the beautiful series of stamps paying tribute to the French *haute couture*, silk and fragrance industries in the 1950s. At that time, "luxury goods" meant "Made in France."

Those days are gone. Mauboussin, place Vendôme jeweler since 1827 and one of the temples of French luxury, recently acknowledged that some of its products are made in China. Mauboussin is not alone in this. There are powerful economic reasons driving this uncontainable process. It is happening not only because the "luxury" label has taken a much less selective meaning, but also because North African, Eastern European and Asian countries are now able to offer unbeatable cost/quality ratios and have established themselves as the biggest manufacturers of luxury goods.

Since the end of the 1990s, Louis Vuitton and Dior handbags and small leather goods have been manufactured in the Loewe factories in Spain. Hogan, Bruno Magli and Gucci shoes are today manufactured in Eastern Europe; Prada, Bally, Clergerie and Kelian shoes are stitched in Eastern Europe, the Maghreb or India; certain Armani clothes are assembled in Eastern Europe; in men's ready-to-wear, Valentino is partly sewn in Egypt, and Hugo Boss in Turkey; Lancel and Longchamp small leather goods are made in North Africa, etc. The list is long.

If "delocalization" it is no longer a taboo among the brands, it remains one with the luxury customer. Knowing this, the brands try to maintain the legitimacy of the "Made in France" or "Made in Italy" label by completing the final assembly of the products themselves, even if most parts are manufactured abroad. U.S. brands may be less sensitive in this regard. For the past 10 years, Coach has been manufacturing its leather goods entirely in China, India and the Dominican Republic and its business has been thriving in Japan.

Prada's president, Patrizio Bertelli, has suggested that a label "Made in Prada" would be more meaningful than anything related to geographical area. He rightly argues that it is better to have a higher-quality product made abroad with all the necessary inspections on materials and manufacture, than a poorer-quality product made at home. The Hong Kong brand Shanghai Tang used to put "Made by Chinese" labels in its clothes.

The trend toward relocating manufacturing to China and other Asian countries is going to continue unabated for a while, making a logistics office in Hong Kong or Shanghai an absolute necessity for most luxury brands.

Anticipating a time when low costs would no longer be sufficient, China has improved the quality of its manufacturing dramatically in the past few years. It has also developed global sourcing knowledge, such that it can supply luxury shoe brands with information on where to locate the best components and where best to have specific parts of the process completed.

The learning curve logic is implacable: the more the Chinese produce, the better they are at it; the less the Europeans produce, the weaker their skills become until luxury Chinese brands start selling everywhere in the world, as their silk and chinaware did between the sixteenth and eighteenth centuries.

LICENSING

While nobody cares to mention the fact, these days licensing is the name of the game in the luxury industry. Almost everybody in this industry deals with licenses and license contracts. There are exceptions of course: Louis Vuitton, Hermès and smaller brands like Robert Clergerie. (Cartier might be included on this list of exceptions, but its cigarettes are manufactured by a sister company in the Richemont Group.) For many years, Chanel had no licensing arrangements but today, it has a licensing contract with Luxottica in Italy to develop optical frames.

By "licensing" we mean the subcontracting of manufacturing and distribution of a branded product. When a luxury company subcontracts just parts of its production, we refer to this as "manufacturing subcontracting." When a company farms out its distribution in a given territory, we call it an "exclusive distribution" contract or a "franchising" agreement. In this section we confine ourselves to circumstances in which a firm farms out both production and distribution to one licensee, who therefore has complete control over product development and of all marketing and commercial activities, including advertising, promotion and public relations.

This licensing activity is sometimes a major source of income for a brand. In the case of Courrèges or Balmain, for example, license royalties account for more than 50% of all revenues. If they were to cancel all licensing deals, they would be forced to close down.

In fact, licensing agreements are the best way for a brand to develop activities in product categories that are outside its core competences. This is certainly true for optical frames, which need a specific industrial expertise, specialist optical outlets and professional sales teams. This is also the case for perfumes that are sold in specialist stores around the world and require specialists in the manufacture of fragrances.

The licensing process
Selecting a licensee
In selecting a licensee, a brand needs someone who can develop a new product and distribute it everywhere in the world. Because the licensee is, in fact, investing its own money in such a venture, it must have sufficient financial resources to do so.

Product development can be quite expensive. A complete set of glass and plastic molds to create a full line of perfumes, together with its alcoholic line (perfume extracts and eau de toilette– fragrances diluted in alcohol) and its bath line (soap, talc, powder, liquid soap, body creams and so on) can cost up to €1 million. This amount must be spent upfront, before any sale can materialize. Similar figures are also necessary for the development of a new line of watches before the first product reaches the stores. And this is just the tip of the iceberg.

Most of the investment to launch a perfume, a watch or a new line of optical frames is a commercial one. Given that the original advertising and promotional investment can be huge and initial success is by no means guaranteed, the brand has to consider whether a potential licensee has the financial wherewithal to absorb any losses and invest in a second project. It goes without saying, of

luxury **brand** management

course, that the licensee will have access to the best raw materials and have its own production facilities capable of producing goods that meet all the requirements of quality and brand identity.

Product development under license

Developing a product to the required standard may take 12 to 18 months. Distributing that product around the world may take a further 18 months. This obviously requires a long-term commitment from both parties. For products such as perfumes, contracts are sometimes effected for periods of 20–25 years. For watches, nothing can be achieved in less than seven to 10 years. So a licensing contract is almost always a long-term commitment for the licensee and a major long-term risk for the licensor.

What are the rewards? As a rule of thumb, a licensee pays royalties amounting to a standard 10% on the wholesale volume sold. There are exceptions: perfumes can be very large businesses and royalties are generally between 3–5% of wholesale and export volume. Products that are difficult to develop and to sell—men's and women's ready-to-wear, for example—can command royalties of 6–8%. On the other hand, products that are quite far removed from the licensor's usual universe or do not add much to the brand's overall image can sometimes justify licensing contracts with royalties of up to 12%. In addition, the brands may impose minimum sales (or at least minimum royalties) and minimum communication budgets per year.

It is important to differentiate the investment categories (perfumes, watches, optical frames or ready-to-wear, for example)— activities that should improve the status of the brand—from the consumption categories (belts, underwear or handkerchiefs, for example), which consume the brand image without bringing much additional value to it. A good license portfolio should have a balance of "investment" and "consumption" activities.

A perfume license deal has another peculiarity: the perfume market is quite large and this product category works on an advertising-to-sales ratio that can go as high as 15%, where that of the ready-to-wear business works generally on a 2–4% ratio. It is therefore quite common for investments in perfume advertising to be several times higher than for fashion. This strong advertising presence in the perfume category can increase brand awareness and help develop a fashion brand. A case in point is Calvin Klein: when Minetonka (since purchased by Unilever) started the perfume license, the fashion brand was almost unknown in Europe. It is the perfume advertising investment that conveyed the message of the brand and helped it in its ready-to-wear activities.

Japan is the number-one source of license income (excluding perfumes and watches). Generally, brands sign a master license agreement with a specialist that, in turn, signs sub-license agreements with different local companies. Table 11.1 shows

Table 11.1: Ready-to-wear licenses in Japan, 2005

Brand	Licensee	Retail value (€ million)
Burberry	Sanyo-shokai	435
Ralph Lauren	Impact-21	240
Daks	Sankyo-Seiko (ladies')	
	Kashiyama (men's)	190
Paul Smith	Joix Corporatic (men's)	235
	Kashiyama (ladies')	
Michel Klein	Itokin	70
Leonard	Sankyo-Seiko	75
Elle	Itokin	70
Marc by Marc Jacobs	Look	50
Courrèges	Itokin	50
Aquascutum	Renown	50
Lanvin	Joix Corporatic	50
Austin Reed	Kosugi-Sangyo	50
Sonia Rykiel	Kashiyama	45
Mila Schön	Ronna	30
CK Calvin Klein	Kashiyama	20
Castelbajac	Raika	20

Source: Yano Keizai Research

luxury **brand** management

the retail value of the licensed ladies' and men's ready-to-wear categories in Japan. This does not include accessories, but the amounts are still staggering. The retail value is generally double that of the wholesale value and royalties are in the region of 10% of the wholesale. When accessories are added, it is clear that income from royalties can be substantial. In fact, it is estimated that the ready-to-wear categories account for only 10% of the total royalties from textiles, ready-to-wear and accessories. When perfumes and cosmetics are factored in, the rewards the brands reap from licensing arrangements are enormous.

The control of licensees

A licensee will sometimes have a relatively short-term view of the brand: it wants its investment to be profitable. When the licensee is obliged to pay, say, 10% royalties on sales, it may be tempted to understate its sales figures. Licensees sometimes consider, on their own initiative, that income from bargain sales or from factory outlets should not be subject to royalties. It is for this reason that license contracts generally stipulate a minimum royalty level that must be paid irrespective of actual sales. In our experience, for most contracts this is the only amount that will ever be paid.

Sometimes licensors find ways to control the volume manufactured under their brand: they may decide that they will control the printing of all labels bearing their name and the quantity of such labels issued to a licensee will be restricted to the licensee's specific volume needs. The licensor may also include in the label a water mark or other such device that makes it difficult to reproduce, in much the same way as central banks do with the notes they issue.

But control is not confined to financial matters. Licensors must control the style and the quality of the final product, including the quality of the packaging and all aspects of the product environment— from presentation of the goods to warranty arrangements to after-sales service.

Many top brands provide a complete design and sometimes a real prototype of the product to be manufactured and distributed under license. Less-sophisticated brands sometimes leave their licensees to develop the product as well as they can on their own. When this happens, of course, the licensor has no real control over what goes on afterwards.

It is extremely important that brands understand just how important it is for the licensee to respect and enhance the licensor's brand identity. In the mid-1990s, for example, Ferragamo contracted a German company to develop its first fragrance under a license agreement. The contract had taken time to negotiate as the brand was quite rigorous in respect of its identity. Despite numerous attempts by the licensee's creative teams, they were never able to come up with a concept, bottle and name that the Ferragamo family found coherent with the brand identity. After several years of effort, both parties agreed to cancel the contract and Ferragamo made a joint venture with Bulgari to develop its fragrance business.

When they provide the prototypes, licensors can control the product environment and insist on quality control of the final item. They must also control the product distribution. They sometimes specifically determine the distribution channels, if not the actual points of sale. They can also define prices and tariffs with the licensees.

That licensors and licensees can work together to develop different products under the same brand is underscored by the success of the German brand Joop, which has almost all of its activities under license and is doing extremely well.

Different phases of licensing activities

Any criticism of the licensing concept seems to center around the experience of Pierre Cardin. Cardin develops very few products and seems to specialize in lower middle-range license deals for suitcases or medium-quality kitchenwares. But, as we saw with the example of Joop above and in Chapter 5, there are other ways to develop products under license.

To clarify the issue and to ascertain the real value of licensing activities, it is necessary to consider this activity over the lifecycle of a luxury brand.

Phase 1

As it gets started, a brand needs visibility. As it first sells its product, it must build awareness and its identity among a large group of consumers. Licensing deals are an effective way for a brand to increase its activities and general exposure.

At this very early stage, potential licensees will be reluctant to take on a brand that lacks sufficient awareness to help in the launch of a new product category. But if a ladies' ready-to-wear brand can sign a license contract for men's suits, this is certainly a good opportunity, provided that the brand identity can legitimize the new product category and that the product is of very good quality. It would also be an opportunity to establish major license deals for watches, costume jewelry or optical frames.

For European brands at this early stage, license deals in a specific territory can help the brand's development at home and increase its visibility abroad. Asia, and particularly Japan, has been an El Dorado for brands looking to raise their visibility or simply looking for cash. Japanese companies are very interested in licensing activities and have developed very specific and successful product categories (ladies' handkerchiefs with printed versions of larger scarves, for example) for their home markets.

In Japan, luxury brands often use a "master licensee" who, in turn, signs sub-license contracts with many manufacturers. It is possible to have a large number of license operations in Japan, including a bridge line (a new, less-expensive line) of ladies' ready-to-wear and a full collection of accessories that can add to the brand's presence in the country. These contracts are generally limited to the Japanese territory.

In some cases, activities licensed in Japan do not exist in Europe. In the 1980s and '90s, for example, Lancel had a full collection of ladies' and men's ready-to-wear and accessories. Rochas, Paco Rabanne and Revillon, too, had a full range of licenses for products that then did not exist in Paris. This is a very profitable activity, but it makes sense only if the royalties are used to develop a real brand presence in Europe, with free-standing stores and ladies' ready-to-wear fashion shows.

In the past decade, though, such arrangements have become a little more difficult to sustain, as people travel more and expect to find in Paris or Milan products that are similar to those they have seen in Japan. So, little by little, these license businesses have become less active, although they still constitute a major source of income for many brands.

As interest in master licenses has waned a little in Japan, China has stepped in to take up the slack.

Phase 2

When a brand develops and becomes more successful at home, it is time to launch another phase of licensing activity.

When the awareness of the brand makes it possible, worldwide license deals for such things as perfumes and cosmetics, watches, writing instruments and costume jewelry become imperative.

It is through developing such licenses that the brand will increase its presence and its awareness. As mentioned earlier, advertising budgets for perfume are much larger than those for fashion, and having a perfume bearing its name gives a brand greater credibility. Lolita Lempicka is probably better known for its perfume license than for its fashion, and Guy Laroche is better known for L'Oréal perfumes than for fashion.

The selection of a perfume licensee is a very important part of the development of a brand. When Louis Féraud signed a perfume license contract with Avon cosmetics for the United States, it made a big mistake. The perfume would be sold mainly from door to door and therefore would not get strong advertising support in major magazines. The fact that Avon was stronger in the United States than in Europe also made it difficult for the brand, which had its origins in Paris. Féraud would probably have done much better if it had entered into a licensing deal with L'Oréal or with Cosmopolitan cosmetics.

Phase 2 is the perfect time to develop a brand through licensing. Aside from these major worldwide licensing arrangements, it might also be possible to sign specific agreements in Latin America, where licenses can be developed. This is also the case in Korea and, to a lesser extent, Thailand. However, in developing these secondary markets, it is important to ensure that any local deals do not conflict with the terms of existing worldwide licenses.

Through developing perfume deals in this second phase, a brand can establish a worldwide presence and develop additional business. If Azzedine Alaïa had developed a successful perfume license, his fashion business would be much stronger today and better known by a wider range of consumers. An Azzedine Alaïa perfume brand would be sold in duty-free stores everywhere in the world, thus raising overall brand awareness. An Azzedine Alaïa luxury watch range would have reinforced the creative talent of this exceptional designer and transformed his image into a fully fledged luxury group identity.

It is when a brand starts to become well known that the launch of a perfume license makes most sense and can work as an amplifier and an accelerator for the brand. But this should not happen too early. When Christian Lacroix launched his first perfume, *C'est la vie*, in 1990, it was only two years after he created his fashion house. His name was very well known in Paris and New York, but much less so in Düsseldorf, Manchester or Geneva where his perfume had to be sold and purchased. The timing of this acceleration is critical to a brand's development. Christian Lacroix is still affected by that failure in 1990. If it had waited another five years, who knows?

Phase 3

As a brand develops through different phases, the next step is to open free-standing stores in the major cities of the world. But this objective can sometimes be in direct conflict with the development of licenses that have, by definition, a much larger distribution network. If a brand already has licenses selling underwear, belts, scarves and leather goods in department stores and in multi-brand stores, it will have difficulty selling the same products in its own boutiques, especially when department stores may be selling those same products at a discount. This type of uncoordinated distribution could send confusing and damaging signals to consumers.

Confusion would arise, too, if the brand had specialist boutiques that sold only, say, its ready-to-wear collections and left the accessories to a larger network of stores. And brand boutiques offering only a limited selection of products would have difficulty breaking even.

Phase 3 therefore represents a major change in policy direction. Brand managers must reduce the number of licenses so that individual stores can be opened and developed. But brands should not rush into this. It does not make sense to negotiate the immediate cancellation of exiting licenses at great cost (as YSL found out when it was purchased by PPR Gucci). The move away from a strong license business to a strong boutique structure is not always easy, but it can be done, as the experience of Christian Dior shows.

Christian Dior was a very strong license brand in Japan until 2002. Dior management had probably been preparing for the shift years in advance. It opened free-standing stores, which could then not be profitable because of competition from its own licensed activities in major department stores. But when the "master contract" of the licensee, Kanebo, expired, it was not renewed and the brand was able to introduce, very successfully, the direct import of its ready-to-wear and accessories. But the groundwork for raising awareness of the Dior brand had been done over many years through the licensing arrangement with Kanebo.

Timing is of the essence: too early and the brand lacks the necessary awareness; too late and it has already lost momentum.

Phase 4

When a brand has its own stores in major cities in the world, this does not mean it should stop all license activities. If it has a strong perfume activity under license, it should go on as usual and this would be an additional resource. If it has licensing agreements for

luxury **brand** management

ties and optical frames, and its boutique stores cater primarily for women, again there is no reason not to go on with these license activities for men.

We mentioned earlier that even Chanel has a license contract. But Valentino and Moschino also have license contracts. Moschino's handbags and leather goods are made by an Italian licensee, Borbonese. This is the new balance that must be developed in Phase 4.

So licensing, at every stage of brand development, is necessary and is part of the global financial and identity balance. Those who speak against licenses have failed to understand that in this activity timing is almost everything: what is useful or even necessary at a given period may be useless at a later time. The subject is very important and requires sensitivity and a good sense of timing and execution.

For every step in the development of a luxury brand there are different types of licensing activity that are all capable of generating profits and brand awareness and of reinforcing brand identity.

The next chapter will give us a methodology to ensure that brand identity remains at the heart of most decision-making processes.

luxury **brand** management

chapter 12

THE
Brand
AUDIT

Having described the characteristics of the luxury business and reviewed the particularities of the various functional areas of the management of luxury brands, we can now assemble all these considerations into a coherent methodology, one that can increase the probability of success and that can be applied to any brand in any business sector.

Although a "universal formula" has yet to be constructed, in this chapter we present the broad outlines of a method whose aim it is to ferret out examples of faulty brand management that can prevent a luxury brand from achieving success. This method is drawn from our individual and combined experience of having to verify—often under pressure—the expressed and potential strengths of various brands.

The pragmatic aspect of this approach must be underlined: its concrete, practical usefulness counts for more than its theoretical value when it comes to getting results. Our point of view remains that of practitioners, not theoreticians. In any case, there is no miracle method. As we have had occasion to say elsewhere, formalization makes for a clearer picture and a more rational approach to the factors at stake. It is a major advantage for a manager. But it is no substitute for creativity, both individual and collective, which is, in the final analysis, the real foundation of any brand's strength.

Our basic idea is that any specific methodology must focus on the coherence, effectiveness and relevance of the communication of the brand's identity. To structure our approach, we will begin with the chain of communication.

THE CHAIN OF COMMUNICATION

The aim of this simplified representation is to show the path the brand's message takes, from its source (its identity) to its logical culmination (the act of purchase). The principle is simple: the brand expresses its identity through varied manifestations—its products, its communication and the behavior of the people, both inside and outside the company, who work in the company's name. These manifestations are perceived variously by the different market segments, and the perceptions created in consumers result in acts of purchase that together make up the sales volume.

Figure 12.1 comprises four states and three transitions between them. Throughout the process, numerous and complex phenomena take place. (This is a simplified version of Figure 8.1 presented in the chapter on communication.)

For the brand manager, each transition calls for controls that can only be enacted after the fact, once the transition has been made.

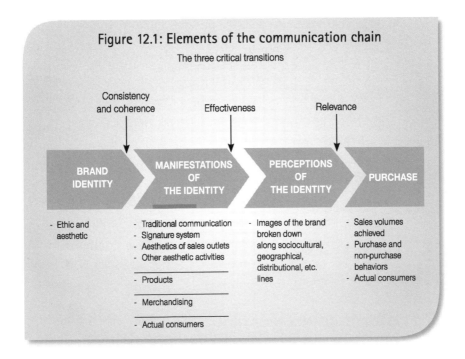

Figure 12.1: Elements of the communication chain

The three critical transitions

Consistency and coherence

Effectiveness

Relevance

BRAND IDENTITY → MANIFESTATIONS OF THE IDENTITY → PERCEPTIONS OF THE IDENTITY → PURCHASE

- Ethic and aesthetic

- Traditional communication
- Signature system
- Aesthetics of sales outlets
- Other aesthetic activities

- Products

- Merchandising

- Actual consumers

- Images of the brand broken down along sociocultural, geographical, distributional, etc. lines

- Sales volumes achieved
- Purchase and non-purchase behaviors
- Actual consumers

The brand's identity

We have already defined brand identity in Chapter 6. Any company that has made a serious study of its brand identity will have built up a whole series of documents examining this to varying degrees and depths. These documents are not limited to a simple description of the brand's ethical and aesthetic invariants, such as can be obtained using the tools we outlined earlier—the hinge, the semiotic square or the narrative schema. These are mere points of departure for collective reflection. Generally, the project of defining an identity involves the principal directors, and then moves on to a broad-ranging internal discussion. All the results are then added to, and enrich, the basic data.

For example, Figure 12.2 is a document Taurus used to disseminate its brand identity internally. Beyond the content specific to the brand, note the format used here. The most technical and semiological concepts have been converted into simple, concrete recommendations. The result is a document that is much

Figure 12.2: Taurus: Brand identity

What it is/what it isn't

A brand with a history...not a traditional brand

A luxury house...not a fashion brand

A luminous, classical aesthetic...not baroque and somber

A brand rooted in its country of origin...not folkloric

A marque associated with refinement...not meaningless sophistication

Rare products...but not inaccessible and outrageously expensive

more accessible, one that can be distributed broadly, throughout the company, because it's important that everyone agrees on the final assessment. This dimension of internal agreement is an essential condition for the emergence of a brand identity.

The manifestations of the identity

The ethics and aesthetics of the brand's identity form the framework within which all the creators and communicators working on the brand—whether dedicated to products, advertising or any other aspect—must create, innovate, invent and develop. It is on this framework, therefore, that the manifestations of the brand's identity will be based.

We have seen how the brand identity affects all aspects of a company's strategy to varying degrees. The manifestations of brand identity can be split into four distinct categories.

The general aesthetic

This covers the activities that would normally be under the direct control of the person in charge of the brand's identity and include:

- Traditional communication: advertising, press relations, organization of events.
- The signature system (the brand's graphical identity): logo, store signs, product labeling and packaging, letterheads, and so on.
- The aesthetic activities related to points of sale: the architectural concept of the stores and showrooms, window displays, interior displays, staff uniforms, methods and style of sale.
- Other aesthetic activities: architecture of the offices, the tone and style of all public contact (receptionists, hostesses, managers, directors, the president's sartorial style, and so on).

When IBM CEO Lou Gerstner arrived at the company, his decision to wear sky-blue shirts was a real revolution in a company where the norm had long been white shirts. This minimal change had a major impact on the perception of the brand by all the players in the market and, above all, by the employees.

When Diego della Valle, president and founder of the Tod's brand, wears his button-down shirt unbuttoned, he promotes the easy elegance typical of the postwar Italian lifestyle that is intrinsic to the Tod's brand ethic.

For all these manifestations of an aesthetic nature (in the broad sense of the term), there should be "briefs" prepared by the person in charge of managing brand identity, which makes their management easier. These documents are written for the creative people, in their own language. Tables 12.1 and 12.2 provide a few examples taken from the Taurus case, which stemmed directly from the work done on defining the identity.

Table 12.1: Taurus: Advertising brief

1. Illustrate a lifestyle.

2. Suggest the characteristics of that lifestyle by stressing individual values:
   - freedom, autonomy, personal projects (but not rebellion, anticonformism, adolescence)
   - breaking with the daily routine, intense emotions
   - generosity, frankness
   - refinement, assumed sensuality
   - combining values of energy and refinement, urban life and the outdoors.

3. Snapshots or visuals that suggest movement and dynamism in a classical context. Invent a neoclassicism that comprises modernity, innovation, and surprise, without losing sight of the best of tradition.

4. Bring out the link between technological innovation and refinement in the product.

5. Suggest the richness and coherence of the brand universe without giving the impression of a "panoply of signs" or a label brand.

Table 12.2: Taurus: Store architecture brief

1. Place less importance on the store and more on the product offering. Use verticality, the expression of energy and vitality.

2. As for the products, take particular care with combinations of materials to suggest refinement, a taste for the rare and the beautiful. Use of glass, wood, and steel.

3. Define traffic patterns and store fittings that encourage handling and touching the products.

4. Design furnishings that transmit identity:
   - lamp
   - armchair, table
   - lectern for presentation of historic products
   - framing for documents related to the history of the brands (old advertisements, posters, photos with celebrations, etc.).

5. Stress light and transparence. No closed display windows. The store interior has to be visible from the street.

luxury **brand** management

Products

This category concerns all the aesthetic and tangible aspects of the products: colors, materials, shapes, cut, style, quality, durability, performance and so on. The product remains the most important medium for communicating the brand's identity. It's clear that style, applied to products, is an essential component of identity. And everyone knows that the worst thing that can happen to a brand is for it to disappoint its customers with the quality or performance of its product: the perception of the brand's identity is immediately affected.

This means that both expectations and their implementation must be managed. For example, Volvo products must clearly express the brand's fundamental value: safety; Hermès products, the ultimate in quality and refinement; Audi, a combination of design and performance.

Product design, development and production are also dealt with in initial briefs. Table 12.3 provides another example from Taurus. Again, note the positioning of this type of document: vague

---

Table 12.3: Taurus: Brief for product development

1. Assertion of luxury status: work more on design than on fashion effect. Focus on accessories and gift items.

2. Design details that identify products (buckles, buttons, stitching, chains).

3. Extend the logo through a whole series of products. Invent a "logomania" fabric.

4. Define several chromatic ranges inspired by nature in light shades for application to scarves and necklaces.

5. Extend iconic products into ranges of colors, materials and a "logomania" fabric.

6. Redefine standards of quality for gilding to improve the quality. Make customers aware of the finish.

7. Seek to innovate with leather in general, stressing tactile qualities (suppleness, softness, etc) and visual ones (pleats, waves, etc.) and creating new associations of materials.

8. Evoke active, even athletic, lifestyles.

9. Intensify efforts to find new materials to promote a more modern image.

generalities (such as "elegance" or "conviviality") are eliminated, but the concrete recommendations do not go so far as to hamper the work of the designers. For example, no particular color or shape is imposed. An accurate perception of the brand's invariants allows a strict framework to be drawn, within which the designer's creativity is free to express itself.

Such creative briefs endure beyond seasonal changes. They don't replace the more detailed documents—drawn up in collaboration with the designers—that affect development for each season.

Merchandising

This category essentially defines the structure of the product offering, prices, the stocking policy and the inventory of the sales outlets. The fundamental decision is to define what product the brand will offer, where, to which customers, at what price and at what time. This is a question of basic strategy and of merchandising in its literal sense (what the "merchants" decide).

These decisions are of paramount importance for the brand's positioning, and therefore for the way in which its identity will be perceived. Mercedes-Benz's decision to develop the Class A and the Smart Car or Porsche's decision to enter the 4X4 segment have had a considerable impact on their identity. Presenting three groups of four handbags does not project the same brand identity as presenting 12 groups of three.

The consumer

This is the only category of manifestations that is not under direct management control, but it is by no means the least important. The people seen wearing or using the brand's products—and this extends to all the people who are talking about the brand—are part of the processes that build market perceptions of the brand.

In any strategy worthy of the name, an attempt is made to define the ideal consumers to whom the brand aims to sell its products— not only because creation, communication and distribution are entirely oriented toward these target customers, but also because

luxury **brand** management

the products being worn, driven or used by a certain type of person contributes strongly to the perception of the brand's identity. As we saw in Chapter 8, Lacoste experienced the way this works when its shirts and sweat-suits suddenly became wildly popular among inner-city youth. Bentley and Krug experienced similar problems when their respective products were embraced by hip-hop stars. The question is whether the emergence of these "unplanned" consumers will have a detrimental impact on the perception of the brand among its core consumers.

This reality remains valid even if the "mood marketing" we mentioned earlier is used. If the market is segmented by mood, it is important to know what moods are being aimed at. The target consumer can be seen as a "potential manifestation of the brand" until its real manifestation—the actual customer—is revealed via the audits and regular controls all companies conduct.

The consistency and coherence transition

This transition aligns with the first critical point at which the brand's success is at stake. Any activity that influences the perception of the brand's identity—any manifestation of the brand—must contribute to strengthening that identity, and must therefore be consistent with it. If this first condition is fulfilled, all these manifestations should be consistent with each other. Nevertheless, the transition from being a brand identity described purely in terms of its specific ethics and aesthetics to one whose manifestations are visible and tangible represents such a creative leap, and the activities involved are so diverse, that it becomes vital to ensure consistency.

High-quality champagnes such as Dom Pérignon or Krug are not distributed in supermarkets and hypermarkets, even though these distribution channels sell the highest volume of this type of product. They are found only in specialist stores—wine stores and gourmet groceries. Customers who buy these products would be shocked to find them on the shelves at Wal-Mart. This example illustrates the necessary consistency between price, quality and positioning of the product and its sales outlets.

At this stage, before the necessary studies on actual customers have been conducted, the target customer (as the potential manifestation of identity) is used to verify the consistency of this profile with the rest of the manifestations. It is also important to make sure that all the components of the strategy are compatible and in phase with the brand's identity. It would make no sense to take Hermès as a competitor of reference if you produce your leather bags in Asia or distribute them in supermarkets. Or so you might think, but such was the fate that awaited Louis Vuitton and Hermès in Japan, in spite of their efforts. In 2001 the French Carrefour chain has been offering their products in its Japanese stores. It acquired them from Japanese wholesalers, or possibly through parallel-market buyers such as those that can be seen outside brand stores in Europe trying to persuade passers-by to buy their products instead.

This is a major controversy when you realize that, in Europe, luxury brands have won, via the courts, the right to choose their retailers in order to prevent their products from appearing on supermarket shelves. The Carrefour case in Japan is worth watching.

Perceptions of identity

Above all, we must not expect potential customers, once in contact with the manifestations of the brand, to become conscious of its identity in the same terms that led to its development. Few consumers carry analysis beyond the concrete aspects of the product, or the emotions (and the causes of these emotions) aroused by a particular purchase experience.

As we've already said, we must not expect a monolithic perception of the brand. Perceptions vary depending on culture, on each customer's personality, on the competitors present, on the duration of the brand's presence and so on. The difficulty is in evaluating the compatibility of these differences with the brand's development strategies.

There are several approaches to the analysis of consumer behavior, and it is possible to focus on this notion of perception

luxury **brand** management

more clearly. One possibility is to use a model called the "hierarchy of effects," which suggests how, based on the reception of messages, the consumer first becomes conscious of the existence of a brand, then defines an attitude toward it, then changes that attitude into a preference, and finally moves from preference to actual purchase.

The effectiveness transition

This transition correlates with a second critical point in a brand's development. Do all of the manifestations of the brand reach the consumers they target? And do these consumers perceive them in a way that is aligned, in a broad way at least, with the brand's identity? These are the two types of effectiveness that are expected of any communication. To use a ballistic metaphor, we might use the terms "precision" (of aim) and "impact" (the effects caused by the missile).

After it has been verified that effectiveness with target consumers is satisfactory, the actual coherence of the brand's manifestations can also be tested authentically through their perception.

The act of purchase

This time the actual consumer is analyzed in order to get the best possible understanding of the mechanisms that led her or him to make a purchase. Of course, the market is always partly shrouded in mystery, and everybody is quick to come up with explanations for a success after the fact. Still, understanding past successes is essential in explaining the functioning—and the dysfunctions—of the chain of communication.

Differences—if they exist—between the target consumer and the actual consumer need to be analyzed.

Survey techniques can also be used to isolate a crucial aspect of the chain of communication: non-purchase by the target clients. This information is often more useful than what is known about actual purchasers because it can be used to isolate major dysfunctions in the chain of communication.

The relevance transition

Communication can be completely successful—that is, can be fully perceived and understood by the consumer—and not set off a sufficient number of acts of purchase. The chain of communication can function in a fluid way up to the stage of perception. The message can faithfully reflect the brand's identity and make the product highly desirable—but the consumer's intentions to purchase never become concrete. In the interests of simplification, we have left out an intermediate transition in the chain of communication, between perception and the act of purchase: desirability. We deal with the concepts of desirability and accessibility as one. This can be because there is inadequate distribution, or because poor logistics result in the product being repeatedly out-of-stock, or because the prices are unaffordable. Another possibility, and one that is much more difficult to manage, is that the brand has less relevance than its competitors. Its identity gets across well to the consumers, but it is based on values that interest them less than others.

Obstacles to the full realization of the brand's potential fall into several categories:

- merchandising problems: the structure of the offering in relation to number of groups of products at the sales outlets, price and margin policies
- problems of operational execution, which stem from difficulties at the level of production, logistics or organization
- problems related to the brand's identity being out of phase with the mood of the market—or, at least, having become less desirable than that of its closest competitors.

BRAND AUDIT METHODOLOGY

The methodology we recommend takes three areas into consideration:

- The chain of communication described above. By underlining the difficulties inherent in the transition from one phase to another, from brand identity to the act of

luxury **brand** management

purchase, it presupposes the analysis of the consistency, coherence, effectiveness and relevance of the communication.

- The competitive context in which the chain of communication operates. The brand is obviously in competition, not only with its competitors of reference (the ones that were used as an aid in seeking differentiation of the brand's identity), but also with the "noise pollution" of all the brands that are constantly vying for the consumer's attention. As illustrated in Figure 12.3, this media bombardment contributes to creating the consumer's perception of the brand, even if this is sometimes fragile and elusive.

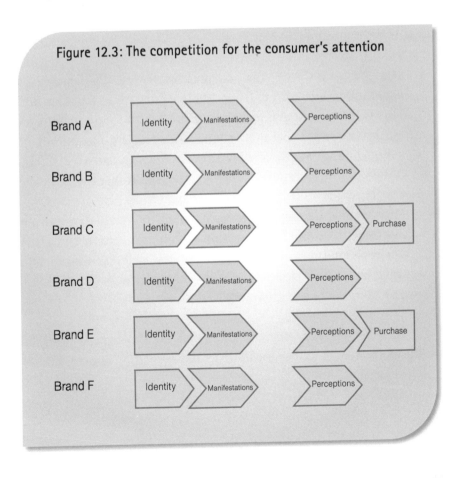

Figure 12.3: The competition for the consumer's attention

We have insisted on the comparative and competitive dimension of the concept of brand: there can be no identity without differentiation. It follows that there can be no identity without the elements of comparison provided by the competitors of reference. For example, in its re-launch (described in Chapter 6) Bally defined Louis Vuitton, Gucci, Ferragamo and Prada as its competitors of reference.

- Finally, the consumer. All communication is built on hypotheses of perception and reaction on the part of consumers. In the context of an audit, these hypotheses need to be verified.

The methodology of the brand audit, as presented in Figure 12.4, is built around three phases:

- The "snapshot" of the current state of the chain of communication, through the four states that make it up. This is the longest and most costly stage of the audit. It calls on market research techniques and requires the absorption of a large quantity of data, which are not always easily accessible. It includes three types of analysis, focused respectively on the company, the consumers and the competitors.
- The verification of what we have called the "transitions" from one state to another in the chain of communication.
- The recommendations for change, which are broken down into three functional categories: identity management, merchandising, and operational and organizational processes.

We will look at all the phases and transitions described in the audit methodology in Figure 12.4.

luxury **brand** management

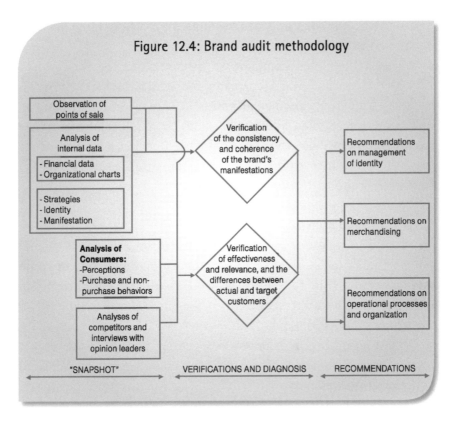

Figure 12.4: Brand audit methodology

Observation of points of sale

All brand audits begin with several days of observation of what is happening at the brand's points of sale, and also at those of its competitors of reference. The purpose of this is to form a personal opinion of the brand's degree of differentiation, of the products, the behavior and type of customers, and finally the environment and atmosphere of the points of sale. This experience is fundamental, and we cannot stress strongly enough the importance of this initial observation, especially before any close contact is made with the personnel of the brand being audited. After all, the points of sale are the places where the brand's destiny is being decided.

Financial and management data

These are the basic data needed to locate the brand in its lifecycle and measure its strength for the different product categories, distribution channels and geographic zones. This study must be conducted in terms of volume and margin.

The deliverables comprise a formalization of the brand's lifecycle: business volume (corrected for retail value), expenditures on communication, number of points of sale, operational margin, operational cash flow and share value (if applicable) are traced back over the previous years. All this is done in a homogeneous way, to take into account brands that operate in several market segments or product categories.

Organizational charts

To avoid a complete review of the organization, the focus should be on the brand's nerve centers: the communication, creation and merchandising functions, as well as all the mechanisms of coordination and arbitrage between the functions that control all the brand's manifestations.

Most problems of coherence of brand identity arise at the level of organization (and process). The managers of the different functions involved have different training and different specialties. The merchandiser/commercial director wants to sell now; however, the identity manager cultivates the brand for the long term. The production manager wants to reduce costs; the brand identity manager always looks to improve quality, and so on.

It frequently happens that the product design function is dissociated from the traditional communication function, and that the latter is dissociated from the function of development of the architectural concept of the points of sale. Yet all three come under the heading of "aesthetic" management of the brand. The ultimate director of the brand's identity, and this is particularly relevant for the luxury sectors, is often the CEO, because he or she is the only one who can settle all conflicts.

The techniques used are simple interviews with the managers concerned and study of the documents supplied by the human resources department. The deliverables are:

- organizational charts of the first two levels of the structure
- complete organizational charts of the creation, communication, and merchandising functions
- a description of the mechanisms of coordination between the managers of the brand's different manifestations.

Strategies and brand identity

The aim here is to compare the version of the brand's identity as it is known and used by the managers with the official version, if such a version exists. Very often, different vocabularies are found from one company to another, and even within the same company ("brand image," "image characteristics," "brand philosophy," "brand essence," "genetic code," and so on). Often there is confusion between the notion of image and that of identity.

The brand auditor, if he or she has access to no existing formalization of the identity, will have to synthesize the opinions of the principal managers. The audit can reveal an identity that is vague, confused and poorly defined. If a more in-depth study of a semiotic nature is felt necessary, it cannot be done in the context of the audit and will take the form of a recommendation.

The degree of formalization of the brand's identity in ethical and aesthetic terms is always an indication of the quality of the management of its communication.

Since the brand's identity is a "subset" of the overall strategy, care should be taken to also study the documents that formalize the company's strategies in respect of target consumers, communication, structure of the product offering, distribution, production and culture to ascertain whether there is a strong coherence between them and the brand's identity.

The techniques used are classic interviews with the principal managers and the study of the existing documents. The deliverables are:

- The brand's identity in terms of its ethics and aesthetics, in its official form (if the brand has produced such a document), or failing that, in the form of a synthesis compiled by the auditor. At this stage, it is ascertained whether the identity as expressed has the necessary competitive characteristics, such as differentiation from the competitors of reference, and constancy or continuity of a brand ethic and aesthetic over time.

- A synthesis of the expression of the brand's identity as understood by the managers. Particular attention will be paid to analyzing the degree of homogeneity of the managers' comprehension of the identity, and any areas where they are out of phase with each other or with the official version.
- The company's strategies. Possible incompatibilities between strategies and identity will be pointed up. For example, is the presence of Chanel perfumes in department stores such as JC Penney compatible with the brand's luxury positioning?

Manifestations of the brand's identity

The aim is to take a "snapshot" of all these manifestations so as to focus on the consistency of these manifestations with the identity, and on the coherence of the various manifestations. Depending on the type of industry, the following material will be gathered for the four categories of manifestations we have identified.

For the first category (**the general aesthetic**), under the direct control of the person in charge of management of the identity:

- All the briefs (if they exist). Evaluate the level of detail, the coherence of the creative directions and the degree of consistency with the identity. These briefs are especially important because they are the official relay between the identity and its manifestations. Generally, they are not sufficiently formalized.
- All the audiovisual material relative to traditional communication—for example, the six or eight latest advertising campaigns, the communication program, the media plans, and videos of events (product launches, galas, fashion shows and so on).

- A sampling of all the elements of the signature system. The corporate graphic chart, if it exists.
- If applicable, the plans for the architectural concept and photographs (interior and exterior) of the points of sale.
- Photographs of the most recent window-display concepts.
- The training manuals for the sales personnel and the internal merchandising rules.

For the second category (**products**):

- All the products (or photographs of them) offered over the past two years. The best-and worst-sellers should be identified by geographical region, by distribution channel and so on. This is one of most significant processes, and also one of the easiest to carry out.

For the third category (**merchandising**):

- Programs for product launches, and plans for the structure of the product offering with lists of consumer prices (the collection plans).

For the fourth category (**the consumer**):

- The definition of the target consumers, which should be part of the strategies.

Observations of the behavior and appearance of all the persons who are the interface between the company and the outside world (from the receptionist up to the CEO, and including the sales personnel) should be organized.

Deliverables are:

- Formalization (if not already existent) of all the briefs for the first category of manifestations.

- Formalization of the structure of the product offering (development plan for automotive industry, launch plans for detergents, collection plans for accessories and ready-to-wear), viewed as the initiating document of the brand's merchandising.
- An assemblage of the brand's entire "iconographic corpus" and all the material collected.
- A synthesis of the degree of familiarity with the constituent elements of identity on the part of the various people in charge of the brand's manifestations, and of their strategies.

Verification of consistency and coherence

The work on consistency and coherence begins with the hypothesis that the more the manifestations tend to send a "compact" message, the greater its chances are of being perceived. Using the documents and conclusions assembled during the preceding activities, each of the manifestations is compared with its objectives, or directly with the documents that express the brand's identity. Generally, the most flagrant "inconsistencies" (manifestations that blatantly contradict the values or the aesthetic the brand wants to promote) quickly come to light.

This verification is coupled with an evaluation of the coherence of the manifestations among themselves. Of course, if the verifications point to a high degree of consistency with the brand identity, the coherence of the manifestations among themselves should be automatic. However, this is an area where personal opinions and intuitions can take precedence. So it's a good idea to maintain the coherence criterion as an additional control.

All the material assembled under the "deliverables" category for the brand's manifestations is studied to measure the coherence of all these elements among themselves. The communicative content of each object, each advertisement and each store is a specific experience in itself. This experience carries within it numerous messages that generate emotions of varying intensity. The delicate process of evaluating coherence is of the same nature as evaluation of consistency with identity, but in a much broader field.

luxury **brand** management

Absence of incoherence is the easiest stage to measure; it is a positive aspect in itself. At the optimal stage, each manifestation is both a relevant and an effective expression of the brand identity, and at the same time reinforces the impact of the other manifestations.

The volume of work involved in such an analysis can be staggering. It is better, therefore, to give priority to working on the manifestations that have the greatest impact: products, traditional communication, and points of sale, if applicable.

The scale of importance of the brand's manifestations can vary from one industry to another, but it has been shown that the experience of the product, coupled with that of the point of sale, remains essential to transmitting the brand's identity. Then come street communication (display windows, billboards and so on) and the social experience—consumer word of mouth ("That's a great tie. Where did you find it?"). The accent should be placed on the products, product merchandising and aesthetics, the aesthetics of the points of sale, and the target consumers. Deliverables are:

- Diagnosis of the consistency of its manifestations with the brand's identity, and their internal coherence; description of the causes of inconsistencies and lack of coherence; and classification of these problems according to the nature of the recommendations they prompt (identity, merchandising, organization and process).

Analysis of consumers

Two parallel analyses must be conducted if the target customer and the actual customer are substantially different. The differences will be analyzed closely. What are studied above all are the actual customers' reasons for purchase, and the reasons target customers fail to purchase. In the interest of simplicity, we will use the hypothesis here that the target customer is also the actual customer.

Traditional quantitative and qualitative techniques should suffice to cover both the aspects of perception and of purchase or non-purchase behavior. Each respondent falls into one or the other category. An attempt will be made to get the best possible picture of the following aspects:

- the consumer's familiarity with the brand and his or her consciousness of its different manifestations: products, characteristics, benefits related to products, aesthetics, materials, price, points of sale, service, accessibility, advertising and so on
- the consumer's perception of the brand's identity in terms of originality, aesthetics, significance and so on
- the consumer's idea of the brand's ideal customer
- whether the consumer wants the products, and the reasons motivating this desire/absence of desire
- the reasons for the purchase/non-purchase
- the frequency and amount of the consumer's purchases over the previous two years
- who the consumer thinks are the competitors of reference
- the competing brands the consumer buys and the reasons for doing so
- the consumer's recommendations for making the brand more competitive.

Deliverables comprise a synthesis of all the differences noted between the brand's objectives and actual results: between the desired identity and its perception; between the various perceptions of identified segments; between target and actual consumers; between the competitors of reference chosen by the brand and those perceived by customers. This will point up the brand's degree of familiarity and the attractiveness of its products against the competitors of reference, and any problems of product accessibility.

Analysis of competitors and interviews with opinion leaders

An analysis of the competitors of reference is done in part at the start of the audit, through observation of the different sales outlets. What was learned needs to be complemented by studying the other manifestations of the brand's competitors: advertising, press clippings and financial data (if accessible). If the competitors perceived to be most significant by target consumers (and

luxury **brand** management

purchasers) are different from the competitors of reference defined in the brand identity, those brands will also have to be studied.

Interviews with leaders of opinion, who generally come from the world of the press or economics, serve as a kind of safety net to confirm the impressions and facts collected during the audit.

This will serve to point up the strategic and operational differences from competitors, and above all, the degrees of differentiation of the brand's identity.

Verification of effectiveness

Using all the material assembled concerning the differences between the planned and the real, the mechanisms that led to these differences are dissected in order to identify the source of the difficulties. Since problems of coherence have already been dealt with, the only remaining matters should be those related to:

- The effectiveness of the resources chosen for communication. This applies more particularly to traditional communication methods.
- Cultural differences between segments. The different perceptive realities can be characterized by the differences still existing between best-sellers and worst-sellers as a function of geographic region. At Bally, in October 1999, this exercise—conducted on the five best-selling shoes in Japan, Hong Kong, the United States and Switzerland—showed that these regions had only 20% of these products in common. In studying the different perceptions of the brand, care needs to be taken to evaluate their relative importance and degree of compatibility.
- The identity itself. Often it can be perceived in a vague way because of a lack of a clear definition at the outset. Or, more frequently, the brand proves not to be sufficiently differentiated from its most significant competitors. What difference do consumers see between a Pilot ball pen and a Pentel, both of modern design and manufactured in Japan? Or between one brand of rice and another?

This verification exercise will provide answers to the following questions:

- Has the communication directed at the different segments reached and hit its targets? This is the measure of the effectiveness of the resources used.
- Have the messages contained in the communication been received? This is the degree of awareness of the brand's existence.
- How have the messages been received? This is the perception of identity.

This will also provide a list of the causes of disruptions to the transmission of identity.

Verification of relevance

The market itself is, in fact, what verifies the brand's relevance. An analysis of the brand's desirability compared with its close competitors is used as measurement. If my brand interests people less than others, it's because the brand experience I offer (visits to the store, use of the product, contact with its advertisements and so on) doesn't do as good a job of reaching their sensitive spots and generates less emotion.

Being in phase with the mood of the moment without betraying the invariants of the identity requires talent, intuition and processes that are difficult to rationalize. It is at this level that creativity and market intuition make the difference.

Thanks to their experience and their intuition, the product marketing teams at Renault thought that if their Espace model was a success, there would be room for a much smaller car that would have the characteristics of a small family monovolume vehicle. Who could have predicted that this model alone would account for almost half of the sales of the Mégane line since its launch? It would have been difficult, too, to predict the success of the Swatch watch when it was launched. It was not an obvious move, on the face of it, to launch a plastic watch with a plastic band and a very plain case, and make it a worldwide success. The relevance of the concept was based on a sense that the market was waiting for such a product. And how to account for the weaker performance of the S.T. Dupont brand against that of competitors like Montblanc and Cartier? Is it because of its strong positioning in cigarette lighters, which symbolize an activity contemporary society strongly condemns? Or is it related to a somewhat vague and poorly differentiated brand identity?

All these examples illustrate the difficulty, for the auditor, of getting a handle on the notion of relevance. It is in this area that semiotic tools can be of great help. The semiotic square (presented in Chapter 6) can be used to classify brands into two major categories (see Figure 6.13):

- "Substance" brands (which produce their own meaning), which ride society's groundswell trends—Chanel, at the appearance of the women's liberation movement; Volvo, with the trend toward automotive safety.
- "Sign" brands (which are interested in more short-term trends)—Zara, for whom reactivity is the core competency; Louis Vuitton, the majority of whose sales volume is generated by various versions of the "monogram" fabric.

But the relevance transition, as we have seen, can also be hampered by numerous obstacles related to merchandising or operational execution. Therefore, all the problems related to accessibility of the products are studied, pointing up the operational difficulties that prevent the brand from realizing the sales potential its degree of attractiveness should generate. These difficulties generally come out in the internal interviews and, above all, in customers' comments. They can be of various types:

- A distribution network that is not dense enough, or points of sale that are poorly located, compared with the competition.
- Inadequate delivery systems. This is a recurring problem in the fashion sector where, too often, the advertised products

arrive in stores a month after the advertising appears.
- Lack of certain sizes, colors or models, or insufficient quantities to meet demand.

While discovering these problems is relatively easy, diagnosing their causes is not always simple. The real causes are often related to the processes of monitoring the markets, design and development of the products themselves.

This analysis will deliver a diagnosis of attractiveness (summarizing the principal differences noted in comparison with competitors) and of product accessibility (with the problems classified by type and importance).

Recommendations

The recommendations for resolving all the problems encountered during the audit fall into three categories: those relating to the brand's identity, for improving its coherence, its relevance, and the effectiveness and the consistency of its communication; those to do with merchandising, to improve the product offering in the broad sense; and recommendations concerning organization and operational process.

In this, the company's priorities, the feasibility of implementing the recommended actions and the time needed to do so will be taken into consideration.

The limits of the audit

The methodology we have just described can give a considerable tactical advantage to management teams or brand managers. It constitutes a "dictionary" of all the aspects to be taken into account. It requires analysis of all processes, from creation through purchase, and identifies the weaknesses: lack of coherence, a difficult transition from one state to another, shortcuts, or glaring omissions in a key point in the chain of communication.

In all of this, though, it is essential not to forget that, sometimes, creativity or the power of seduction is better than a

luxury **brand** management

systematic approach and too-rigid procedures. The audit remains an introspective and analytical tool, not a creative operation. It has to be appreciated for what it is. It often allows proper assessment of the problems, but solving them will depend on individual talents. It's one thing to identify recommendations and another to put them into practice.

Still, as in painting or music, it makes sense to analyze the work of your predecessors and to construct rules from it, but be prepared to break your own rules in the cause of creativity. Personal expression always increases in relevance and maturity from such an exercise. Similarly, on the battlefield, the most thorough strategic reflection must not smother the crucial dimension of opportunistic improvisation; in fact, it feeds on it. Clausewitz, the great theoretician of the Napoleonic wars and the founder of modern military strategy, never forgot what he had learned on the ground.

For these reasons, a relevant audit must make clear, both to the client and to the auditor, its own strengths and limitations. Nothing is worse than to lose focus in the face of the mass of data collected, or to imagine that all the solutions will naturally flow from the assessments made from them. Nevertheless, a problem whose outlines are clearly drawn is always better than a latent problem; it's also better to study the reasons for a success or a failure than to sit back and rely on the "mystery of creativity." And if each stroke of genius is accompanied by systematic organization of the actions to be undertaken, the results can only be better.

We might describe this little extra dose of rationality that leaves nothing to chance as being like the double zero on European roulette wheels, which guarantees that the casino will have slightly higher gains than the players. It's a very necessary, if never sufficient, tool, all the more so because in its strictly analytical dimension it is not immune to criticism. Its main weakness is that there is no real methodology for studying in detail problems related to the brand's relevance.

Major market or social trends can be overlooked or the analysis of consumers may fail to take account of ever-changing consumer behavior and requirements: because they have longer vacations, they travel more and hotels in certain tourist destinations are full; because they are better fed and their average weight is increasing, more of them want to lose weight and turn to diet-food products; because they spend more time on leisure, they buy more Jeep and SUV-type vehicles. The success of the cell telephone can be explained, in retrospect, by the desire to stay in contact with one's "tribe" at all times and the need for greater mobility. Yet nobody was predicting, just a few years ago, that there would ever be more cell phones than fixed-line phones in the developed countries. Clearly, certain external elements determine the success of a product or category of products, but they are not always easy to identify.

For certain simple cases, however, anticipation is fairly easy. Now that cell phones are so prevalent, it's possible to predict a reduction in calls made from telephone booths and thus that booths will be less profitable or less well maintained, if not disappear altogether in some places.

This type of concern is not new. Books on strategy always start with "analysis of the environment" to evaluate the potential of a market. Are the general conditions of the environment favorable to the development of a certain market or product? But there are sometimes sudden changes that are difficult to predict. Marketing strategists today talk about "windows of opportunity," which implies that, as for the launch of a rocket, favorable conditions are very circumscribed.

Some 25 years ago S.C. Johnson, which specialized in the production of household cleaning products, considered the long-term future for its furniture polish and floor-care products. The assessment was simple: the percentage of working women was increasing, so women would have less time to devote to the upkeep of their houses. Household income was on the rise, and people would invest more in leisure. Eventually, sales of household-care products could run into problems. The company, therefore, launched an energetic diversification campaign, creating a "leisure" division and buying

luxury **brand** management

companies that made equipment for outdoor leisure activities. These activities did develop, but much more slowly than household-care products. S.C. Johnson would certainly have been better served had it stuck to its core business and bought companies that made innovative household products, rather than tents and canoes.

To sum up: the audit is a rapid-verification tool that complements other necessary studies, which are more costly and of longer duration, into the evolution of the market as a whole.

CRITERIA FOR GOOD BRAND MANAGEMENT

September 11, 2001 and the invasion of Iraq have not helped a world economy already on the verge of recession and threatened by deflation. Yet several brands seem better equipped than most to survive the downturn: Ralph Lauren, Tod's, Hermès, Audi, Camper, Burberry, Armani, Hugo Boss, BMW, Coach, Puma, Louis Vuitton and a few others.

What these brands have in common is that they are all in a growth phase or in early maturity. They all know the importance of their brand, and sell substantial quantities of recognizable products of unchanging quality. Beyond these shared points, each has its own history, its own way of doing business and staying competitive.

Having a recognizable product is the central element for successful brands, but it is only the tip of the iceberg, the final crystallization of complex processes. The major brands are characterized by:

- a product that is recognizable, popular and the basis of its own brand awareness
- an identity that is well differentiated, relevant and well managed
- an effective organization and processes
- a culture of innovation, attentiveness to the markets and rapid reaction to change.

The product

We have already stressed the fundamental importance of the product. It is the most visible and most tangible component of a brand and it is the instrument of both revenue generation and communication about the brand itself.

Expertise

The product is the foundation of the brand's legitimacy in a specific sector. It is proof of expertise in a business area (the client is rarely aware of licensing or franchise agreements and is only marginally interested in them) and guarantees the substance and authenticity offered by the brand.

The principal dimension of creation and innovation

It is on the product that the bulk of research and creativity are concentrated. It is also where they are most visible. Stylistic and technological research go hand in hand. Audi is perhaps one of the brands that have succeeded best in concentrating their efforts in both areas, with tangible results.

Its own best advertising

We have stressed the fact that the product itself is the most effective manifestation of the brand's identity. It is advertising in its most direct, evident, multi-sensory form, generating immediate impressions. It is also the foundation of brand awareness. The more it is sold, the better it is known, especially if it is identifiable from across the street. This explains the use of logos, materials, colors, metal accessories and other style codes that are aimed at facilitating identification.

'The search for new elements of recognition must be continuous, even for established brands. Prada, which already had its use of black nylon and its triangular metal plaque as elements of recognition, then launched the little red rectangle to set off the Prada Sport line.

The product must be managed with full awareness of its impact on communication. Never kill a best-seller: *restyle* it.

luxury **brand** management

The automotive industry has been successful in this regard—the Volkswagen New Beetle and the new Mini Cooper (BMW group) are good recent examples. Canceling groups of products that sell well, on the grounds that they no longer fit a style or a new brand identity, shows a lack of respect for the market. It amounts to a massive "layoff" of customers who could have become spokespeople for the brand's change had it been carried out progressively and intelligently. Certain brands have tried it and regretted it.

The key to the relationship with the consumer

The product is the source of repeat purchases, of the confidence or the disillusionment that is created between the consumer and the brand. The product spends a lot of time with its owner. An "affective" tie develops. Brands of cars, motorcycles, perfume, shoes and coffee know this well.

Except in certain extreme cases, bad advertising rarely deters a faithful customer, whereas poor quality in a product always will.

The basis of economic results

The product will have the same rank as the brand's identity, at the center of all processes and all reflection.

Identity

All brands that succeed have an identity that is well differentiated; in the public eye, and thus visible; and relevant, because they sell. In short, they are the result of an identity that is well managed.

A differentiated identity

The product brings more than purely tangible benefits. It carries with it a panoply of images, emotions and representations. The brand's ethic and aesthetic must define a vision of a specific world, yet its seasonal products must offer, in the shorter term, originality and innovation within the framework of that vision. What Burberry, Puma and Coach have done in recent years embodies this ability to innovate and differentiate while preserving an identity.

A perceived identity

Successful brands know how to talk. Consumers listen, and they understand. This is proof of the effectiveness of their communication in the broad sense. The more coordinated and effective the manifestations of brand identity, the stronger their impact will be. This is why there is constant attention given to coordinating all the functions that contribute to the brand's manifestations. It's why fashion and luxury brands have a growing preoccupation with controlling their distribution. It represents one of the essential manifestations of their identity.

Gucci's success in the late 1990s lay in the fact that Tom Ford not only controlled all aesthetic aspects of brand, but that he was also a great retailer and merchandiser. This allowed him to coordinate all aspects of the product and most of the brand manifestations.

A relevant identity

Successful brands sell because they interest the people who buy the products. This critical transition, as we have seen previously, is the most difficult one to plan. It requires sales genius and intuition about where the market is going. Faced with the mysteries of the market, the only constructive, rational attitude that can be taken is to watch it very closely, remaining ready to react as quickly as possible to significant signals. This requires systems for ongoing observation of markets, and operational processes oriented toward rapid response.

A well-managed identity

A well-managed identity requires strategies that are in phase with the brand's identity. It requires a corporate culture with real awareness of the concept of identity and all its operational implications and an understanding that identity management works on two different time scales: the middle term, when dealing with the invariable components of the brand ethic and aesthetic; and the short term for everything to do with the manifestations of the brand identity.

To sum up, managers of brands that want success will be as aware of the concept of identity as a major component of the company's strategies as they are of the product itself. The brand will have a relevant identity that will be communicated (in the broad sense of the term, that of entering the chain of communication) effectively and coherently. Managers will be constantly attentive to consumers and to their competitors of reference.

Organization and operational processes

We too often forget that behind a product and a brand there is a physical performance. When Coca-Cola decided to sell its Minute Maid fruit juices in Europe, it met with real difficulty. Its trucks were not refrigerated and therefore unable to distribute fresh fruit juices. To achieve its aims, it had to associate itself with Danone.

Two imperatives will govern the structure of the organization and the operational processes: putting the company in a position to react as quickly as possible to market signals, and coordinating the manifestations of identity as well as possible in order to maximize communicative impact.

Logistics

Today, the effectiveness, reliability and reactivity of the logistical chain have become decisive competitive elements in nearly all industrial sectors. The right products, delivered at the right time, and available in the right places, are the ones that sell well and whose presence and quality the consumer appreciates.

The principal points of sale need to receive deliveries almost every day, and the major retail chains bill their suppliers for delivery delays and inventory shortfalls. This is also the rule for luxury goods—particularly fashion products. A week's delay in shipping equates to an average loss of 2% of seasonal sales.

Logistics is only one of the elements that make it possible to respond rapidly to signals from the market. The essential yardstick here is time-to-market—the time between the product concept and its availability to consumers. Short development times make it possible to stay with the market and react more quickly to the competition's innovations. As mentioned earlier, the luxury industry has seasonal development times of nine to 12 months. For apparel items, Zara has reduced this to 10 days, from the initial sketches to the presence of the product in the stores.

Organization

For a brand to succeed, the organization of the company has to be up to the challenge. The company culture and, in particular, the coordination of its different functions, will play a determining role. With increased competition comes the need for the cultural attitude of the company to be closely in tune with market conditions. A company that thinks it has the key to consumers' expectations and can sell them whatever it offers will have a tendency to feel it doesn't need to meet all their requirements. We believe it is essential to develop a culture of respect for the market and its mysteries.

The second element comprises all the mechanisms of integration or coordination of the functions that oversee the brand's manifestations: committees, regular meetings, specific reporting. Nothing is more efficient than having a common manager for the design and merchandising functions, as we saw in the Gucci example earlier. The difficulty lies in finding the right individual, someone capable of using both hemispheres of the brain. This rare animal is sensitive both to the rationality of figures and to the aesthetic of the products; someone who has an enquiring mind and an understanding of human behavior.

For organizations that are not structured like consumer-products companies and have no product managers assigned to each brand in their portfolio, we recommend the creation of the position of brand–identity manager. The brand–identity manager will have control over all the functions aligned with the aesthetic aspects of the company's activity—from the design of the products to the uniforms worn by the receptionists to in-store window displays to traditional communication activities.

Other elements—computer systems, for example—also play an essential role in competitiveness, operating in tandem with logistics and the real-time circulation of data needed for rapid reaction.

luxury **brand** management

INNOVATION, ATTENTIVENESS AND REACTIVITY

As we have already noted, in addition to the product there are many other possible axes through which innovation is expressed: advertising, events, distribution, human resources management and so on. Management of human resources holds one of the keys to innovation. For there to be innovation, people must first be empowered to innovate. This means venturing into new territory and not being afraid to make mistakes. In a word, people need to be encouraged to take risks. This requires developing a corporate culture where certain types of risks (and thus also errors) are permissible. This means defining those errors that are not admissible.

At Bally, in 2000, at a point when risk-taking was being encouraged in each employee's field of endeavor, a list was sent out giving the outlines of a typology.

It is impossible to create an environment that encourages initiative and new ideas without encouraging transparency, curiosity, the right to ask questions, and a certain tolerance toward certain kinds of errors. Certain things should never be tolerated, however. These include making the same mistake twice; a lack of effort and a rejection of the principle of continuous improvement; concealment and non-communication; lack of interest; and refusing to accept responsibility commensurate with ability.

In the same way, if we are convinced of the need to be attentive to the market, we must develop a culture of respect for consumers, systems for listening to them, a process for transmitting data to the appropriate decision-makers, and a whole series of rapid-reaction procedures.

RECAPITULATION

We have examined the four elements on which the success of a brand is based:

- a recognizable product
- a well-managed identity
- an innovative organization

- effective operational processes that allow rapid reaction to signals from the market.

Figures 12.5 and 12.6 provide a simple graphic illustration of these essential points where a brand's success is built. They also let us reposition the different transitions in the chain of communication.

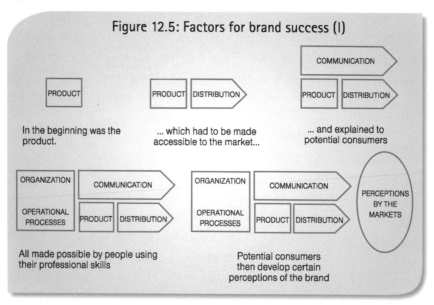

Figure 12.5: Factors for brand success (I)

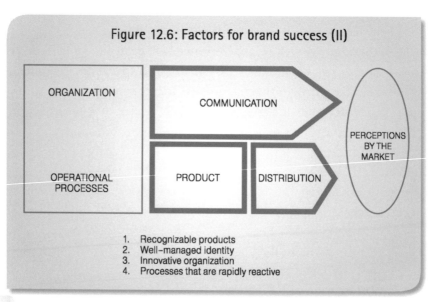

Figure 12.6: Factors for brand success (II)

1. Recognizable products
2. Well-managed identity
3. Innovative organization
4. Processes that are rapidly reactive

luxury **brand** management

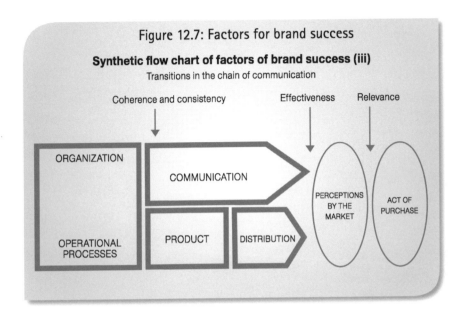

Figure 12.7: Factors for brand success

Synthetic flow chart of factors of brand success (iii)
Transitions in the chain of communication

To conclude this chapter, we must reiterate the pragmatic nature of our approach. In these pages we have tried to set out as clearly as possible a set of reflections and suggestions, a "toolbox" in which we hope brand managers will find inspiration for their work. If the formal structure of our arguments calls on various disciplines (semiotics, in particular), it is because in our experience its application in the field has produced good results.

Just as a semiological study of brand identity translates into very pragmatic recommendations, the methodological recommendations we have made in these pages lead to commonsense suggestions. But our presentation, we feel, has the advantage of painting an overall picture of brand management, one in which no aspect has been neglected. Having said that, it remains our fundamental conviction that the important events and decisions that affect a brand happen "on the ground." This is why we advocate so strongly for a responsive and "humble" attentiveness to the market, where too-rigid formalisms will always fall short and opportunistic ingenuity and creativity are always needed.

index

A

A. Lange und Söhne, 74

Absolut, 62–7, 87, 111, 113, 175, 195, 218, 235, 286, 293, 336, 361

Accessible luxury, xi, 170

Accessories, 9, 21, 28, 34, 42–4, 78, 107, 123, 130–4, 138, 158, 159, 167, 195

Acquascutum, 7, 15, 40, 90, 364

Ad!dict, 276

Adeline André, 94

Adidas, 143, 147, 210

Adolfo Dominguez, 41, 170

Advertising, xii, 2, 10, 14, 16, 19, 38, 40, 49, 50, 51, 56, 58, 59, 67, 94, 98, 101, 106, 124, 127–9, 131, 155, 159, 171, 173, 181, 183, 186, 192, 195, 200, 202, 213, 215, 219, 221, 223, 225, 229, 230, 240, 243, 244, 251, 258, 259, 261, 266, 268–70, 274–80, 284, 286–8, 290, 299, 302–6, 309, 314, 341, 345, 347, 348, 362–4, 368, 376, 378, 390, 394, 398, 402, 403, 407

Advertising agencies, 183, 279

Advertising brief, 277, 377

Advertising budget, 40, 50, 51, 276, 280, 302, 303, 305, 306, 309, 368

Affordable luxury, 49, 273, 346

Agnès B., 39

Akris, 41

Alberta Ferretti, 39

Alessi, 253

Alexander McQueen, 29, 54, 143, 179

Alien, 254

Allied Domecq, 65, 84

American Express, 285

Amica, 275

Angelo Tarlazzi, 38

Ann Demeulemeester, 41

Apple, 101

Aramis, 53

Armand Thierry, 246

Armani, vii, xii, 13, 15, 18, 23, 30, 35–8, 41, 43, 46, 50, 51, 53, 70, 76, 82, 86, 87, 91, 93, 96, 104, 123, 130, 131, 159, 167–70, 187, 188, 228, 243, 246, 247, 261, 286, 332, 344, 360, 401

Arthur Andersen, 141, 147, 288, 289

Asprey, 78

Aubade, 187

Audemars Piquet, 74

Audi, x, 187, 287, 379, 402

Austin Reed, 384

Avon, 368

Azzaro, 51, 54

Azzedine Alaïa, 38, 369

B

Baccarat, 16

Bailey's, 62, 63

C

luxury **brand** management

luxury **brand** management

G

Galerias Preciados, 140
Galeries Lafayette, 128, 140
Gallo, 61, 62
Gap, 2, 22, 210, 242, 280
Gatorade, 210
Gauloises, 145
Geographical expansion, 125, 127–9
Gillette, 140, 209, 210
Girard-Perregaux, 74
Givenchy, xiii, 7, 27, 51, 53, 94, 155, 179, 295
Glenmorangie, 65
Global brand, 85, 95, 143–5, 147, 200, 280
Globalization, 94, 144, 147
Gordon Gin, 62, 63
GQ, 275
Grammy award, 283
Grey market, 299, 315–9, 339, 349
Gucci, xiii, 5, 12, 13, 15, 16, 19, 20, 23–5, 29, 30, 35, 36, 38, 50–3, 72, 76, 86, 87, 93, 97, 103, 107, 115, 118, 119, 124, 131, 142, 143, 155, 167–70, 188, 204, 228, 238, 243, 277, 285, 348, 358, 360, 370, 386, 404, 406
Guerlain, vii, 17, 46, 50, 51, 53, 98
Guy Laroche, 6, 53, 350, 368

H

H&M, ix, 242, 243, 246, 259, 280
H.Stern, 69, 73
Habitat, 253
Hamilton, 283
Handbag, ix, 15, 16, 36, 42, 47, 48, 113, 114, 149, 150, 152, 159, 169, 187, 236, 238, 239, 250, 339, 317, 318, 328, 357, 371, 380
Harley Davidson, 107, 132, 348
Harry Winston, 72, 74, 76

Haute couture, xi, 8, 34–7, 94, 123, 152, 359
Havana Club, 65
Heinemann, 313
Helmut Lang, 193
Hennessy, 27, 62, 64, 65, 86–8, 291, 311
Hermès, vii, xii, 4, 23, 24, 30, 38, 40, 51, 75, 82, 86–9, 96, 103, 107, 121, 149, 163, 165, 167, 168, 174, 187, 189, 194, 222, 282, 283, 330–2, 342, 343, 345, 347–50, 353, 356–8, 361, 379, 382, 401
Hervé Léger, 38
Hogan, 360
Holland and Holland, 54
HP, 107
Hugo Boss, vii, viii, 40, 50, 51, 53, 167, 168, 170, 247, 360, 401

I

IBM, 101, 377
Idea Como, 11
Identity prism, 186, 188, 189
Index of attractiveness, 326
Inditex Group, 129, 271
Innovation, 123, 124, 130, 179, 189, 196, 200, 205, 208, 220, 228, 233, 275, 287, 343, 378, 401–3, 406, 407
Intel, 107
Intelligible dimension, 192, 195, 196, 268
Inter Parfums, 54–5
Interbrand, 83–8
Intermediary luxury, xi
Intramuros, 276
Invariant, 18, 91, 96, 136, 145, 185, 192, 210, 215, 216, 221, 222, 237, 375, 380, 396
Inventory, 8, 252, 298, 317, 327, 335, 336, 338, 349, 380, 405
Inventory turnaround, 327
Issey Miyake, 51–2, 54

luxury **brand** management

M

luxury **brand** management

luxury **brand** management